Up and Running with Affinity Designer

A practical, easy-to-follow guide to get up to speed
with the powerful features of Affinity Designer 1.10

Kevin House

BIRMINGHAM—MUMBAI

Up and Running with Affinity Designer

Associate Group Product Manager: Pavan Ramchandani
Publishing Product Manager: Ashitosh Gupta
Senior Editor: Mark Dsouza
Content Development Editor: Divya Vijayan
Technical Editor: Shubham Sharma
Copy Editor: Safis Editing
Project Coordinator: Manthan Patel
Proofreader: Safis Editing
Indexer: Pratik Shirodkar
Production Designer: Roshan Kawale

First published: August 2021

Production reference: 2031221

Published by Packt Publishing Ltd.
Livery Place
35 Livery Street
Birmingham
B3 2PB, UK.

ISBN 978-1-80107-906-8

www.packt.com

To my wife, Sherry, for your boundless enthusiasm and for letting me keep my crayons; to my son, Keaton for teaching me how to be a very proud dad; and to my parents, Betty and Kevin, who encouraged a quiet kid who liked to draw.

Contributors

About the author

Kevin House, also known as Kevin Creative, has an award-winning design and illustration studio located on the west coast of Canada. Before becoming a freelance designer and illustrator, he spent a few years in advertising agencies and design studios as a graphic designer. Those demanding, creatively fruitful years gave him the experience and confidence to set up a freelance business in 2006. Today, his clients are small to mid-sized creative studios and his focus is on illustration and logo design. Since 2014, Kevin has been using Affinity Designer almost exclusively for his 2D illustration work and loves the ease of use and array of creative options it brings to the table.

This book wouldn't have been possible without the assistance of a great many people. I would like to thank all of the team at Packt for not only suggesting this book and encouraging me to write it but also for everyone who guided me through the process, answered my questions, and were nothing but patient and helpful to this first-time author.

About the reviewer

Benet Zaganjori is an experienced graphic designer and illustrator from Florence, Italy. With a background in art history and design studies, he started working as a freelancer in 2018.

Inspired by his love for tattoos and classical art, he began providing vector-based designs for different types of projects, from printing to multimedia. He has worked for local and international businesses, clothing brands, and established software development companies and publishers. In 2019 and 2020, he collaborated with Serif Ltd as a freelance artist and has been published on the Affinity Spotlight website.

Benet's work distinguishes itself with a surreal mix of reality, fantasy, and color combinations, while his love of fine art is scattered throughout with the inclusion of elements drawn from mythology and the classical period.

Table of Contents

2

Getting Familiar with the Three Personas of Affinity Designer

3

How to Customize Your Affinity Designer Workspace

Section 2: Deeper Exploration of Affinity Designer's Documents, Tools, and Workflow

4

Document Setup and Modification

7

Tools – Pixel Persona

8

Tools, Panels, and Process – Export Persona

9

Workflow: Layers and Objects

10

Workflow: Symbols, Assets, and History

Section 3: Bringing It All together

11

Creating a Professional Logo

12

Creating Astronaut Ricky and Sidekick K9

13

Rocketing into the Pixel Cosmos

Other Books You May Enjoy

Index

Preface

Welcome to *Up and Running with Affinity Designer*.

Affinity Designer is a relative newcomer in the world of creative design software. Its ground-breaking vector and Pixel Persona workflow is attracting more and more users who are looking for alternative options and fresher thinking when it comes to their creative toolset.

Through discussion, visual examples, and practical exercises, this book explores Affinity Designer's methodology, processes, and the features that make it unique.

Who this book is for

Artists, designers, illustrators, and enthusiastic hobbyists will find this book of interest.

Up and Running with Affinity Designer is for beginners, intermediate users, or anyone who is interested in learning the fundamentals of Affinity Designer. From the basics to more advanced real-world exercises, whether you're just starting out or are looking to explore new techniques, there's something here for everyone.

What this book covers

Chapter 1, Getting Familiar with Affinity Designer's Interface, introduces Affinity Designer's interface.

Chapter 2, Getting Familiar with the Three Personas of Affinity Designer, provides an overview of the Designer, Pixel, and Export Personas.

Chapter 3, How to Customize Your Affinity Designer Workspace, looks at personalizing your experience through keyboard shortcuts, preferences, and workspace customization.

Chapter 4, Document Setup and Modification, covers file creation, document presets, and working with artboards.

Chapter 5, Main Studio Panels and Managers, explores the main studio panels' and managers' behavior, uses, and functionalities.

Chapter 6, Tools – Designer Persona, looks at the Designer Persona's tools, uses, and options.

Chapter 7, Tools – Pixel Persona, looks at the Pixel Persona's tools, uses, and options.

Chapter 8, Tools, Panels, and Process – Export Persona, looks at the Export Persona's tools, uses, and options.

Chapter 9, Workflow: Layers and Objects, studies workflow and best practices using layers and object behavior and management.

Chapter 10, Workflow: Symbols, Assets, and History, studies workflow and best practices using Symbols, Assets and History.

Chapter 11, Creating a Professional Logo, looks at how to create a fun, space-themed logo (Beginner).

Chapter 12, Creating Astronaut Ricky and Sidekick K9, looks at how to create the astronaut Ricky and her sidekick, K9 (Advanced 1).

Chapter 13, Rocketing into the Pixel Cosmos, looks at how to create a rough-and-ready rocketship (Advanced 2).

To get the most out of this book

The idea of this book is that, although it eventually does explore some advanced concepts and techniques, even if you have no prior knowledge at all of Affinity Designer, you should be able to start from *Chapter 1* and be able to complete the three practical chapters.

Intermediate users or those with some familiarity with Affinity Designer may choose to review the earlier chapters or skip ahead to the more advanced content.

Software/hardware covered in the book	Operating system requirements
Affinity Designer 1.10	macOS, Windows

The content of this book was created and written on a Mac OS desktop using a Mac desktop version of the software. We used a three-button mouse, however, any mouse will suffice and a drawing tablet can also be used but is not mandatory. Some aspects of the interface, methods, options described, menu items, shortcuts, terminology and processes demonstrated in this book may be different on a Windows system. That being said, the overall core concepts, explanations, fundamentals and exercise outcomes are the same. Whether you are on a Mac or Windows system you should be able to follow along.

Download the example code files

You can download the example code files for this book from GitHub at `https://github.com/PacktPublishing/Up-and-Running-with-Affinity-Designer`. If there's an update to the code, it will be updated in the GitHub repository.

We also have other code bundles from our rich catalog of books and videos available at `https://github.com/PacktPublishing/`. Check them out!

Download the color images

We also provide a PDF file that has color images of the screenshots and diagrams used in this book. You can download it here: `https://static.packt-cdn.com/downloads/9781801079068_ColorImages.pdf`.

Conventions used

There are a number of text conventions used throughout this book.

Bold: Indicates a new term, an important word, or words that you see onscreen. For instance, words in menus or dialog boxes appear in **bold**. Here is an example: "Select **System info** from the **Administration** panel."

> **Tips or important notes**
> Appear like this.

Get in touch

Feedback from our readers is always welcome.

General feedback: If you have questions about any aspect of this book, email us at customercare@packtpub.com and mention the book title in the subject of your message.

Errata: Although we have taken every care to ensure the accuracy of our content, mistakes do happen. If you have found a mistake in this book, we would be grateful if you would report this to us. Please visit www.packtpub.com/support/errata and fill in the form.

Piracy: If you come across any illegal copies of our works in any form on the internet, we would be grateful if you would provide us with the location address or website name. Please contact us at copyright@packt.com with a link to the material.

If you are interested in becoming an author: If there is a topic that you have expertise in and you are interested in either writing or contributing to a book, please visit authors.packtpub.com.

Share Your Thoughts

Once you've read *Up and Running with Affinity Designer*, we'd love to hear your thoughts! Scan the QR code below to go straight to the Amazon review page for this book and share your feedback.

https://packt.link/r/<1801079064>

Your review is important to us and the tech community and will help us make sure we're delivering excellent quality content.

Section 1: Getting Familiar with Affinity Designer's Interface and Layout

Each journey starts with a first step. Our first step will be to take a look at the landscape of Affinity Designer's UI. Knowing the general layout and where things are will give you the confidence to take on the chapters that follow.

This section comprises the following chapters:

- *Chapter 1, Getting Familiar with Affinity Designer's Interface*
- *Chapter 2, Getting Familiar with the Three Personas of Affinity Designer*
- *Chapter 3, How to Customize Your Affinity Designer Workspace*

1

Getting Familiar with the Affinity Designer's Interface

Welcome to the first chapter of *Up and Running with Affinity Designer*.

Success when learning any new software application is to know enough to be able to get it to do what you need it to do. Starting out, you don't necessarily need to know every aspect of the interface, just enough to help you to take that next step. The goal of this chapter is to get you comfortable with the layout and location of Affinity Designer's main interface panels, toolbars, and menu items. Later, we will be discussing each of these areas in more detail, either in a dedicated section or as part of the three practical exercise chapters.

In this chapter, we're going to cover the following main topics:

- What is Affinity Designer?
- What's new in 1.10.x
- Understanding the user interface and its menu
- An overview of the Menu bar
- Main tools – Tools panel overview

- Toolbars – overview
- Studio panels – overview
- The document view and artboards – overview
- Navigation tools – overview

Technical requirements

To follow along with the chapter and to get the most out of this book, it is recommended that you have an installed copy of Affinity Designer. Affinity Designer is available for Mac, Windows, and iPad and can be purchased, or a trial version can be downloaded, from the Serif online store `https://affinity.serif.com/en-gb/store/` or from the Mac App Store. The exercises, examples, and screenshots in this book were created using a Mac desktop setup with an extended keyboard and mouse.

What is Affinity Designer?

Affinity Designer is a modern, state-of-the-art vector design and illustration application. It's used in everything from logo and illustration work to websites, advertising, UI/UX, and icon work. Since its introduction in October 2014, Affinity Designer's popularity has grown steadily and despite it being a relative newcomer to the creative industry, it is fast becoming a go-to, high-performance alternative for creative professionals, teachers, students, and enthusiastic hobbyists alike.

The future is very bright for Affinity Designer and since its introduction, the team at Serif, the creators of Affinity Designer, have also introduced Affinity Photo and Affinity Publisher, two companion applications that run seamlessly alongside Affinity Designer as part of the Affinity range of professional creative applications. Now is an excellent time to get to know Affinity Designer and add it to your creative toolset and with *Up and Running with Affinity Designer*, we're going to discover together why you should consider adopting it as a permanent part of your creative arsenal.

What's new in 1.10.x

The most recent update to Affinity Designer version as of this writing is 1.10.x. It is basically a performance and stability update with little to no real new features added. Since the initial 1.10 update there have been incremental updates 1.10.1, 1.10.2, 1.10.3… each addressing bug fixes and general improvements. Rather than listing all of them here as they are dynamic in nature and keep being added, please visit the Affinity user forum News and Updates page for the most recent up to date information.

```
https://forum.affinity.serif.com/index.php?/forum/4-news-and-
information/
```

Serif, the makers of Affinity Designer, themselves described the 1.10.x update in an online News and Update post on August 5th 2021 saying that *"We're proud that the Affinity apps already offers class-leading speeds in many tasks, and for our latest update, we wanted to take a step back and really see what further levels of performance we could achieve"*. - Ashley Hewson, Managing Director Serif.

With 1.10.x they have undertaken a complete re-visit of memory management. This is apparently most noticeable when working in larger more complex files with higher numbers of layers and thousands of objects. These improvements are consistent across all apps and platforms. Windows, Mac, and iPad.

This update, while not sounding very exciting, is actually a good thing. By taking the time now to really look into performance and stability improvements they are setting the application up or laying the ground work for hopefully some exciting things to come down the road. Ideally in the not too distant future with version 2.0. Also remember Affinity Designer is not just a standalone vector illustration and design application. It's also the third part of a suite with two other applications (Affinity Photo and Affinity Publisher) that are designed to work as seamlessly together as possible, even sharing the same file formats. So, performance is crucial for a smooth experience moving between applications and within each application.

As outlined in their update post on July 28th, 2021, below are some other areas that have seen improved performance or have been added with the 1.10.x update:

- Improved performance when using linked placed images
- Improved performance with text
- Improved performance with embedded documents
- Improved performance with low memory conditions
- New selection options – Parent, Top and Bottom
- Improved IME text editing for Japanese and simplified Chinese languages
- Improved SVG import and export
- Added support for most emoji
- In the Resource manager, there is a new "Relink" option for missing resources, a new added "File Type" column and a new ability to link EPS files

- Assorted other small fixes

- Help and localization improvements

From the Stock Panel, Unsplash, the stock photography service has been removed due to a new licensing fee. Currently there is still Pixabay and Pexels stock photography services available.

The new update is free to existing customers of Affinity Designer. Each app in the suite has their own update versions found for all three Windows, Mac and iPad platforms on the online Affinity user forum.

Understanding the user interface and its menus

Before diving in too deep when picking up any new application, it's always good practice to get familiar with the broad landscape or "lay of the land" somewhat. To start with, in this section, we're going to take an overall look at the **User Interface (UI)** and learn where the important menu commands, panels, and toolbars are located. This way we can get a sense of how the application is set up and start to get acquainted and take advantage of some of its unique UI conventions.

Skipping ahead

Try to resist the urge to skip ahead if you can in these first few sections. Believe me, I understand the desire to get creating – it's what drove me to pick up the application to begin with, but you really don't want to miss out on something here that may prove invaluable down the road and a good grounding of the interface will help build your confidence when you do start creating that masterpiece.

Let's get started exploring the UI by opening up a new file. Launch Affinity Designer and go to **File | New**. Choose any page size from the available options (I chose letter size but for this, it really doesn't matter) and then click **Create**. You should be presented with a centered blank white page. Now if you have already opened the application and have been playing around and moving various panels about, you may want to set up your layout to look like mine, shown in the user interface screenshot in *Figure 1.1*, to follow along. To change to the same layout seen here, go up to the top menu, click and hold on **View**, navigate to **Studio**, and select the last option at the bottom of the flyout, **RESET STUDIO**. This will reset the Affinity Designer interface to its default layout and it should look pretty much the same as mine.

Figure 1.1 – Affinity Designer light interface

The preceding screenshot shows the light interface version while the next is the dark interface version. Both are screenshots of the Affinity Designer default interface.

A note about the screenshots in this book

Screenshots that don't need to be printed in color are printed in black and white. Screenshots that are best shown in color will be in color. In some screenshots the UI type will be too small to read, however if the information or concept being discussed requires readability every attempt at enlarging it will be made. That being said, there are limitations to resolution and the size of some UI elements.

Figure 1.2 – Affinity Designer dark interface

In practice in my day-to-day work, I find the light version a bit too bright for working with so I normally work in the dark interface mode. However, we will be using the light interface for all of the screenshots in this book for the main reason that they are easier to read at the sizes they are reproduced here. If you would like to change your interface to the light or dark interface option, go to **Affinity Designer | Preferences** (Mac) or **Edit | Preferences** (PC), locate the **UI Style** option, and select **Light**:

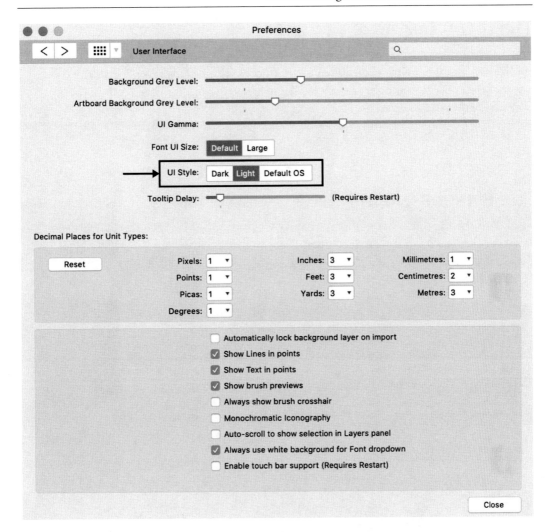

Figure 1.3 – Preferences panel – user interface

We will be discussing many of the user interface areas in more detail in *Chapter 3, How to Customize Your Affinity Designer Workspace*, but for now, let's just get familiar with the overall footprint of Affinity Designer's default setup. Let's begin with a quick tour of the interface.

The menu bar

Looking around the screen, we can see in the top left a horizontal bar containing a typical application menu bar with drop-down menu items: **Affinity Designer**, **File**, **Edit**, **Text**, **Layer**, **Select**, **View**, **Window**, and **Help**. We will cover these in more depth in the *An overview of the menu bar* section.

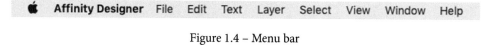

Figure 1.4 – Menu bar

The Persona toolbar

Just below the top menu bar and still on the left-hand side of the layout, you will see the three Persona icons for the **Designer**, **Pixel**, and **Export** Personas. This is called the Persona toolbar. See *The Persona toolbar* section for a more in-depth look at the Persona toolbar.

Figure 1.5 – Persona toolbar with the Designer Persona active

Toolbar

Continuing along the same horizontal bar and just to the right of the three Persona icons is an area known simply as the Toolbar. See the *The Toolbar* section for a more in-depth look at the Toolbar.

Figure 1.6 – Toolbar

The context toolbar

Just below the Toolbar is the context toolbar. See the *The context toolbar* section for a more in-depth look at the context toolbar.

Figure 1.7 – The context toolbar

The Tools panel

Moving over to the left-hand side of the layout, we find the Tools panel. See the *Navigation tools – overview* section for a more in-depth look at the Tools panel.

Figure 1.8 – Tools panel (Designer Persona)

The document view

The central workspace area containing my white page is known as the Document View. The dark gray area around my page also contained within the document view is called the Pasteboard. See *The document view and artboards – overview* section for a more in-depth look at the document view and pasteboard.

Figure 1.9 – Document view and pasteboard

The Right Studio

The last area of the default interface to cover is the wide column along the right side of the layout. The area is known as the Right Studio. See the *Studio panels – overview* section and *Chapter 5, Main Studio Panels and Managers,* for a more in-depth look at the Right Studio.

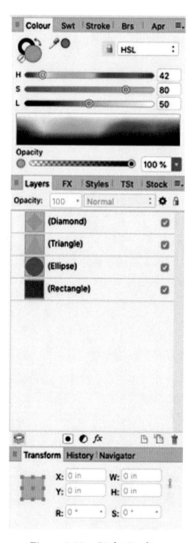

Figure 1.10 – Right Studio

Now that we have seen where the main areas of the interface are located in the default layout, let's begin to take a look at some of these individual areas a little more closely, starting with the top menu bar.

An overview of the menu bar

No chapter entitled *Getting Familiar with the Affinity Designer's Interface* would be complete without a quick look at the interface's top menu bar. As this is an overview, a lot of these menu items will be covered or touched on as we go through the book, especially in the three practical exercise chapters (Chapters 11-13). Once again, these menu bar items and the drop-down menu lists that follow are from the macOS desktop version of the software. There may be some slight differences in the Windows version, but overall, most are the same.

Figure 1.11 – The menu bar

> **Keyboard shortcuts**
>
> You may notice that the menu bar dropdowns in the following screenshots display some existing keyboard shortcuts that are already assigned here for many functions. Most are assigned by Affinity Designer while some are shortcuts that I have assigned for my personal workflow. We will cover assigning keyboard shortcuts in *Chapter 3, How to Customize Your Affinity Designer Workspace*, after which you will know how to create your own shortcuts that make sense to your working style.

The Affinity Designer menu

The drop-down sections of this menu are as follows:

- **About**: Here you'll find the current splash screen with the Affinity Designer version number.

- **My Account**: A quick link to register or sign in to your account.

- Check for **Updates**: Use this to see if your version of Affinity Designer is the latest.

- **Personas**: Personas that are not currently active. Selecting one makes it the active persona.

- **Preferences**: Various Affinity Designer preferences.

- **Services**: macOS services.

- **Hide/Show All**: Hide or show Affinity Designer or other applications.

- **Quit**: Quit the application.

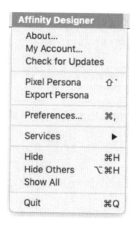

Figure 1.12 – The Affinity Designer menu dropdown

The File menu

The drop-down sections of this menu are as follows:

- **New**: Create a blank new file or a new file from Affinity Designer artwork that has been copied to the clipboard from another Affinity Designer file.

- **Open**: Opens a previously saved file or a recently saved file.

- **Close**: Closes the current file.

- **Save**: Saves the file or saves a new file with a different name.

- **Save as Package**: Saves a separate "Package" file format containing all of the file's relevant resources and fonts.

- **Save History With Document**: Saves the current file's history.

- **Edit/Reveal**: Allow editing in Affinity Photo and Affinity Publisher. Reveal the file's location in the Finder.

- **Place**: Places an image in the file.

- **Export/Share**: Export the file in a variety of formats, including templates. Share the file using email or messaging, or add to libraries.

- **Document Setup/Print**: Edit or review the document setup. Print the document.

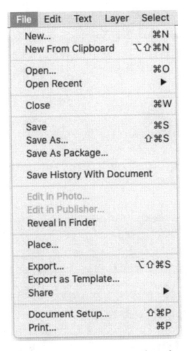

Figure 1.13 – The File menu dropdown

The Edit menu

The drop-down sections of this menu are as follows:

- **Undo/Redo**: Undo or redo operations performed.

- **Cut/Copy/Paste/Duplicate/Delete**: Cut and copy with paste options as well as duplicate and delete.

- **Defaults/Create Style**: Define element defaults. Create styles from a selection.

- **Dictation/Emoji & Symbols**: Start dictation. Create styles from a selection. Browse text emojis.

Figure 1.14 – The Edit menu dropdown

The Text menu

The drop-down sections of this menu are as follows:

- **Show**: Show text-related panels.
- **Character**: Adjust character options and positioning.
- **Alignment**: Adjust alignment and spacing.
- **Styles**: Create and adjust character and paragraph styles.
- **Insert**: Insert lines, dashes, spaces, and hyphens.
- **Spelling**: Check spelling and spelling options.

Figure 1.15 – The Text menu dropdown

The Layer menu

The drop-down sections of this menu are as follows:

- **Group**: Group or ungroup selected or all objects.

- **Compound**: Create compound shapes (shapes with holes).

- **Positioning/Editing/Transforming**: Options for arranging, editing, and transforming objects.

- **New Layer** types: New vector layer, new pixel layer, new adjustment layer

- **Lock**: Lock or unlock object options.

- **Hide/Show**: Hide or show object options.

- **Find**: Manually find the selected object in the layer stack. This can be changed to automatic.

- **Convert**: Convert/rasterize options for objects or text.

- **Convert Artboard**: Converts an object to an artboard or an artboard to an object.

- **Fill Mode/Layer Effects**: Fill mode for self-intersecting shapes and the Layer Effects panel.

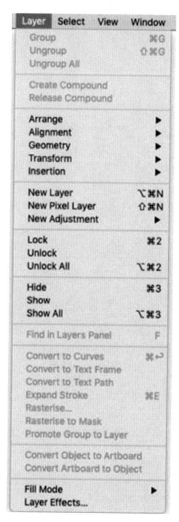

Figure 1.16 – The Layer menu dropdown

The Select menu

The drop-down sections of this menu are as follows:

- **Select**: Select all, deselect all, or invert the pixel selection.
- **Select Next/Select Previous**: Select the next object or select the previous object.
- **Select Same/Select Object**: Select the same object attributes. Select specific types of objects.

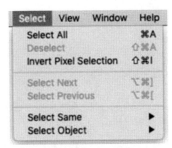

Figure 1.17 – The Select menu dropdown

The View menu

The drop-down sections of this menu are as follows:

- **Zoom**: Document zoom options.
- **Rotate**: Document rotate options.
- **View Mode**: Document view mode options.
- **Views**: Create new views. Browse saved views.
- **Show/Hide**: Grids, guides, bleed, margins, and rulers.
- **Lock Guides**: Lock or unlock guides toggle.
- **Studio**: Drop-down list of all studio panels.
- **Studio Presets**: The ability to save and choose custom studio panel setups.
- **Managers/Color Picker**: Five document managers; the Apple Color Picker.
- **View Point**: Browse the next or previous saved viewpoints.
- **Show/Hide Context Toolbar**: Context toolbar toggle.

- **Show/Hide/Customise Toolbar**: Toolbar toggle. Customize Toolbar

- **Show/Hide/Dock/Customise Tools**: Tools panel toggle/docking. Customize the Tools panel.

- **Toggle UI**: Hide or show all UI panels.

Figure 1.18 – The View menu dropdown

The Window menu

The drop-down sections of this menu are as follows:

- **Modes**: Normal mode or separated mode. Merge windows in separated mode.

- **Minimize/Zoom**: Choose whether the document fills the screen or is minimized to the dock.

- **Fullscreen**: Expand the window to fullscreen and hide the application menu bar.

- **Floating Windows**: Repositions floating windows.

- **Filename(s)**: List of open Affinity Designer files.

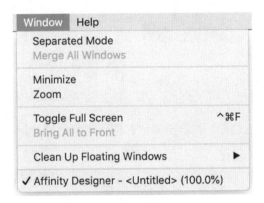

Figure 1.19 – The Window menu dropdown

The Help menu

The dropdown sections of this menu are as follows:

- **Search**: Menu bar search for a keyword.

- **Help**: Launches the Affinity Designer application's help topics browser.

- **Welcome…/Tutorial…**: The former launches the welcome splash screen. The latter launches the tutorial website.

- **Support**: Launches the Affinity online user forum website.

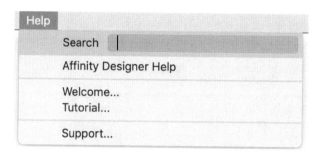

Figure 1.20 – The Help menu dropdown

With the main menu bar overview covered, let's focus a little more closely on some of Affinity Designer's Tools panels and toolbars.

Main tools – Tools panel overview

In the default interface layout, the Tools panel is located as a column of vertical icons on the extreme left side of the window. Depending on which Persona is active, the tools displayed will change in appearance, as shown here:

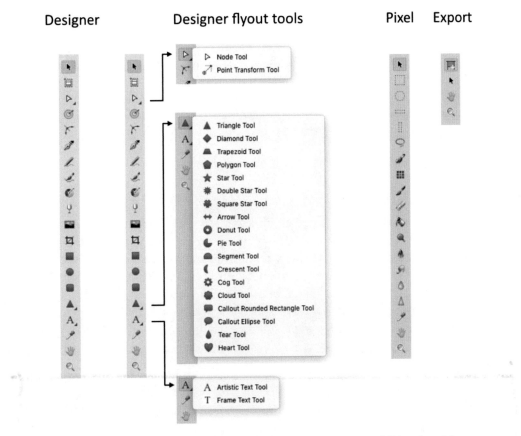

Figure 1.21 – Three Persona tool panels with the Designer Persona additional tool flyouts

If you look carefully, you'll notice in the case of the Designer Persona tool panel in the default setup, there are some nested tools indicated with flyouts below other related tools. The **Pixel and Export Personas** currently do not have any default flyout tools, although this may change in future updates.

The default order of the tools is set up for them to logically work with one another. The types of tools or tool groupings are as follows: **Design** tools, **Shape** tools, **Text** tools, **Selection** tools, **Retouch** tools, and **Export** tools. The specific tools for each Persona will be covered in full detail in *Chapter 6, Tools –Designer Persona, Chapter 7, Tools –Pixel Persona*, and *Chapter 8, Tools, Panels, and Process –Export Persona*. As with many interface elements in Affinity Designer, you can customize how or which of the tools for each persona are shown, and you can even change the order if you wish. We will discuss this in much more in detail in *Chapter 3, How to Customize Your Affinity Designer Workspace*.

Toolbars – overview

In the default interface layout, the toolbars are located directly below the menu bar as two horizontal bars containing commonly used options, settings, and functions depending on what Persona you are currently in, what is currently selected, and what tool is currently active. They consist of the Persona toolbar, the Toolbar, and the Context Toolbar.

Figure 1.22 – The Persona toolbar, the Toolbar, and the Context Toolbar

The Persona toolbar

As touched on earlier, the Persona toolbar allows you to select between the Designer, Pixel, and Export Persona workspaces. The ability to work in a dedicated vector, pixel, and export environment in one application is a definite advantage and is one of the strengths of this application. The seamless integration between Personas allows you to concentrate on creating instead of jumping in and out of different applications to achieve results. In some cases, the pairing of pixels and vectors together permits you to do things that are simply not available in other similar applications, such as pixel painting inside a vector shape with ease.

The type of project you are creating will determine which Persona you will want to work in. You will most likely be spending most of your time in the Designer Persona or the Vector Persona, which take advantage of Affinity Designer's excellent vector toolset. If you prefer more of a painting working style, you may spend more of your time in the Pixel Persona. If your work involves web design, UI/UX, or icon work, then chances are you'll be spending more time in the Export Persona. Generally, a combination of all three will come into play over the course of your work in Affinity Designer.

The Toolbar

Along with the Tools panel, the Toolbar just to the right of the Persona toolbar is full of settings and functions you will use consistently over the course of a project. Most or all of these options can also be assigned hotkeys. Here you will find the options outlined in the following sections.

Synchronize default settings

The ability to synchronize object defaults allows you to change your default stroke or fill. The first icon when selected will adopt the current selected object's stroke and fill. The second icon will revert to the application default.

Figure 1.23 – Synchronize default settings

Viewing modes

You are able to toggle your viewing mode from Pixel to Retina or Outline views. Pixel and Retina will display your vector artwork as pixels. This is handy when you want to see what your work will look like as pixels without having to export it. The Outline view will display all vector artwork as paths only, which is very handy when you need to see just the raw vector paths for precise adjustments.

Figure 1.24 – Viewing mode options

Order

Each object or element in Affinity Designer is placed on its own separate layer (layers are covered in detail in *Chapter 9, Workflow: Layers and Objects*). When an object is created or placed into your document, it can be positioned in front or behind an existing object, commonly referred to as the stacking order. The **Order** toolbar options allow you to reposition an element's stacking order or where it's positioned in relation to other objects' positions. To reposition an object, the object must be selected and more than one object can be repositioned at a time.

The options are as follows – left to right:

- **Move to back** – the selected object moves to the bottom of the layer stack.
- **Back one** – the selected object moves back one layer.
- **Forward one** – the selected object moves forward one layer.

- **Move to front** – the selected object moves to the front layer.

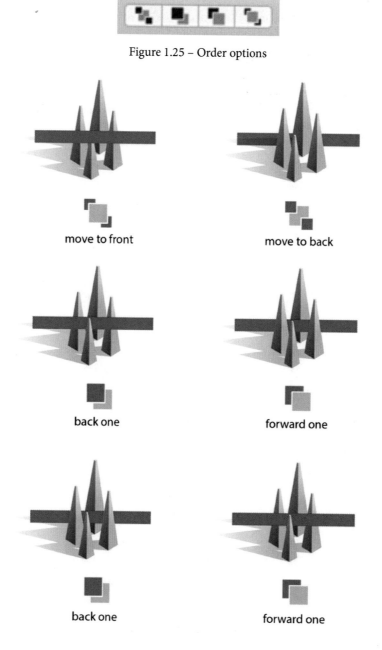

Figure 1.25 – Order options

move to front

move to back

back one

forward one

back one

forward one

Figure 1.26 – Order options show the pink rectangle moving front to back, backward, and forward

Transforms

These four options allow you to quickly transform a selected object or objects by flipping it horizontally, flipping it vertically, rotating it counter-clockwise, or rotating it clockwise.

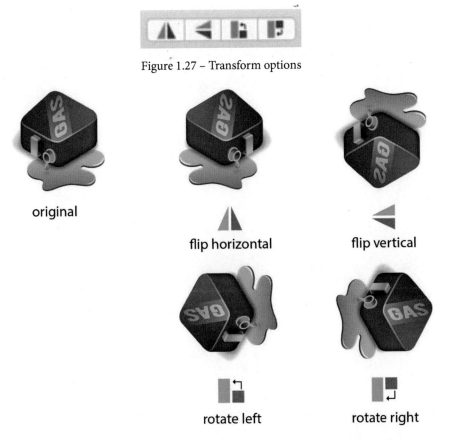

Figure 1.27 – Transform options

original

flip horizontal

flip vertical

rotate left

rotate right

Figure 1.28 – Transform options – flipping horizontally and vertically and rotating left and right

Document title

This is where your saved document title is located and the current zoomed view percentage. An asterisk will appear to the right if the file has not been saved.

My Document (100.0%)

Figure 1.29 – Document title

The next set of icons along the right of the Toolbar are **Distribute**, **Align**, and **Space**. They allow you to reposition multiple objects quickly and in predictable ways that might be difficult to achieve one at a time or only by sight. I encourage you to create and experiment with multiple shapes to really grasp these concepts.

Distribute

The options in this group of icons allow three or more selected objects to be distributed as follows – left to right:

- Left edges – the selected objects are distributed equally to the left.
- Horizontal centers – the selected objects are horizontally distributed centrally.
- Right edges – the selected objects are distributed equally to the right.
- Top edges – the selected objects are distributed equally to the top.
- Vertical centers – the selected objects are vertically distributed centrally.
- Bottom edges – the selected objects are distributed equally to the bottom.

Figure 1.30 – Distribute options

Align

The options in this group of icons allow two or more selected objects to be aligned as follows – left to right:

- Left edges – the selected objects are aligned to the left.
- Horizontal centers – the selected objects are horizontally aligned centrally.
- Right edges – the selected objects are aligned to the right.
- Top edges – the selected objects are aligned to the top.
- Vertical centers – the selected objects are vertically aligned centrally.
- Bottom edges – the selected objects are aligned to the bottom.

Figure 1.31 – Align options

In order to provide some clarity between the distribute and align functions, here are two instances of each that may help to visually explain how they are slightly different from one another. Compare the original element positions on the left to those on the right.

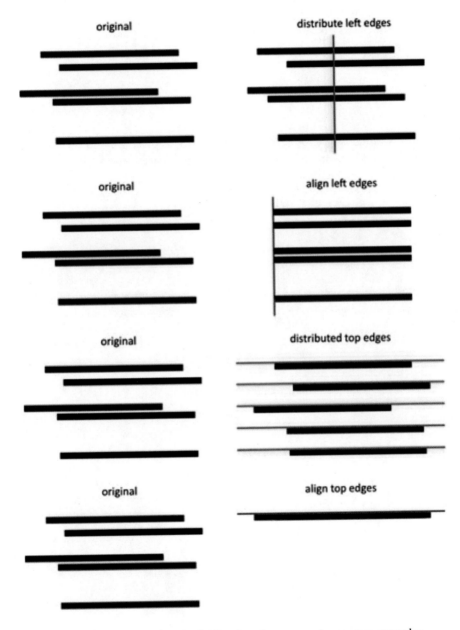

Figure 1.32 – Distribute and Align function comparisons – two examples

Spacing

These two options in the default Toolbar setup work similar to **Distribute Horizontal Centers** and **Distribute Vertical Centers** by adjusting the Vertical or Horizontal spacing between two or more selected objects.

Figure 1.33 – Spacing options

Snapping

Affinity Designer's robust and extensive snapping options come in handy when the type of work you are doing requires precise movement, sizing, or positioning. The options are as follows – left to right:

- **Force Pixel Alignment**: Snaps vector objects by full pixels as opposed to half pixels, when moving, creating, or editing.

- **Move by Whole Pixels**: Constrains the movement of objects, nodes, or vector handles to full pixels.

- **Snapping**: When enabled, objects will snap to the settings specified in the snapping drop-down panel. See *Figure 1.35* for the many options available.

Figure 1.34 – Snapping and pixel alignment options

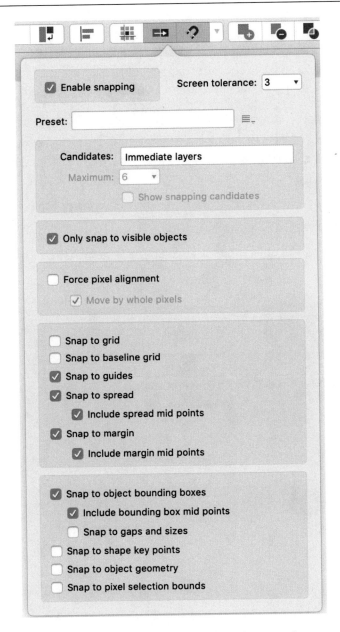

Figure 1.35 – Snapping options drop-down panel

Boolean operations

Affinity Designer offers a standard range of Boolean operations. These options allow you to combine, slice up, or make holes in overlapping objects in order to make new objects. See *Figure 1.37* for a simple visual depiction of Boolean operations. The options are as follows – left to right:

- **Add**: Objects are combined to make one new object.
- **Subtract**: The objects in front or higher in the stack will cut out the object on the bottom.
- **Intersect**: A new object is created where objects overlap or intersect.
- **Xor**: Creates holes in objects where two objects overlap.
- **Divide**: Slices up all objects into separate pieces where they overlap.

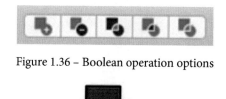

Figure 1.36 – Boolean operation options

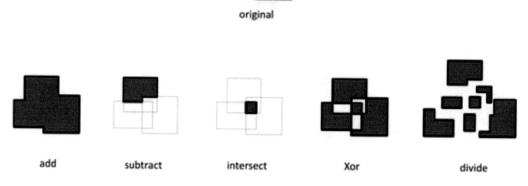

Figure 1.37 – Three objects displaying the Boolean operation options

Insert Target

Earlier, we discussed the stacking order and how we can re-order or re-arrange objects with the **Order** options in the Toolbar. With **Insert Target**, when you create a new object, it's possible to target where your new object will be placed in the stacking order or even whether you would like to nest that new object inside of another object. The options in *Figure 1.38* are as follows – left to right:

- **Insert behind selection**: Objects are placed behind the selected object when created.

- **Insert at the top of the layer**: Objects are placed at the top of the layer when created.

- **Insert inside selection**: Objects are placed inside the selected object when created.

Figure 1.38 – Insert Target options

My Account

This icon will open the **Register your App** splash screen. It allows you to register, or if you are already registered, it will allow you to sign in and offer you further options or app-related news.

Figure 1.39 – My Account link

With the Toolbar covered, let's take a look at Affinity Designer's Context Toolbar.

The Context Toolbar

The Context Toolbar sits just below the Toolbar and as its name implies, it displays options based on the context of whatever is selected. Text or shape options will differ from path or placed image options, for example. One thing to note: most of these options may be accessible in other panels as well, depending on what is selected.

The Context Toolbar is really just a convenient spot for quick access to the most commonly used options for the currently selected object and may not display all of the available options for each item. To access those, you will need to further navigate to the selected object's relevant panels or related menu items. For example, to add an *Effect* to a selected object, you will need to use the **Effects** panel.

In order to demonstrate the basic options presented by the Context Toolbar, I created a simple document with a variety of typical shapes you will likely use at one time or another inside of Affinity Designer. The document contains the word type, a couple of shapes, and an open path and a placed image.

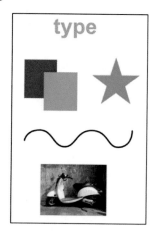

Figure 1.40 – Simple elements to demonstrate the Context Toolbar

Type options

When **type** is selected, the Context Toolbar editing options, available from left to right, are: font family, font weight and size, color, style – if applicable, paragraph justification, bullet or numbered listing options, line spacing or leading amount, and ligature information.

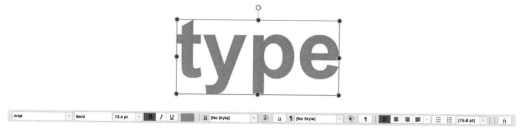

Figure 1.41 – type selected with type options in the Context Toolbar

Shape options

When a shape is selected, the editing options in the Context Toolbar, available from left to right, are: fill and stroke color; if it has a stroke or border, the stroke weight option will be available; for shapes that have corners like this rectangle, you will have options to have a single type of corner radius or different types for each corner, as well as size as a percentage of the overall shape's size or absolute-sized corners based on the measurement system you have set up (inches, centimeters, or pixels, and so on…). There are also options for the type of corner – **square**, **rounded**, **straight**, **concave**, or **cutout**. The next batch of icons from left to right are enable transform origins, hide selection while dragging, show alignment handles, transform objects separately, cycle selection box, and convert to curves.

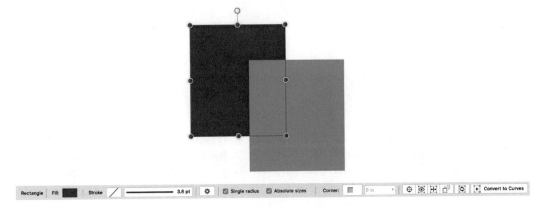

Figure 1.42 – A selected pink rectangular shape with options in the Context Toolbar

Some shapes will have special options depending on the underlying parametric structure of the shape. Refer to *Figure 1.21, the Tool Panels* for a look at the current lineup of Affinity Designer's 18 different parametric shapes in the Designer Persona. For example, the **Star Tool** options, from left to right, are fill and stroke color, stroke width, icon for different star shape presets dropdown, curved edges, number of points on the star, inner radius size, outer and inner circle sizes, the same transform icons from the previous rectangular shapes options, and convert to curves.

> **Convert to curves**
>
> Convert to curves will convert a Shape tool to its base curve paths, losing the ability to change some of the above options, such as the number of points on a star. Unless you absolutely need to edit the paths of a shape, it's usually best to not convert it to curves so you can go back at any time and make shape adjustments if you need to. However, if you want to create a custom shape based on a Shape tool, you will have to convert it first to have access to the base curve paths.

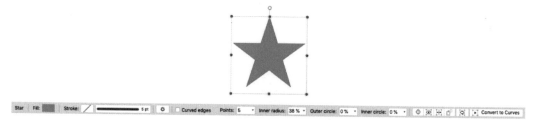

Figure 1.43 – A selected star shape with options in the Context Toolbar

Curve options

When a curve, also referred to as a path, is selected, the Context Toolbar displays the editing options available. Depending on whether you have used the Move tool (black arrow) from the Tools panel or the Node tool (white arrow), different options will present themselves.

With the Move tool, the options from left to right are fill and stroke color and stroke weight.

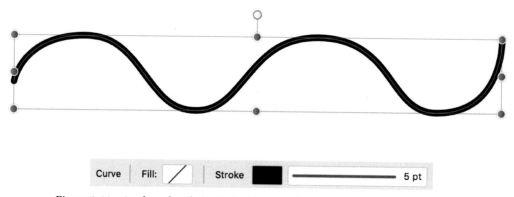

Figure 1.44 – A selected path (with the Move tool) options in the Context Toolbar

With the Node tool, the options from left to right are fill and stroke color and stroke weight, convert the node type (sharp, smooth, and smart), and actions options to edit the curve (break curve, close curve, smooth curve, join curves, and reverse curve). The final option is transform. If two or more nodes are selected and the transform node icon is selected, a transform widget will be activated and will allow you to edit the node's position and rotation independent of the unselected nodes.

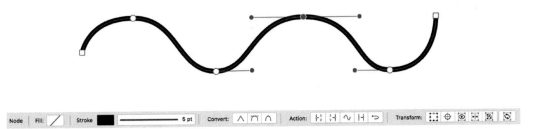

Figure 1.45 – A selected path (with the node tool) options in the Context Toolbar

Image options

When a placed image is selected, the Context Toolbar displays the image name, the image size, a button to replace the image, whether the image has a fill or a stroke, and if it has a stroke, there will be stroke options presented in the dropdown.

Figure 1.46 – A selected placed image with options in the Context Toolbar

Studio panels – overview

In the default interface layout, the studio panels are located on the right-hand side of the screen, in the area mentioned earlier called the **Right Studio**. They are stacked on top of one another with only their tabs displayed in the top row of the panels. *Figure 1.47* shows a view of the **Designer Persona Studio Panels**, which have been dragged out of the stack and arranged so we can get a look at them. Some of the panels shown here are **Color**, **Swatches**, **Text**, **History**, **Brushes**, **Layers**, **Effects**, and **Glyphs**.

In order to see a list of all of the studio panels available in a particular Persona, go to **View** and navigate to **Studio**, and in the flyout, you will see all of the available panels. The panels with a checkmark beside them are already onscreen and should be viewable unless they are hidden behind another panel. In which case, just select the top tab and it will pop to the front.

We will be taking a closer look at all of the studio panels and their options and functions in *Chapter 5*, *Main Studio Panels and Managers*.

As of the writing of this book, there are 26 panels in total over the 3 Personas.

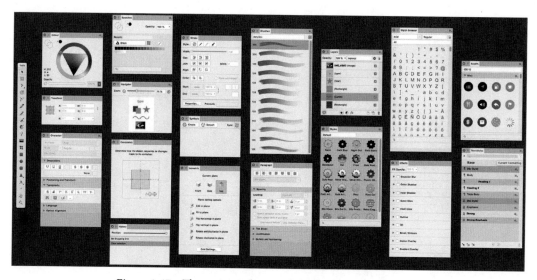

Figure 1.47 – The main studio panels in the Designer Persona

The document view and artboards – overview

The document view is the large central area where you will bring your artwork or designs to life. The document is surrounded by a pasteboard area where you can place elements or references you use over the course of a project that will not be printed or get exported in the final file. Additionally, elements that spill over the document view border into the pasteboard will be clipped at the edges and the areas that lie within the pasteboard will not appear in the printed or exported artwork. It's important to note that any elements that are in the pasteboard area will be saved in your file.

When setting up a new file, Affinity Designer gives you the option of a single-page document, as shown in *Figure 1.48*:

Figure 1.48 – Document view – a single-page document

Or if you prefer, you can set up your file to work with multiple "pages" called artboards, as shown in *Figure 1.49*:

Figure 1.49 – Artboards – a multiple artboard document with elements on the pasteboard

The type of work you do with Affinity Designer will determine whether you should work with single-page or multiple artboards. You can always start out with a single-page document and add artboards later if you wish.

The next three options are options that fall under what I like to call "design aids." They allow you to quickly reconfigure your interface to suit your needs as you work.

Toggle UI

Sometimes you just want to view your document uncluttered and without the UI. A fast way to hide all of the panels and tools is to press the *Tab* key. This will hide all of the UI except for the top menu bar and leave just your document's content. Pressing *Tab* again will unhide the UI. Toggle UI can also be found in the top menu bar, under **View** | **TOGGLE UI**, right down at the bottom of the **View** menu dropdown.

Figure 1.50 – Toggle UI – Document view with hidden UI tools and panels

New View

Affinity Designer allows you to have multiple views of the same file open in the same document. Imagine you are working in a zoomed-in area of your document but would also like to see the whole document in another window. This is possible with New View. Go to **View** | **NEW VIEW** to create a new view of your current document.

Window modes

So far, we have only shown the user interface in Normal mode. Affinity Designer also has Separated mode. In this mode, all of the toolbars and panels are basically floating on the screen. See *Figure 1.51*. This mode can be handy if you have two or more documents open and you want to see them all at the same time. Go to **Window | SEPARATED MODE**.

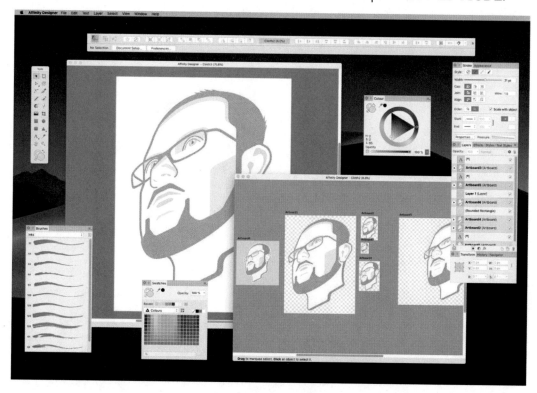

Figure 1.51 – Separated Mode – Document view with floating UI tools and panels

Next, we'll cover the basics of getting around in your document. The things you'll find yourself doing quite often and will soon become second nature.

Navigation tools – overview

Navigation involves moving around in your document by panning, zooming, and rotating.

Panning

To pan your view in a document, choose the move tool, which looks like a hand, second from the bottom in the Tools panel. The default shortcut for the move tool is *H*. This will select the hand tool. If you press *H* again it will toggle it off and revert to the previous tool you had selected. Another way to achieve this is to simply press and hold the spacebar, which is also a toggle shortcut for the Move tool. Once you let go, it will toggle you back to the previous tool. Alternatively, if you have the Navigator panel on the screen (**View | Studio | Navigator**), you can also click and drag within this panel to pan the view.

Figure 1.52 – View tool

Zooming

There are a few different methods to zoom in and out of your document in Affinity Designer. Through experimenting with each of these methods, you will find what works best for you. I generally use a combination of a few of them.

> **Fun fact**
> The makers of Affinity Designer state that zoom levels of 1,000,000% are possible with this application (!).

Zooming – the Zoom tool

To zoom the view of your document in or out choose the zoom tool, which looks like a magnifying glass and is located at the very bottom of the Tools panel. The default shortcut for the zoom tool is *Z*. This will select the zoom tool. If you press *Z* again, it will toggle it off and revert to the previous tool you had selected.

Figure 1.53 – Zoom tool

> **Power zoom**
>
> In general, when zooming in or out, you can either click once each time to
> zoom in or out in 50% increments or you can click, hold, and drag out an area
> to quickly zoom right into that specific spot. As you drag, a semi-transparent
> blue rectangle will show you the bounds of what will be zoomed in when you
> let go. This is much quicker than multiple clicking and fills the document view
> with the area you specifically zoomed in on. Note this clicking and dragging an
> area behavior only seems to work when zooming in. If you try it with the zoom
> out tool, it will continue to zoom in.

Zooming – keyboard shortcuts

By far, you'll most likely prefer keyboard shortcuts for zooming in and out as you will be
doing it repeatedly over the course of your time working in Affinity Designer and you'll
want to keep it as efficient as possible:

- **Zoom in/out**: With the zoom tool active, its default is to zoom in. You can
  temporarily zoom the view out by pressing and holding the *option* key (Mac) or *Alt*
  key (Windows).

- **Zoom in/out**: While any tool is active, you can temporarily enable zooming by
  pressing the spacebar plus the *command* key (Mac) or *Ctrl* key (Windows) to zoom
  in. Or, zoom out by adding the *option* key (Mac) or *Alt* key (Windows) to that key
  combination. Letting go of these keys will revert the tool to what it was.

- **Zoom in/out**: With the zoom tool active or inactive (in other words, at any time),
  the (Mac) *command* key plus the + sign or (Windows) the *Ctrl* key plus the + sign
  together will temporarily zoom in the view, while the *command* key (Mac) plus the
  – sign or *Ctrl* key (Windows) plus the – sign will temporarily zoom out the view.

- **Zoom to fit**: The *command* key plus *0+* or the *Ctrl* key (Windows) plus *0* will zoom
  in the view to include everything on the document or artboards.

- **Zoom to 100%**: The *command* key (Mac) plus *1+* or the *Ctrl* key (Windows) plus *1*.
  Depending on your document's unit settings (inches, pixels, and so on…), this will
  zoom in the view to where the document's size matches the screen pixels size.

- **Zoom to Selection**: The *command* key (Mac) plus the *option* key, plus *0+* or the *Ctrl*
  key (Windows) plus the *Alt* key, plus *0* will zoom your selection to fill the document
  view. If you are working with artboards, clicking on the artboards title in the
  document window, then choosing the Zoom to Selection method will center your
  artboard in the document window.

- **Zoom to Actual DPI Size**: The *command* key plus 8+ or the *Ctrl* key plus 8 will zoom your selection to the **DPI** (**dots per inch**) or print resolution set up in your document setup.

- **Zoom to Actual Pixel Size**: The *command* key plus 9+ or the *Ctrl* key (Windows) plus 9 will zoom your selection to the Pixel (pixels per inch) or pixel resolution set up in your document setup.

Zooming – mouse scroll wheel

Another way to zoom your view in and out is by using a mouse with a scroll wheel. This method can be fast as you don't have to click a shortcut key or the zoom tool in the **Tools** panel. To do this, you must have the **Use mouse wheel to zoom** option checked in **Preferences | Tools**. See *Figure 1.54*:

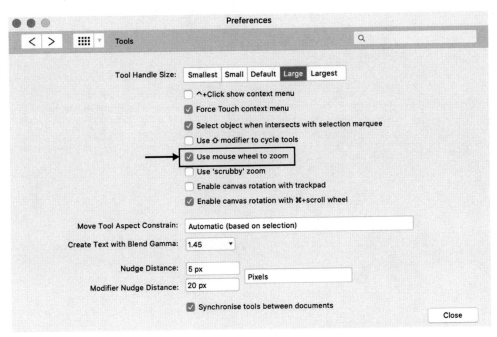

Figure 1.54 – Preferences panel – mouse wheel zoom enabled

As with the zoom tool methods described above, zooming occurs from your mouse position. In other words, wherever your cursor is located in the document view, Affinity Designer will use this location to zoom in or out from.

Zooming – 'scrubby' zoom

Another way to zoom your view in and out is by enabling **'scrubby' zoom** in **Preferences | Tools**. Scrubby zoom gets its name from the movement of panning or "scrubbing" your cursor left and right with the zoom tool active or temporarily enabled by the various methods described previously. Scrubbing left zooms out and scrubbing right zooms in. One thing to note with this method is that you will no longer be able to **Power Zoom** as described earlier in the callout as this **'scrubby'** method overrides the ability to drag out a rectangular area to zoom in on. See *Figure 1.55*:

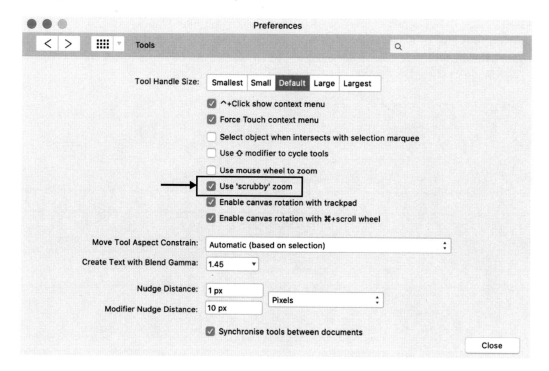

Figure 1.55 – Preferences panel – 'scrubby' zoom enabled

Zooming – the Context toolbar

In the context toolbar, there is a field that indicates the current zoom level of your document in percentage points. Entering your desired zoom level here is another way to zoom in and out.

Figure 1.56 – Context Toolbar zoom level

Zooming – the Navigator panel

Finally, the Navigator panel, which we haven't talked about yet, is another way to zoom your document view in and out. Go to **View** | **Studio** | **Navigator**. There is a slider at the top of the panel that starts at a zoom level of 1% and goes up to 1,000%. It can go higher if you click the + button on the right side.

Another great feature of the Navigator panel is the document thumbnail view, which gives you not only great visual feedback on the zoom level but when you're really zoomed in, it allows you to navigate or pan your document without having to zoom back out to see where things are located. You can stay at the current zoom level and get to other areas of your document while still zoomed in. The transparent gray rectangle in the document thumbnail indicates the position and size of the main document window.

Figure 1.57 – The main document window and the Navigator panel

Rotating

One of the great things about using Affinity Designer is the ability to rotate a document. This allows a more organic workflow similar to working with pencil and paper, especially when painting or freehand sketching in the Pixel Persona using a tablet or a pen display.

Rotating – menu/shortcut

To rotate a document, go to **View** | **ROTATE LEFT** or **ROTATE RIGHT**. This will rotate your document in 15-degree increments. Just below is the option to reset the rotation. If you find you are rotating your work on a regular basis, I would highly recommend you set keyboard shortcuts for each of these options for more enjoyable and efficient work sessions.

Rotating – scroll wheel

Another way to rotate a document is to use your mouse scroll wheel and the *command* key (Mac) or the *Alt* key (Windows) to rotate the document around the mouse location. Adding *Shift* will rotate around the document's center.

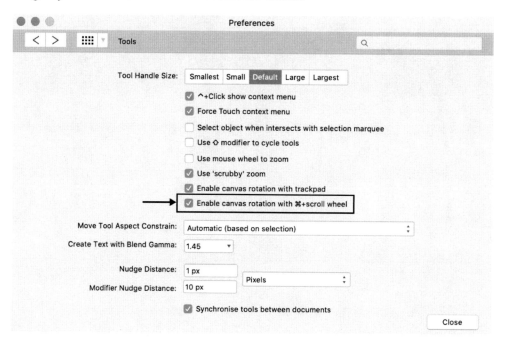

Figure 1.58 – Preferences panel – enable canvas rotation with the command key and scroll wheel enabled

The result looks like this:

Figure 1.59 – A rotated document

Summary

In this chapter, we've become familiar with Affinity Designer's default interface and touched on many key components of the software that we will continue to explore in more depth in the upcoming chapters. We explored the layout, tools, toolbars, and studio panels. We learned about the document view and how to navigate, zoom, pan, rotate, and generally get around in the application. In short, the knowledge acquired in this chapter will set you on a path of further exploration in the chapters to come and give you the familiarity and confidence to dig a little deeper into what Affinity Designer has to offer.

In the next chapter, we'll be looking at Affinity Designer's three Personas – **Designer**, **Pixel**, and **Export**, and see just what makes them so unique and powerful. We'll discuss the difference between vector and raster artwork, and finally, we'll have a look at options to export our artwork out of Affinity Designer.

2
Getting Familiar with the Three Personas of Affinity Designer

Welcome to the second chapter of *Up and Running with Affinity Designer*.

Affinity Designer has the unique ability to work both in vector and raster environments in one application. In this chapter, you will be introduced to Affinity Designer's unique concept of **Personas**. Almost like having three different applications in one, each Persona offers its own distinct set of tools and workflow. The goal of this chapter is to provide an overview of the three Personas and their general uses. We will cover the specific tools and panels of each Persona in more depth in subsequent chapters. Here, we'll touch on the basic differences and advantages of the Designer and Pixel Personas and when you should choose one over the other, or use a combination of both, in your projects. We'll also take a look at the Export Persona and its unique features for exporting your artwork out of Affinity Designer.

In this chapter, we're going to cover the following main topics:

- Vector and raster – the power behind the Personas

- Designer Persona overview

- Pixel Persona overview

- Export Persona overview

Vector and Raster – the power behind the Personas

Affinity Designer has the unique ability to work both in vector and raster formats. But why is this a big deal, and what are the advantages over other similar drawing applications that don't have this ability? Well, to start off with and to help provide a bit of a foundation for what we're going to discuss, let's take a quick look at the main differences between vector and raster art.

In short, vector art is art that comprises or is derived from bezier curves or paths, which are themselves based on a mathematical grid. Because they are built upon math, they can be resized or repositioned and will be recalculated to retain their appearance. Because of this, vector art is called resolution independent, meaning art created entirely of vector information can be scaled up or down without any loss in clarity or sharpness. This is ideal for logo design or specific types of projects that need to retain their sharpness at any size.

Raster art on the other hand is based on a horizontal and vertical grid of square pixels, and those pixels are of a certain fixed size. This means that they are resolution dependent. If you have ever zoomed in close on a pixel-based photograph, for example, you'll notice that the closer you zoom in, the fuzzier the image appears, because you are seeing the individual pixels that make up the image. If you resize a pixel-based image up or down, all of the image's pixels are reassigned, and this degrades the image because each pixel is being reassigned at a different size and you are losing resolution. Generally, scaling artwork up in size is worse than scaling down. The key to getting good results with raster images is having enough resolution (**ppi**, or **pixels per inch**) to achieve the outcome you need. For online or screen usage, a resolution of 72 to 144 ppi is acceptable. For artwork that will be printed, you'll want between 300 to 600 ppi, with some specialty printers needing an even higher resolution.

Also, curved edges of shapes that are raster based may appear jagged, depending on the resolution, because square pixels are being used to attempt creating round edges, as shown in the following screenshot:

Figure 2.1 – The vector (left) is smooth, while the raster (right) is jagged

So why isn't everyone using vector art instead of pixel based art? Because there are advantages to using pixel based art that vector art's sharp resolution independent nature can't easily achieve. Soft transitions, realistic shading, and naturalistic styles of art are what raster images excel at. This is why photographs are always in raster form, or pixel based. It's capable of all of the subtleties and nuances, highlights, and shadows required to trick our eye.

For our own practical purposes in Affinity Designer, we can take advantage of both vector and raster benefits, as shown in *Figure 2.2*:

Figure 2.2 – Vector and raster art used in the same illustration

This illustration uses both vector and raster techniques and displays the basic differences and the advantages of having the ability to partner up using both in one application. I've circled a couple of areas in the preceding illustration. The left circle is an area of detail showing nice clean vector work as seen in *Figure 2.3*:

Figure 2.3 – Clean and sharp vector art using the Designer Persona

The right circle indicates an area where the painting features of the Pixel Persona really shine as seen in *Figure 2.4*:

Figure 2.4 – Soft values with subtle, textural shaded raster art using the Pixel Persona

This is a great example of why Affinity Designer makes a good choice for digital artists. It gives you the option of both a vector- and a raster-based workflow, which is creatively liberating. You get control and precision alongside rich artistic expression.

To take another look at the illustration to see what's really going on here, I switched to what Affinity Designer calls outline mode and took this next screenshot. To activate Outline Mode, go to **VIEW | VIEW MODE | OUTLINE** or press *Command + Y* (Mac) or *Ctrl + Y* (PC). This changes the display to paths only. In our case, because there are both vector paths and raster art, we see the vector paths and a series of box shapes. The box shapes are the raster painting areas defined by rectangular areas that denote those pixel grids we discussed earlier. As every raster image is made up of pixels in a grid, in this outline view we are presented with their pixel grid boundaries. As you can see, there is more raster work there than there appeared to be at first glance. Outline mode is great when you need to view your work in its simplest form without color or effects:

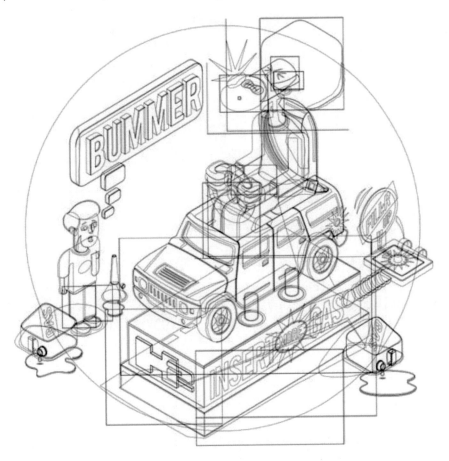

Figure 2.5 – Outline mode

Another view mode is the split view mode, **VIEW | VIEW MODE | SPLIT VIEW**. This view mode presents you with a view of your work with a vertical sliding divider that can be moved to show two simultaneous views that you set up by selecting the appropriate option in the dropdown:

Figure 2.6 – Split view mode

Separate but equal

Affinity Designer is able to achieve a seamless vector and pixel working environment by creating separate layers for each. Every vector object you create exists in its own vector layer, and all pixel-based art resides in its own pixel layer. We will discuss layers in more depth in *Chapter 9, Workflow: Layers and Objects*, but for now just keep in mind that Affinity Designer organizes each element automatically in the layers panel based on what Persona you are currently using.

The type of work you will be creating will, to a degree, dictate how much vector or raster artwork you'll be creating. For example, my workflow is roughly 80% vector or Designer Persona with the remaining 20% as raster or Pixel Persona in the form of shading or texturing.

The best way to explain each of Affinity Designer's Personas would be to actually use them, and that's exactly what we'll be doing a bit later in the book. Before then, however, it's a good idea to just have a quick look at the basic concepts behind each Persona. In the next few pages, we'll discuss some of the characteristics of each Persona and why we might want to use one or the other over the course of our projects, beginning with the Designer Persona.

Designer Persona – embracing the control and precision of a powerful vector workflow

Affinity Designer's main or default Persona is the Designer Persona. It's the Persona you will see when you first open up the application. It's the Persona where you will create and edit all of your vector artwork. The tools and options presented in this Persona are geared toward a drawing-based workflow, and these vector tools and options are only available in the Designer Persona:

Figure 2.7 – Designer Persona icon in the toolbar

Designer Persona workflow

Unless you're strictly creating a raster painting piece, the chances are the Designer Persona is the place where you'll start creating most of your project's basic shapes and elements. The toolset includes a variety of creation and editing options for just about any shape you can think of. This is also where you can add or remove artboards or place an external image or a sketch to aid in the creation of an illustration. If your project contains any kind of text, the Designer Persona is where you'll add, edit, and adjust it. The Designer Persona also has a variety of vector brushes and vector brush tools for vector-style painting. This is not the same as pixel brush painting, but we'll discuss that in much more depth in *Chapter 6, Tools – Designer Persona.*

For an example of the uses of both the Designer and Pixel Personas in practice, let's take a quick look at an actual project I created entitled George and the Dragon.

I started it off as I do with all of my work, developing a detailed sketch based on a fair amount of research and preparation. See a portion of that sketch in *Figure 2.8*:

Figure 2.8 – Designer Persona workflow. Placing a sketch to use as a guide

I then take that sketch, scan it, and place it into my Affinity Designer document. In the Designer Persona, I start to build each shape using the Designer Personas vector toolset using the sketch as my guide as seen in *Figure 2.9*:

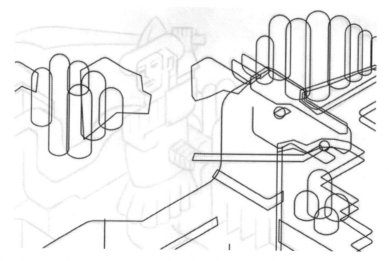

Figure 2.9 – Designer Persona workflow. Building vector shapes based on the sketch

I use a bright color, usually Magenta, to draw my paths so I can see my work as I progress standing out from the sketch, and also, as I start to color in my shapes as seen in *Figure 2.10*. The bright colored paths help me to see what I still need to do:

Figure 2.10 – Designer Persona workflow. Applying flat base color to the vector shapes

It must be said that the Designer Persona alone can achieve much more beyond the path creation and flat coloring we're seeing here. In later chapters, we'll fully explore its unique methods and features for shading with gradients and effects, but for now, let's take a look at the Pixel Persona's role and how it complements the Designer Persona's vector workflow.

Pixel Persona – expanding your creative options with a built-in raster studio

Affinity Designer's second Persona is the Pixel Persona. If the Designer Persona can be thought of as the analytical side of the brain, then the Pixel Persona is surely the artistic side. The Pixel Persona reigns supreme over all things raster based. With its wide assortment of paintbrushes and adjustment tools, the Pixel Persona is where you will add more painterly and textural effects. Its tools are specifically designed for pixel selection, painting, and manipulation:

Figure 2.11 – The Pixel Persona icon in the toolbar

Pixel Persona workflow

This Persona, as hinted at in the heading, is where you can expand or enhance your art to the next level. While the inherent, precise quality of vector art has been accused occasionally as being sterile or stale in its mathematical preciseness, raster art on the other hand has garnered more of an artistic reputation. Fortunately for us, it has never been easier to add these rich aesthetic qualities to your artwork using Affinity Designer's Pixel Persona. While you can, of course, create a piece entirely within the Pixel Persona, you'll most likely be using a combination of the Designer and Pixel Personas.

Continuing with our George and the Dragon illustration example, here we see that the pixel painting shading and highlighting stage has transformed the flat color of the previous step into much more dimensionally shaded objects. Of course, it really depends on you and how far you want to take the shading. For this piece, I was going for a pretty rich feel with lots of depth, and Affinity Designer's Pixel Persona did not let me down. *Figure 2.10* shows the final stage before shading for this piece, with the culmination of all of the drawing and application of flat color in Designer Persona, before going on to a full shading workflow in Pixel Persona. *Figures 2.12* and *2.13* feature the final painting work as well as some key details added in the Designer Persona, specifically the sharp line work helping to define the metal armor:

Figure 2.12 – Pixel Persona workflow. Adding shading/texturing to the vector shapes

The painted shading and highlighting perfectly captures the nice stylized suit of armor feel I was aiming for, as shown in *Figure 2.13*:

Figure 2.13 – Pixel Persona workflow. Pixel painted shading and detailing closer view

I don't think this kind of look would be easily achievable in either the vector or Pixel Personas alone. The following image shows the finished piece, including the dragon:

Figure 2.14 – Pixel Persona workflow. The finished piece, all pixel painted shading

This is a good example of why the Designer and Pixel Personas are such a great team and why Affinity Designer is a standout application in this regard compared to what's currently out there for this kind of work.

Before moving onto the Export Persona, I think I would be remiss if I didn't mention the Pixel Persona's robust color and tonal adjustment tools. Personally, I don't use them very often over the course of my illustration work, but when I do need them I'm glad they are there. They include tools to lighten, darken, blur, and sharpen pixels. Along with the excellent painting features we just touched on, having these adjustment tools is like having a separate photo manipulation suite inside a vector application. We'll look closer at the Pixel Personas tools in *Chapter 7, Tools – Pixel Persona*.

Export Persona – a dedicated exporting environment

When it is time to export your artwork out of Affinity Designer, there are two options available:

- Normal exporting: Using the **FILE | EXPORT** option

- Export Persona: A dedicated Persona with a suite of features and options for exporting single or multiple items with precise control

Normal exporting

Despite having a specific Persona designed exclusively for exporting, you don't have to be in the Export Persona to export your artwork from Affinity Designer. You can also export your art directly from Designer or Pixel Persona by simply going to **FILE | EXPORT**. This is what I use most as I generally just export one full illustration at a time, and these simple export options are ideal for that:

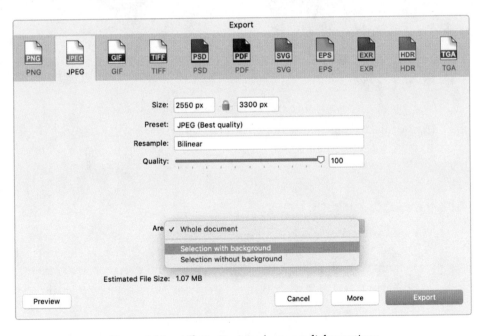

Figure 2.15 – Affinity Designer's export dialog options

The options here, as shown in the *Figure 2.15* allow for a host of output file formats, as well as the option to export the whole document or just the current selection with or without a background, as shown in *Figure 2.16*:

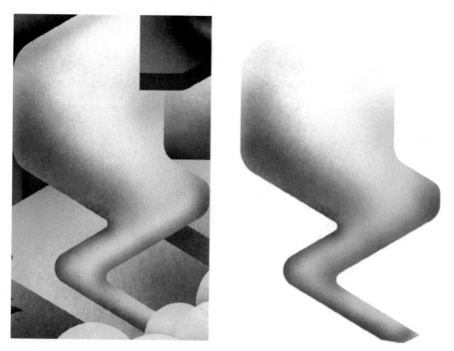

Figure 2.16 – Exporting a selection with and without a background

In *Figure 2.16*, the selected part of the document (the horses leg) will be exported with a white background because it is a JPEG. If you need a transparent background for your export, use the PNG format.

Export Persona workflow

If, however, you find yourself working with multiple artboards or multiple objects that you need to export as separate files (projects such as icons, UX or UI elements, or logos that may contain several different logo options or several different sizes), then the Export Persona will soon become your preferred choice of getting your work out of Affinity Designer:

Figure 2.17 – Export Persona icon in the toolbar

The Export Persona is ideally designed for exporting multiple objects, or slices as they are called in this Persona. As with all of the Personas, the Export Persona comes with its own unique toolset and panels specifically designed for exporting. We will be looking at the specific workflow of this Persona in *Chapter 8, Tools, Panels and Process – Export Persona*.

Until then, and as an overview introduction and to demonstrate the Export Persona basic concept, I created an example file (*Figure 2.18*) with a few different objects in it to explain visually how you can use the Export Persona to export similar types of files. In addition to my corporate face logo in different sizes and colors, I've also dragged out a few of the assets that come included with Affinity Designer and can be found in the Designer Persona via **VIEW | STUDIO | ASSETS**.

Figure 2.18 – Example file showing multiple objects to be exported

The Export Persona is a very advanced yet user-friendly exporting environment that allows you to select each separate object and export them as slices either manually or automatically in 1x, 2x, 3x retina, and other sizes, in many different industry-standard formats, to different file paths on your computer, with tags and/or slice names, as Xcode JSON files, with custom DPI sizes, and either all exported simultaneously or separately with the click of one button. You can also copy presets and settings from one slice and apply to them another completely different slice. The settings are varied and powerful.

Figure 2.19 shows the document objects ready for export alongside the Export Persona's Slices panel:

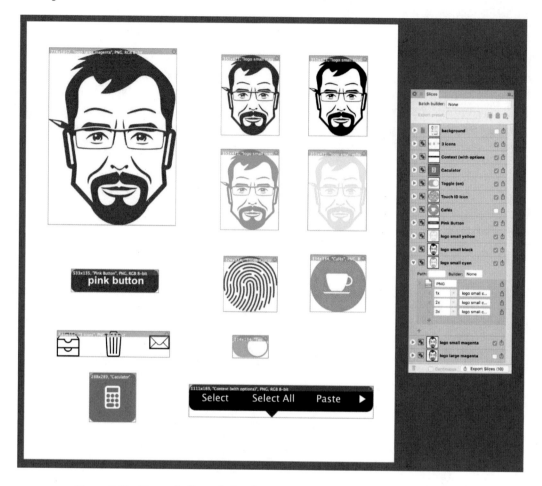

Figure 2.19 – Example file with the Slices panel and the objects set up for export

Hopefully, this brief look at the Export Persona and Affinity Designer's exporting options in general has given you some idea of what you can expect from this application when exporting your artwork. Whether you work with single documents, as I do, or many artboards with scores of separate elements, Affinity Designer's got you covered when it comes to exporting.

Summary

In this chapter, we began by discussing the concepts of vector and raster art and the differences and unique characteristics of each and where to use them. We talked about how this is related to Affinity Designer's workflow with the introduction to Personas. We explored the differences between the Designer and Pixel Personas while covering the advantages of each and the working relationship between them. With visual examples, we got a sense of the workflow from vector drawing to pixel painting, and we talked a little bit about the Pixel Persona's tonal adjustment features beyond its painting abilities. Finally, we learned a couple of ways to export your work from Affinity Designer with an introduction to the Export Persona and why it's best suited for exporting multiple objects.

In the next chapter, we'll be looking at customizing your Affinity Designer experience. We'll cover preferences, keyboard shortcuts, and workspace, tool, and toolbar customization options.

3

How to Customize Your Affinity Designer Workspace

Welcome to the third chapter of *Up and Running with Affinity Designer*.

As you get more familiar with Affinity Designer, you may find instances where you will want to make adjustments to parts of the interface, assign keyboard shortcuts, or just generally set things up to personalize your experience a little bit more to suit your personal working style. We'll cover setting/changing application preferences, customizing the workspace, and how to access and tailor keyboard shortcuts to suit your personal working style.

In this chapter, we're going to take a look at the following main topics:

- Affinity Designer preferences

- Keyboard shortcuts – a closer look

- Workspace customization – Studio panels

- Workspace customization – the Tools panel and Toolbar

- The Clip to Canvas feature

Affinity Designer preferences

Affinity Designer has many ways for you to make the application both feel better and work better for you. You may be coming from another similar type of software and want to ease that transition by assigning familiar keyboard shortcuts. Or perhaps there is a certain workspace layout that enables you to work faster or more efficiently. In any case, Affinity Designer is well equipped to let you customize your user experience.

To locate Affinity Designer's application preferences, go to **Affinity Designer | Preferences** on a Mac or **Edit | Preferences** on a PC. Here, you will find a panel with eight separate areas to be able to make adjustments to.

We won't cover each and every preference here as there are far too many and some are truly best explored on your own. Following the list here, we will help you take a closer look at those that are most relevant to get you up and running with the application. This includes certain preferences that shouldn't be missed and will come in handy throughout the course of the lessons in this book and hopefully will make it a little easier for you to get up to speed with the application. Admittedly, throughout my time using Affinity Designer, I have left a lot of these preferences as the application defaults, but there are a few that are important for our workflow and I will point them out to you here when we come across them in subsequent chapters.

The Preferences panel – at a glance

At a glance, the **Preferences** panel includes the following sections:

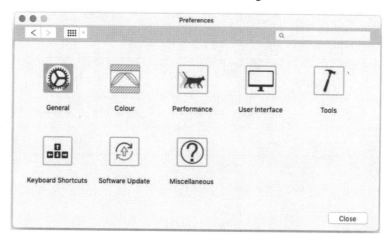

Figure 3.1 – The Preferences panel

- **General**: General options such as file extensions, thumbnail creation, copying to the clipboard as SVG, and language preferences.

- **Color**: Select your color defaults. Choose from **RGB**, **CMYK**, **Greyscale**, and **Lab Color** profiles, as well as many more color adjustments.

- **Performance**: Optimize performance by adjusting the RAM usage, undo limit, hardware acceleration display, view quality, gradient dither, and clipping options.

- **User Interface**: Set UI options such as background and artboard background gray levels, UI gamma and font size, brush cursor display, icon color, and layer panel object selection display.

- **Tools**: Options to control tool behavior such as tool handle size, use of *Ctrl* + click to display the context menu, force touch options, marquee selection behavior, zooming options behavior, trackpad rotation, and nudge distance adjustment.

- **Keyboard Shortcuts**: Options to assign or change keyboard shortcuts.

- **Software Update**: Set a schedule for the application to check for updates.

- **Miscellaneous**: Reset factory defaults for various application options.

As stated earlier, there are a lot of preferences that I leave alone or in their default settings. In the following sections, we won't be going over each and every preference; rather, I will point out which preferences you may want to adjust or be aware of that have become part of my setup and will come in handy for our workflow. Of course, feel free to make your own adjustments as you learn more about Affinity Designer. After all, that is the whole point of the preferences, setting up the application to work for you.

General preferences

See *Figure 3.2* for my **General** settings:

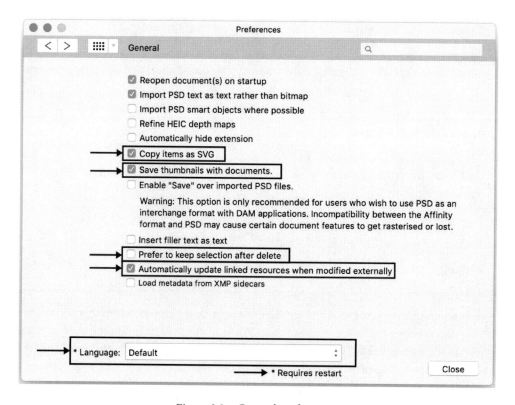

Figure 3.2 – General preferences

The settings of note here are the following:

- **Copy items as SVG**: This means that when you copy vector elements to the clipboard, they are copied in **SVG (Scalable Vector Graphics)** format, enabling the ability to paste into other applications that support SVG.

- **Save thumbnails with documents**: This will assign a document thumbnail to your document, allowing for a quick visual representation of your file in the finder or desktop.

- **Prefer to keep selection after delete**: I deselected this option. If this is selected, when you delete an object in your document, the previous object created in the document history will then get selected. I have accidentally deleted objects with this option on.

- **Automatically update linked resources when modified externally**: This will update any images or resources you have linked in your document if you modify them outside of Affinity Designer. This won't affect embedded images or resources.

- **Language**: For me, it just happens to be **Default**. If you change this to any other language, as indicated by the asterisk, you will need to restart the application to enable it.

Color preferences

As you can tell by the **Color** panel shown in *Figure 3.3*, the options can be quite varied and cover a lot of technical aspects of color profiles, conversions, and configurations. Here are my **Color** settings:

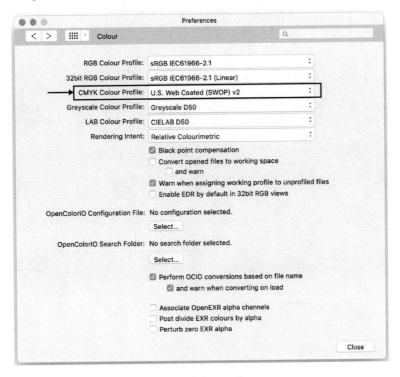

Figure 3.3 – Color preferences

Serious color profile discussion is a deep and wide topic and there are plenty of articles online if you want to know what each of these options refers to. Fortunately, for our purposes, what we need to get up and running is basically ready to go using the application defaults. If you do need a bit more info on these color preferences, you can go to **Help | Affinity Designer Help**, then navigate to the **Extras** flyout (the very last in the list) and click on **Preferences | Color options**.

Affinity Designer Help and Affinity Online Forums

The Affinity Designer Help menu is a great resource that basically covers everything the application has to offer. If you're curious to dig a little deeper into any aspect of the application, the help menu is a great place to start.

For even more resources, the online Affinity forums at `https://forum.affinity.serif.com` are also a great place to learn more about the application, including Affinity Photo and Affinity Publisher. Here, you can ask support questions, read about the latest news and information, discuss new or upcoming features, and view other users' artwork for inspiration.

The only option that I will point out here is the option that pertains to **CMYK** (**cyan, magenta, yellow, and black**), otherwise known as four-color printing. I am in North America so my **CMYK Color Profile** option is set to **U.S. Web Coated (SWOP) v2**; you may need to adjust your CMYK preference depending on where you are located or where you will be sending your files for printing, if applicable.

Performance preferences

When it comes to the **Performance** preferences, there are three in particular that I have discovered to be fairly important. Here are my **Performance** settings:

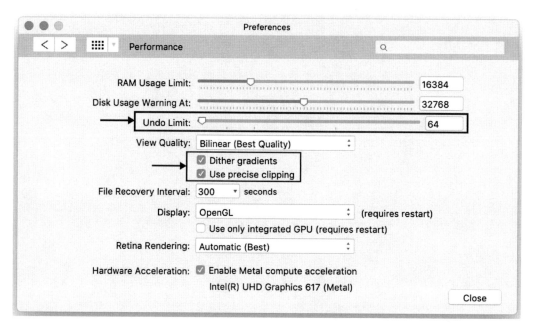

Figure 3.4 – Performance preferences

- **Undo Limit**: This is how many undos you will be able to go back to. Put another way, it's how far back in your document history you will be able to return to. The higher the number, the farther back you can go, but also the more memory your computer will need to store. The default is **1024**, which seems to me to be a bit high. I keep mine at around **64** or **100** and have never had a problem with not being able to undo. Actually, I don't think I have ever had to undo more than 10 or 15 times in a row, so 64 should be more than safe.

- Two other settings that I have highlighted are **Dither gradients** and **Use precise clipping**. Both of these are related to your document's screen preview or how things look onscreen. **Dither gradients** enables any gradients you may have in your document to appear smooth and without any banding. **Use precise clipping** keeps the edges of any clipped artwork nice and smooth.

We will discuss gradients in *Chapter 6, Tools – Designer Persona*, and clipping in *Chapter 9, Workflow: Layers and Objects*, but trust me, you're going to probably want to have these options turned on. They are in the **Performance** preferences panel because they do use up a bit of memory and if they are unchecked may give you a performance boost, especially if you have a fairly complex piece you are working on. That said, I have never experienced any noticeable slowdowns with any of my work with these two options turned on.

User Interface preferences

We have covered a couple of items in the **User Interface** preferences in *Chapter 1, Getting Familiar with Affinity Designer's Interface*, but it's good to remind you of them here again as you may find yourself making changes to this panel of user preferences more often than the others. Again, I am just pointing out the options I think are the most relevant.

Here are my **User Interface** settings:

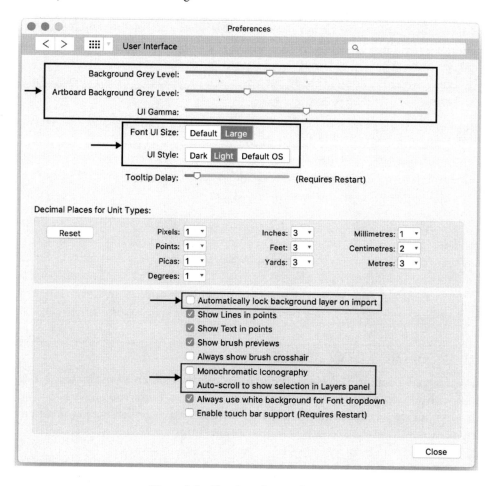

Figure 3.5 – User Interface preferences

In *Figure 3.5*, starting at the top, the first highlighted area refers to the options for the background behind or surrounding your document page. These allow you to lighten or darken the background areas. The only difference between the two is that the first **Background Grey Level** option relates to a file that is a single-page document and does not contain any artboards and the second **Artboard Background Grey Level** option relates to a document that contains artboards. I'm not sure why these are separated out like this as they are technically both backgrounds and should require only one "background" adjustment.

UI Gamma adjusts the lightness or darkness of the UI toolbar and panel backgrounds.

Font UI Size adjusts the size of the UI font. I prefer it to be set to **Large**.

UI Style is where you can choose the **Dark** or **Light** theme. **Default OS** is the light option on my computer. I normally use the **Dark** theme but have chosen **Light** for the book for better readability for the screenshots.

Skipping the next highlighted area for a moment and moving down to the bottom two areas, **Monochromatic Iconography** will change all of your UI icons from color to black and white.

Auto-scroll to show selection in Layers panel can be a very handy option to enable. When an element is selected in your document, this will dynamically select and show it in the Layers panel. If you have a Layers panel that contains hundreds of items, this can save you time if you need to perform any tasks with the selected element's layer. I have it disabled as I found the constant movement in my Layers panel as I selected objects over the course of a project to be a bit distracting. So, I assigned a keyboard shortcut to do the same thing (*f* for find) and now I get access to the feature only when I want it. We will cover keyboard shortcuts later in this chapter.

Going back now to the highlighted **Automatically lock background layer on import** box, I don't have this checked because I've never needed to use it, but basically it's a bit of a misnomer and is somewhat confusing the way it's written, and I wanted to point that out. Affinity Designer doesn't have an import function, or at least there isn't an import menu item. You can place images but you can't import them. So, what does this option mean then? It means that if you open an image from Affinity Designer or you drag an image to your Affinity Designer application icon to open it, this gives you the option of locking that image on its own layer or not; they are referring to it here as a "background layer." The idea is that you can have the option of working over the top of the image on a new layer. If you do a lot of work that requires that sort of workflow, then this might be something you would be interested in enabling. I thought it was worth mentioning as it was not immediately obvious to me at first glance just what this option does.

Tools preferences

Located here are a few items you may want to change from time to time. Here are my four **Tools** settings:

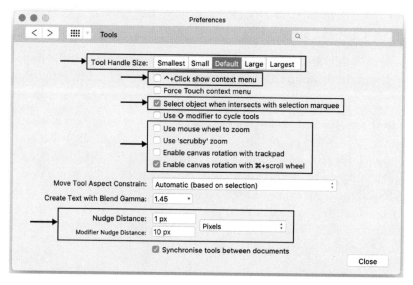

Figure 3.6 – Tools preferences

In *Figure 3.6*, starting from the top down, we first have **Tool Handle Size**. I keep mine at the default middle for the most part. The following are examples of a shape and a path curve showing the differences between the smallest and largest tool handle sizes:

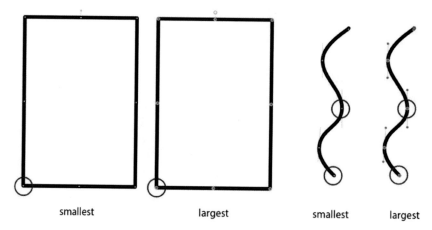

Figure 3.7 – Tool handle sizes

Just below the **Tool Handle Size** options is a macOS-specific option. If you have a mouse with only one button, then you can enable this *Ctrl* + click to show the context menu option to access the context menu for whatever is selected. I use a three-button mouse with a scroll wheel so I have this option deselected.

Select object when intersects with selection marquee allows you to not have to completely surround an object or objects to select them when using a marquee selection. A marquee selection is when you click and drag a selection rectangle over an object to select it as opposed to simply clicking on it. It's used mostly to quickly select multiple objects at once. This option allows use you to just touch an object or objects as opposed to having to completely surround all of the objects you want to select. It's pretty handy to enable.

The next four options deal with zooming and rotating, a subject we covered thoroughly in *Chapter 1, Getting Familiar with Affinity Designer's Interface,* but I thought they were worth highlighting again here in the preferences section.

Finally, the last two areas to look at here are the nudge distances. As their names suggest, these settings allow you to input the distance that you can "nudge" an object with your keyboard's left, right, up, and down arrow keys. These measurements can be set in a variety of units; I have mine set to pixels.

Miscellaneous preferences

The **Miscellaneous** preferences currently are for resetting to the application or factory defaults for a few different options:

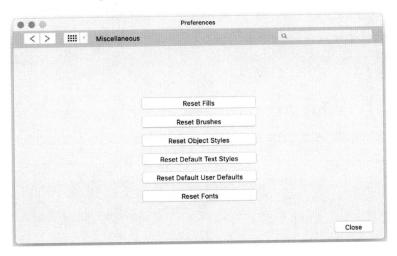

Figure 3.8 – Miscellaneous preferences

This next section will likely affect your workflow like no other. Keyboard shortcuts have the power of becoming part of your muscle memory when used repeatedly throughout your time in Affinity Designer. As in any application, the sooner you start learning and using them, the quicker you will see yourself gaining confidence and efficiency in your work.

Keyboard shortcuts – a closer look

Keyboard shortcuts play a crucial role in any application's workflow and Affinity Designer is well equipped to offer you a great deal of control over how you assign your shortcuts. If you are coming from another application and would like to reassign Affinity Designer's shortcuts to match shortcuts either the same or similar to your previous app, the **Keyboard Shortcuts** panel is where you can do that:

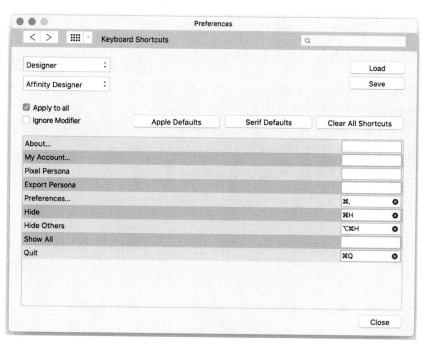

Figure 3.9 – Keyboard Shortcuts preferences

The panel is laid out in such a way that it allows you to choose the area you would like to adjust via drop-down menus on the left side.

If you recall the first chapter, the concept of Affinity Designer's personas is like having three different applications in one. So, instead of just having one set of keyboard shortcuts, we really have three sets, one set for each Persona. This is something to be aware of when assigning or editing your shortcuts. You need to make sure you have selected the Persona first from the upper-left dropdown before editing your shortcuts; otherwise, you may get some unexpected results.

At first glance, it will appear that many of the shortcuts are the same in each Persona. That's because there are many functions that are shared across Personas. These include saving, quitting, panning, and zooming, but as you can imagine, there are many options, features, and tools that are only available in certain personas (for example, pixel painting or vector editing tools); to set a shortcut for each, you will need to select the correct Persona first.

The **Apply to all** option refers to UI-specific functions that you would normally want to be the same across all of the Personas. If this is unchecked, you are able to assign different UI-specific shortcuts per Persona.

So, how does it work? Well, choosing one of the Personas will change the list of shortcuts you have access to, as stated previously. On the right-hand side are the fields where you can add or edit your shortcuts for each section in the dropdown. For instance, in the **Designer** Persona section, you can add a shortcut the takes you from one Persona to another. I prefer to use the three icons in the toolbar for that so my shortcut fields here are empty:

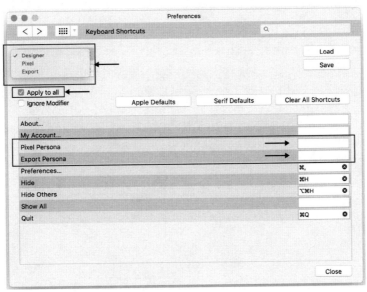

Figure 3.10 – Keyboard Shortcuts preferences showing the Personas dropdown

Once you have chosen the Persona, just below is another drop-down menu list that is separated into four sections. See *Figure 3.11*:

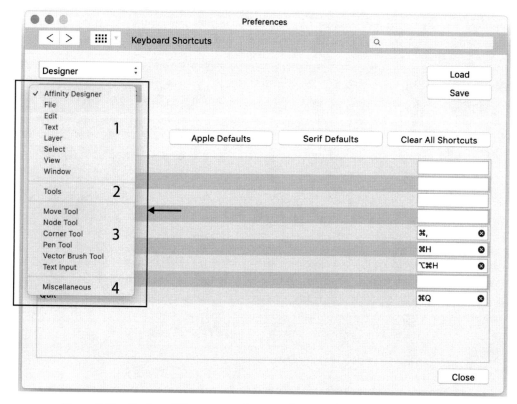

Figure 3.11 – Keyboard Shortcuts preferences showing the categories dropdown

The first section (**1**) corresponds to Affinity Designer's upper menu structure, as follows: **Affinity Designer**, **File**, **Edit**, **Text**, **Layer**, **Select**, **View**, and **Window**. These we discussed in detail in the first chapter. If you recall, I mentioned at the time that there were already some keyboard shortcuts assigned and that we would be able to remove or edit them and even assign new shortcuts. Again, depending on which Persona you have selected, the options will be different.

For example, in *Figure 3.12*, I have selected the **Edit** section. To the right are some of the shortcuts that have been assigned. To remove or change a shortcut, you first need to click on the crosshair or small **x** in the input field to delete the current shortcut. If the input field is already empty, you can simply type in your new shortcut:

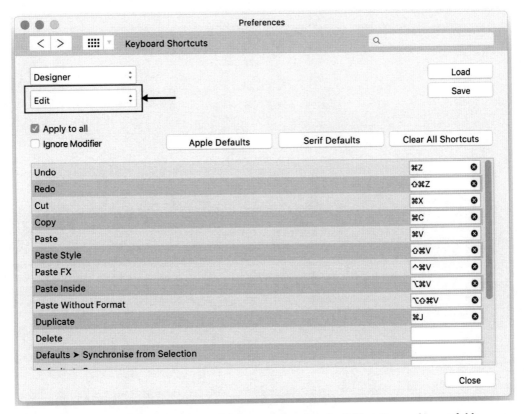

Figure 3.12 – Keyboard Shortcuts preferences showing the Edit section and input fields

Below that is a **Tools** section (labeled **2** in *Figure 3.11*). See *Figure 3.13* for an example of just some of the shortcuts you can assign for your Affinity Designer toolset:

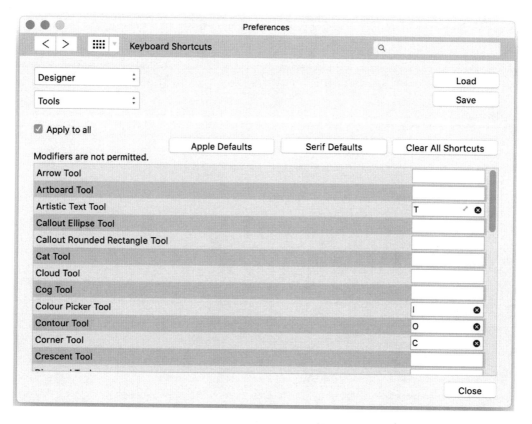

Figure 3.13 – Keyboard Shortcuts preferences showing the Tools section dropdown and its shortcuts and input fields

Below that is a section of options (labeled **3** in *Figure 3.11*) that, as far as I can tell, are listed there because they have secondary shortcuts assigned to them. For example, in *Figure 3.14*, in the case of the Node tool, besides calling the tool with the shortcut *a*, once the tool is active, there are other shortcuts that you can use that enable the tool to do other functions; those functions are listed on the left with their shortcuts on the right:

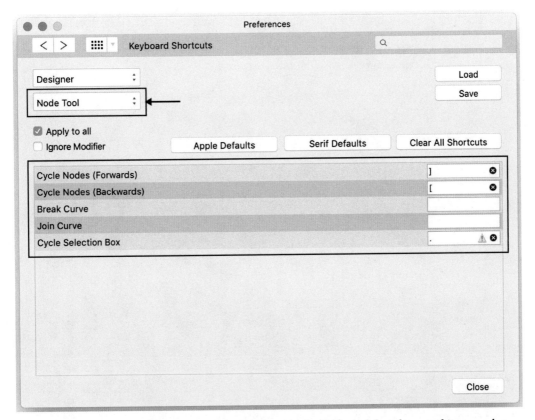

Figure 3.14 – Keyboard Shortcuts preferences showing the Node tool dropdown and its secondary shortcuts and input fields

Last but not least, we have the **Miscellaneous** section (labeled **4** in *Figure 3.11*), containing options that don't fit into the previous category lists, including, yes, you guessed it, yet another way to zoom your document view in and out.

We also have the **Save** button, where you can save your keyboard shortcuts to a file on your hard drive, and the **Load** button to load any keyboard shortcuts you have already saved.

Below that and to the left is an **Ignore Modifier** option. Checking this will enable you to create shortcuts without the usual modifier keys in some of the other shortcuts, allowing you to create single-letter shortcuts. This is similar to the **Tools** shortcuts, such as *P* for the **Pen** tool or *B* for the **Brush** tool.

Just to the right are buttons to reset to either **Apple Defaults** or **Serif Defaults** shortcuts.

Finally, there is a **Clear All Shortcuts** button. Be careful with all three of these buttons as there is no undo if you accidentally click one by mistake!

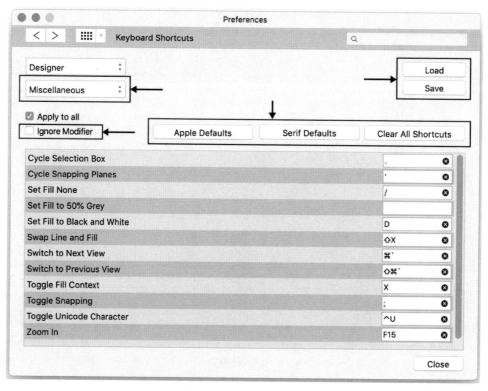

Figure 3.15 – Keyboard Shortcuts preferences showing the Miscellaneous dropdown, the Load and Save buttons, the Ignore Modifier checkbox, the Apple Defaults and Serif Defaults buttons, and the Clear All Shortcuts button

So far, we've explored how to change or add custom keyboard shortcuts to your copy of Affinity Designer, but what if you just want to see a list of the default shortcuts that come with your software? One way might be to go through all of the category dropdowns one at a time but that could take some time. Luckily for us, Serif has furnished a complete list of the default keyboard shortcuts and this can be found by going to **HELP | AFFINITY DESIGNER HELP**; once the Help window pops up, navigate to the bottom of the vertical menu list on the left, and just below the **EXTRAS** flyout, click on **Keyboard Shortcuts** for a full list of all of the default keyboard shortcuts that come shipped with your copy of Affinity Designer.

Now that we have seen where and how to take advantage of Affinity Designer's keyboard shortcuts, I will show you as we progress through this book just how flexible and powerful utilizing keyboard shortcuts can be for a faster and more efficient workflow.

As you get more familiar with Affinity Designer, I encourage you to create your own shortcuts and discover the benefits of how keyboard shortcuts can speed up your workflow. Don't forget to save your shortcuts so you can load them back in if you ever need to.

Continuing on with our customization chapter, let's explore how we can rearrange or reposition some UI elements to set up a custom working environment. Here, we'll be looking specifically at the Studio panels.

Workspace customization – Studio panels

While the default arrangement of the Studio panels that ships with Affinity Designer does give us a good idea of what's available, it isn't set up ideally for anything we would want to use. The panels that are onscreen are all on the right side of the interface in what is called the Right Studio (see *Chapter 1*, *Getting Familiar with Affinity Designer's Interface*) and the application has placed a default group of panels. Some panels we may not necessarily want or need at the moment. Also, there may be some panels that are not shown that we may want to have available for use.

The panels that are onscreen in their default presentation are all nested or stacked on top of one another and that makes it difficult to identify what's available. See *Figure 3.16* for a look at the default setup:

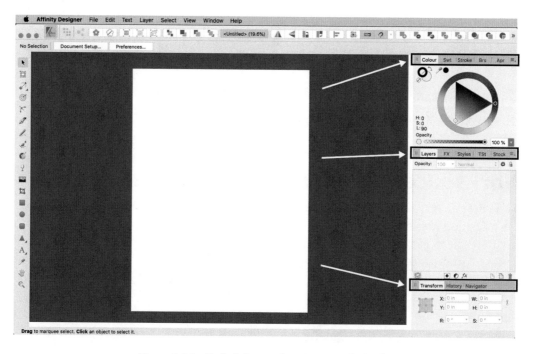

Figure 3.16 – Default layout showing nested panels

Now, some people may prefer this arrangement and that's completely fine, but I would argue that this default setup is not ideal for maximum efficiency. Let's go ahead and have a look at how we can make some simple yet effective changes to get our UI to work better for us.

I'll show you how to do this by showing you my basic setup, but first, let's take a look at the steps it takes to move these panels around. Click and drag on the upper tabs of each of the panels and pull them free of the stack and out into the empty screen area, as shown in *Figure 3.17*:

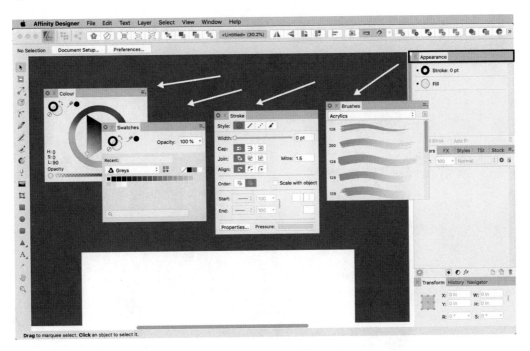

Figure 3.17 – Clicking and dragging out the panels

We are going to rearrange all of the panels into new stacks, so let's drag all of them out of their current stacks. It's only once they are separated like this that their small **x** is showing, enabling you to remove any that you don't want. I will be removing a few that I don't use very often and adding a few that are not onscreen yet. To make it easier to see the panels, I've moved my page document down and out of the way. You should end up with something like *Figure 3.18*:

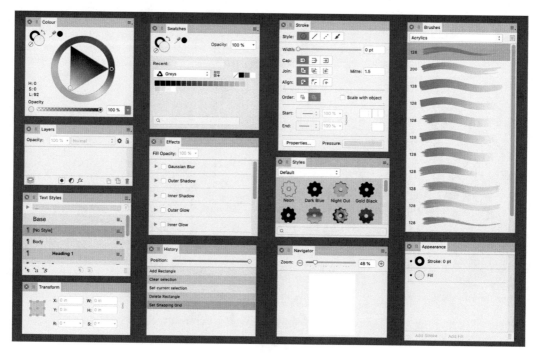

Figure 3.18 – All of the panels dragged out

With all of the default panels out in full view, I can see a few that I'm going to close. Panels that I don't use very often don't need to stay onscreen taking up valuable screen space.

Any panels you do remove you can always add back at any time by going to **VIEW | STUDIO** and selecting any of the panels from the Studio panels flyout list. Close the panels by clicking the little **x** just to the left of the panel's title tab. Feel free to remove whichever panels you want or follow what I'm doing. I'm going to arrange the panel setup that I use for my daily work.

Once the unwanted panels are removed and I've added the panels I want from the Studio panels list, I rebuild the panel stacks on the right and left sides of the document window. To do this, click and drag the panels over to the right and left sides of the UI until a white or light-gray rectangular shape indicates that the panel will be snapped in place along the side of the UI. This is sometimes referred to as docking. Continue to drag each panel into place on both sides above or below the other panels, looking for that snapping rectangle, until you have no more panels floating in the document window. Add or remove panels as desired.

Figure 3.19 shows my basic customized panel setup. This will be more or less the panel setup that I will use throughout the rest of the book. In total, there are 10 or so panels onscreen most of the time. If we need any of the other panels, as we go we can add them as needed.

Notice on the left-hand side I have a couple of panels that are nested. This is a good way to have a panel handy that you don't use as often as the others but you still want to have onscreen for quick access.

The **Layers** panel on the right-hand side is what I consider the real "nerve center" of Affinity Designer. It gets a lot of activity and my illustrations tend to get fairly layer-heavy, so I keep the **Layers** panel close by as a separate floating panel for quick access:

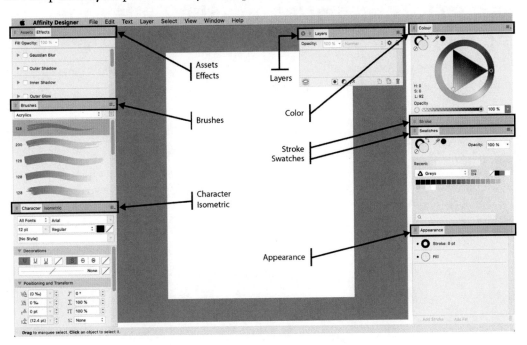

Figure 3.19 – Customized panel layout

Keep in mind that you will need to do this for all three Personas as each Persona will have different panels, so the layout won't be exactly the same but the process is. It might take a few minutes to set up each but once you have, you won't need to do it very often again unless you want to make some changes once you get more familiar with the software.

With that in mind, it's a good idea to save your Studio panels layout as a preset by going to **VIEW | STUDIO PRESETS | SAVE PRESET** and naming and saving your layout preset. You can create multiple layout presets for different types of projects that require different panels to be onscreen. Of course, at any time, you can reset the panels layout back to the default layout by going to **VIEW | STUDIO | RESET STUDIO**. Or, if you want to hide all of your panels, go to **VIEW | STUDIO | HIDE STUDIO**. This isn't the same as pressing the *Tab* key, which will hide the whole UI. **HIDE STUDIO** will only hide the Studio panels, keeping the toolbar, context toolbar, and Tools panel onscreen.

Your UI layout will most likely be completely different from mine and I encourage you to experiment with all of the options available to create your own custom workspace that best suits your needs. I developed this current setup over the course of many projects and a fair amount of trial and error was involved in trying to match up the workspace to my working style and the type of work I do on a regular basis.

Workspace customization – the Tools panel and toolbar

The next two areas we will look at for customizing the interface are the Tools panel and toolbar. The process here is pretty straightforward.

The Tools panel

To customize your Tools panel, go to **VIEW | CUSTOMIZE TOOLS**. This will temporarily expand the Tools panel to show you a view of all of your available tools. Here, you can individually drag any of the tools into your vertical Tools panel, drag any of the tools out of the vertical Tools panel, or even rearrange the tool order in your vertical Tools panel by dragging and moving a tool either up or down to reposition it in the column. See *Figure 3.20*.

For example, if you find you are using the speech bubble geometric shape repeatedly, you may want to make it more accessible by dragging it out of its default nested position and onto the Tools panel directly. Alternatively, you could drag all of the geometric shapes out onto the Tools panel directly; it's all up to you.

To remove the expanded Tools panel, just return to **VIEW | CUSTOMIZE TOOLS** and the expanded Tools panel will disappear, leaving your new Tools panel ready to go:

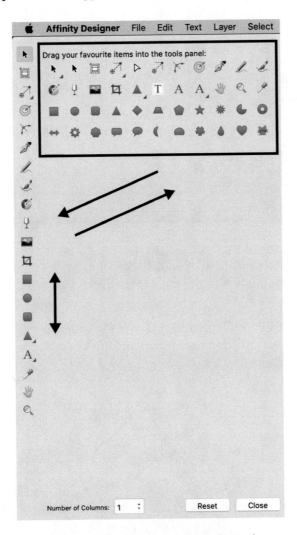

Figure 3.20 – Customizing the Tools panel

The toolbar

The toolbar is customized much the same way as the Tools panel. Go to **VIEW |
CUSTOMIZE TOOLBAR**. A dropdown containing a host of options for the toolbar will
appear. Click and drag the individual options you want to display on your upper toolbar
or alternatively, you can remove items as well by dragging them out of your toolbar. See
Figure 3.21:

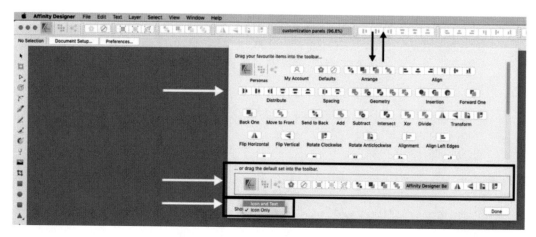

Figure 3.21 – Customizing the toolbar

If you need to reset the toolbar to its default, the section just below all of the individual
icon groups is the default toolbar; just drag it up to the toolbar position and it will replace
everything with the defaults.

One of the options in the lower left-hand corner of the customization panel allows you to
show or hide the names of the icons in the toolbar. This can come in handy, especially for
users just getting accustomed to the interface. *Figure 3.22* shows the toolbar with the icon
names added:

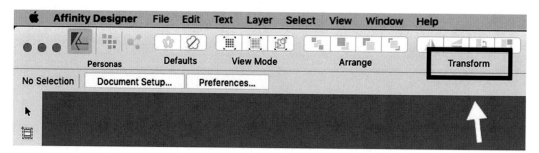

Figure 3.22 – Toolbar with icon names

You may find as you get more familiar with the application that you will be editing the toolbar from time to time. Fortunately, Affinity Designer makes it pretty easy to fine-tune it to get exactly what you need.

The Clip to Canvas feature

The last customization option we're going to cover here is the ability to hide or show what is on your pasteboard. Throughout the course of a project, I can accumulate quite a mass of objects and elements out in the pasteboard area. It's a great place to store elements in case you need them but at times, it can get distracting. Fortunately, Affinity Designer has a feature to reduce the clutter, and that feature is called **Clip to Canvas**. You can find it by going to **VIEW | VIEW MODE | CLIP TO CANVAS**. If the option is grayed out, then your document must contain an artboard as this feature is currently not available in documents with artboards.

Clip to Canvas is switched on by default, so in order to actually be able to use the pasteboard, you will need to switch it off. The default toggle shortcut key for this feature is the \ key.

Figure 3.23 – Clip to Canvas off

Toggle it on and off:

Figure 3.24 – Clip to Canvas on

So far, we have just covered a general interface setup based on the type of work I normally do. Of course, with all of the options available, there are many different interface setups you can create for your own working style or for the type of work you do. The following are two different examples:

Figure 3.25 – Sample interface setups for a typography-heavy workflow and a pixel art workflow

Hopefully, in this chapter, I have demonstrated the flexibility of the UI in Affinity Designer and given you some ideas of how to customize it for your own purposes.

Summary

In this chapter, we have taken a look at a few ways to customize your workflow and your workspace. We first explored the myriad of preferences Affinity Designer has at its disposal, and then we took a deeper dive into its keyboard shortcuts, until finally seeing how to customize its tools and toolbar. I showed you how I set up my UI, with some suggestions on how and why customizing your workspace can be beneficial for a more efficient workflow. Affinity Designer is a pretty impressive package right out of the box, but if you take the time to set it up for a more Personal experience, you will be rewarded with an application that will feel more natural to you.

In the next chapter, we'll cover creating a new document and some of the settings such as document presets, dimensions, resolution, measurement units, color models and profiles, artboards, and document templates.

Section 2: Deeper Exploration of Affinity Designer's Documents, Tools, and Workflow

In this section, we will continue exploring the interface in more depth by creating documents and exploring the panels, tools, and workflow best practices.

This section comprises the following chapters:

4

Document Setup and Modification

Welcome to the fourth chapter of *Up and Running with Affinity Designer*.

In this chapter, we are going to cover opening up Affinity Designer for the first time, setting up a new document layout and taking a look at the various settings and presets Affinity Designer has to meet your specific needs. We'll also see how to make adjustments to an existing file's document setup.

In this chapter, we'll be looking at the following main topics:

- Registering Affinity Designer and the welcome panel
- New document setup, editing your current document setup, and New from Clipboard
- Using Artboards

Technical requirement

Before diving into this chapter, you will need a recent copy of Affinity Designer and access to a desktop computer capable of running Affinity Designer. You may be able to follow the core concepts using a tablet but much, if not all, of the interface will be different.

Registering Affinity Designer and the welcome panel

In Affinity Designer, two temporary panels may pop up upon opening the application. One is the registration panel and the other is the welcome panel. Let's take a look at them both:

- **The registration panel**

  The first time you launched Affinity Designer, you may have encountered a registration screen asking you either to register your software or sign in if you have already registered. This is a new feature with version 1.9. It's simply designed to allow you quick access to any past purchases you have made from the online Affinity Store, specific promotions, giveaways, or to make additional purchases from the Affinity Store. You can either **Register**, **Sign in**, or click **Remind me later** to skip it until a later time.

  This is a relatively new feature as of the writing of this book and I imagine Serif will be developing it further to include more and more options as Affinity moves forward.

Internet connection

One thing to note: while you will need to be connected to the internet to register your copy of Affinity Designer or to sign in to your account, Affinity Designer doesn't require an internet connection to run and you don't have to register in order to use your software.

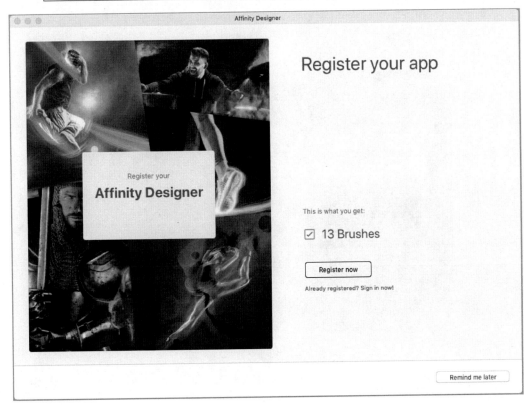

Figure 4.1 – The registration panel

- **The welcome panel**

  Similar to the registration panel, the welcome panel offers you various quick links to Affinity Designer specific tutorials, user sample files that you can download and explore, Affinity Designer user forums, the Affinity Facebook page and Twitter page, plus the Affinity Store and articles related to Affinity Designer in Affinity's Spotlight online series of artist interviews and learning resources. As you may have guessed, the content offered is updated regularly so it's worth checking out from time to time even if you do have the panel disabled on startup:

Figure 4.2 – The welcome panel

With the registration and welcome panels out of the way, let's now take a look at setting up a new document.

New document setup and editing your current document setup

When setting up a new document, you have a few options to consider. These options usually depend on the type of project you are going to work on. You can choose from a host of predetermined presets that the team at Serif has created for you or templates that you can define and save for reuse or entirely custom options you create specifically for each job. Whichever method you choose, Affinity Designer will remember the last settings you used and will present you with them the next time you create a new document, until you make further changes.

The New Document dialog

Figure 4.3 shows the **New Document** dialog. It is split into three separate sections. In **section 1**, you can choose between **Presets** or **Templates**. Choosing one of these will determine what is shown in **section 2** and in **section 3**. For the purpose of this book, we will be just discussing the **Presets** section. For information on templates, go to **HELP | AFFINITY DESIGNER HELP**, navigate to the **Get Started** flyout in the list, and select **Document Setup**. Information on templates can be found there:

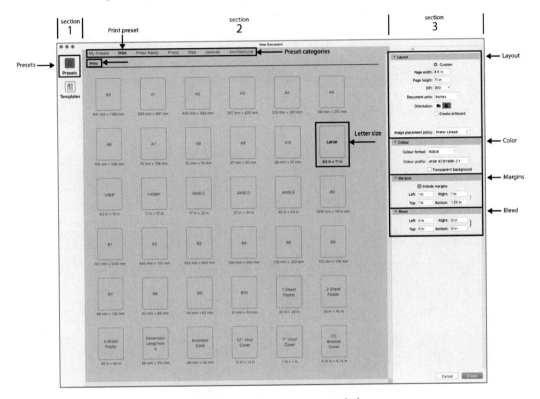

Figure 4.3 – The New Document dialog

In *Figure 4.3*, I have chosen **Presets** in **section 1**, and presented along the top of **section 2** are the current preset categories. Choosing one of these presets will change the options in **section 3**. The preset categories are as follows:

- **My Presets**: If you create any of your own presets, this is where they will be located.

- **Print**: This is the section chosen in *Figure 4.3*. This section contains preset sizes common in RGB desktop printing.

- **Press Ready**: This section contains preset sizes common in CMYK commercial or professional printing. Everything here is virtually identical to the print presets, with the exception of different settings set up in the right section, specifically **DPI** and **Color** settings.

- **Photo**: These presets are for popular photo format sizes and aspect ratios.

- **Web**: Here you will find various web screen resolutions.

- **Devices**: Sizes for iPad, iPhone, Apple Watch, Nexus, Kindle, Galaxy, and Surface Pro devices.

- **Architectural**: Sizes for common architectural documents.

In *Figure 4.4*, we see a closer view of **section 3**, also known as the **Settings** pane. As mentioned earlier, these options will change based on which preset you have selected. For our chosen **Print** preset with the **Letter** size selected, the options are as follows:

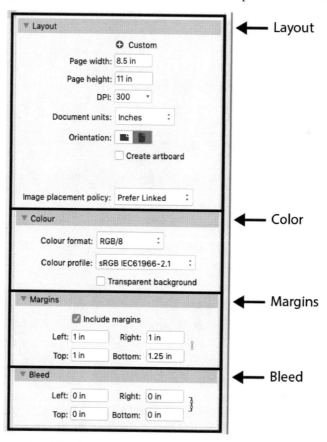

Figure 4.4 – The New Document dialog with a closer view of section 3

- **Layout**: The small plus sign beside the word **Custom** is to add a new preset based on your settings. The new preset will be added to the **My Presets** category. If you find you are using the same settings a lot then it might be a good idea to save them as a preset.

  Next are the **Page width** and **height** sizes. Because this is a North American paper size, the **Document units** are set to **Inches**. You can change the units if you would prefer to work in another measurement system. Your document won't change size, only the units of measurement will change.

  Below this, you can set the **Orientation** to horizontal or vertical.

  Click on **Create artboard** if you want to create your document as an Artboard. There's much more on Artboards in the next section.

  Finally in this **Layout** section, you can specify to Affinity Designer when you place an image into the document whether you prefer it to be **Linked** or **Embedded**. Linked means the application keeps a link to the file on your hard drive and will update the file if you edit the image outside of Affinity Designer. Embedded means it will actually embed the image into your document. Documents with linked files are usually smaller in size than documents with embedded images in them. This is something to keep in mind if you are working with lots of placed images in your documents.

- **Color**: **Color format** will allow you to work in RGB, grayscale, CMYK, or LAB color modes.

  Color Profile changes the color gamut profile to reflect the chosen color format.

  Transparent background allows you to have a document with a transparent background. This can be handy for certain types of projects, such as logos or UI design.

- **Margins**: Here, you can add margin guides to your documents.

- **Bleed**: Here, you can add bleeds to your documents.

Editing your current document setup

Sometimes, after you create your document, you may need to edit some of your document settings. To do this, either go to **FILE | DOCUMENT SETUP** or, with nothing in your document selected, click on the **Document Setup** button in the **Context Toolbar**. If you have something selected, you won't see the **Document Setup** button in the **Context Toolbar** as the **Context Toolbar** will be showing the information for elements that are selected. You need to have nothing selected for the **Document Setup** button to show up. The behavior is the same for the **Preferences** button.

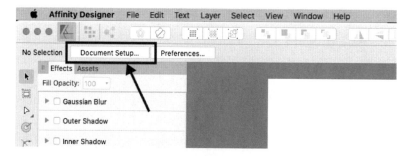

Figure 4.5 – The Document Setup button

When you click on the **Document Setup** button, a drop-down dialog will drop down from the center of the **Context Toolbar** with much the same options as the **New Document** dialog, with the exception of a few more additions.

In the bottom half of the dialog (*Figure 4.6*), you'll find three additional options:

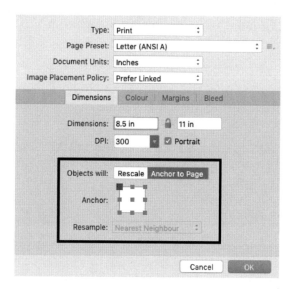

Figure 4.6 – The Document Setup dropdown

The Objects will option allows you to resize your documents by making any objects you may have in your document either **Rescale** by the difference in the page size or **Anchor to Page** when you don't want your objects to scale up or down with a change in your page size.

Below that, because **Anchor to Page** is selected, you have options regarding where to anchor your objects to once the new page size is calculated. If **Rescale** is selected, you will have options on how your objects would be resampled as they are scaled up or down with the new page size.

New from Clipboard

Another way to create a new document is to copy an element or multiple elements from an existing document, then go to **FILE | NEW FROM CLIPBOARD**. A new document will be created with the element or multiple elements you copied to the clipboard pasted into it. The new document will be created to the exact size of the bounds of your copied elements and will have a transparent background. This can be a fast way to create a new document based on elements from an existing document.

Earlier in this chapter and in *Chapter 1, Getting Familiar with Affinity Designer's Interface*, we touched on artboards. In the next section, we'll take a closer look at Artboards, how they work, and when and why you might choose Artboards over a single-page document.

Using Artboards

Artboards are a powerful way to work in Affinity Designer when you want or need to have multiple pages in one document.

Artboards are basically separate pages within one document. They can all be the same size, as in a multipage magazine or brochure design layout, or various versions of the same design in different color schemes. Artboards can also be of varying sizes, for example, for a company stationery package of business cards, letterheads, second sheets, and envelopes, or as an advertising campaign with various ad sizes or concepts.

In short, Artboards are a convenient way to add pages to or organize your multiple-paged Affinity Designer work that are as flexible as you need them to be.

Working with Artboards

Artboards can be created, as discussed in the previous section, from within the **New Document** dialog box by clicking on **Create artboard**, or at any time in an existing document by using the **Artboard Tool** from the **Tool Panel**.

This applies to single-page documents as well. If you are working on a single-page document and you decide that you need more pages, just select the Artboard tool and either go to the context toolbar and click on **Insert Artboard** to create a new artboard that's the same size as the existing page, or simply click and drag a new Artboard into the document at any size you want.

Figure 4.7 shows a typical layout with varying sized Artboards in one document:

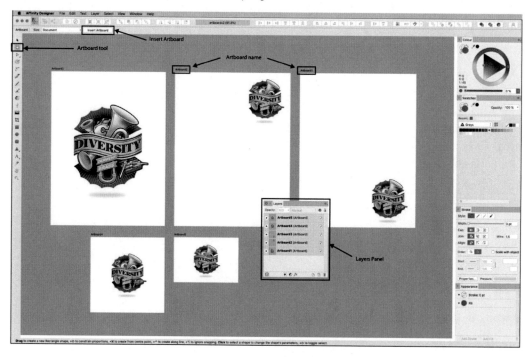

Figure 4.7 – Artboards with the Layers panel

When working with Artboards, there are a few options, features, and best practices available to you for controlling and managing your workflow. Let's take a look at them:

- **Layers panel and Artboards**

    When Artboards are created in your document, they reside and can be accessed through the Layers panel. So, instead of having a separate panel just for Artboards, the Layers panel treats Artboards and their contents similarly to a group of layers. This makes sense as the Layers panel is where you organize your document and where all of the elements in your file can be found.

- **Naming your Artboards**

  Each time you create an Artboard, Affinity Designer automatically uses the naming convention of Artboard 1, Artboard 2, and so on. These names can be seen above and to the left of each artboard. You can rename your artboards by double-clicking on their names in the Layers panel. It's generally a good practice to give your Artboards and layers names that make sense to you as your document gets increasingly more complex with more and more elements. Ten Artboards with the name Artboard 1 will get confusing.

- **Layers panel Artboard options**

  In the Layers panel, you can rearrange or move the Artboard's stacking order or hide or lock an Artboard. You can even apply **Layer Adjustments** such as **Recolor, Levels,** or **Brightness and Contrast** to an Artboard, which will affect everything on that Artboard.

  > **New Artboard in the Layers panel**
  >
  > You can't at this time add a new blank Artboard from the Layers panel. If you click on the add new layer button at the bottom of the Layers panel, it will add a new blank layer to the selected Artboard; it will not add a new blank Artboard.

- **Selecting Artboards – Layers panel**

  To select an Artboard, click on it in the Layers panel.

  To select multiple Artboards, either press *Shift* and click to select adjacent Artboards in the layer stack, or press *Cmd* or *Ctrl* and click to select non-adjacent Artboards in the layer stack.

- **Selecting Artboards – document window**

  To select an Artboard in the document window, select the Artboard tool from the tool panel and click on the Artboard in the document. Press *Shift* and click to select multiple Artboards. Or click on the Artboards title in the upper left corner of the Artboard.

  A marquee selection, as you might do with the move tool to drag and select multiple items, will not work with the Artboard tool. If you click and drag in the document window with the Artboard tool, it will instead create a new Artboard.

- **Moving Artboards**

To move an Artboard, select the Artboard tool in the document window, click on the Artboard to select it, and then hover your cursor on or near the Artboard's edge. When the cursor turns into a small cross arrow cursor, click and drag to reposition the artboard.

You can also click on the Artboards title in the document view with the Move tool to move an unselected or selected Artboard. The Artboard Tool will move it as well by clicking on the title but only if the artboard is already selected. Otherwise it will try to create a new artboard.

Finally, you can also move an artboard by selecting the Artboard itself with the Artboard tool then using the Transform Panel inputs to change its X and Y position numerically:

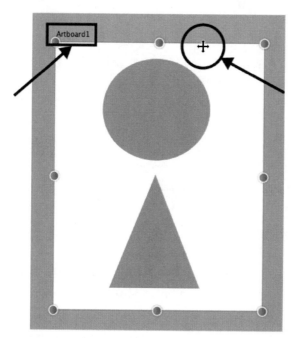

Figure 4.8 – Moving an Artboard: the cross arrows cursor or Artboard label

- **Artboard backgrounds**

You can apply a solid or gradient color to an Artboard that will act as a background always sitting behind any elements you may have on your Artboard. This can come in handy if you want a certain color and don't want to worry about accidentally selecting it while working.

- **Duplicating Artboards – Layers panel**

  To copy or duplicate an Artboard in the Layers panel, right-click the Artboard you want to copy and choose **Duplicate**. See *Figure 4.9 (1)*. This creates a duplicate of the Artboard *exactly on top of the original*. You will need to move it off to see both Artboards.

- **Duplicating Artboards – document window**

  To copy or duplicate an Artboard in the document window, use the same procedure but this time press the *Cmd* or *Ctrl* key while dragging and you will duplicate the Artboard and all of its contents. See *Figure 4.9 (2)*:

  > **Note**
  >
  > When you do either of these two methods of duplication the duplicated Artboard will have the same name as the original. Ideally, Affinity Designer would append a number or the word copy after the Artboard name, but as of this writing it does not, so it's probably a good idea to rename the new Artboard to avoid confusion.

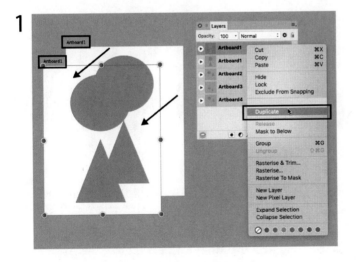
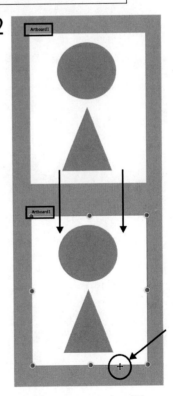

Figure 4.9 – Duplicating an Artboard – In the Layers panel (1) and in the document window (2)

- **Aligning and distributing Artboards**

  You might find that, after you have added or duplicated a few Artboards, you want to clean up your workspace. Artboards can be aligned and distributed just like any other selection of elements in your file. Select all of the Artboards you want to align with the Artboard tool by clicking the first Artboard then pressing *Shift* and clicking on the others you want to align. Then go to the **Context Toolbar** and choose your alignment and distribution options. See *Figure 4.10*:

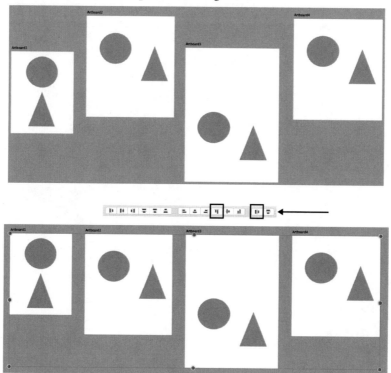

Figure 4.10 – Aligning and distributing an Artboard – Layers panel

- **Scaling, shearing, and rotating Artboards**

  To adjust an Artboard's width and height, select the Artboard with the Artboard tool and click on one of the adjustment circles. Click and drag to make adjustments. If more than one Artboard is selected, it will adjust all of them at the same time as one unit. Use the *Shift* key as you drag to constrain the aspect ratio of the Artboard.

Similar to moving an Artboard using the **Transform** panel, you can also use the Transform panel to scale, shear, and rotate an Artboard. See *Figure 4.11.* Notice, however, that the content of the Artboard does not distort or rotate using this method:

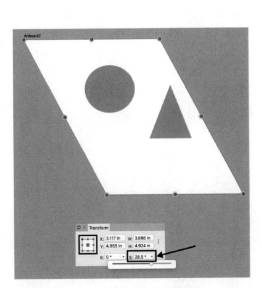 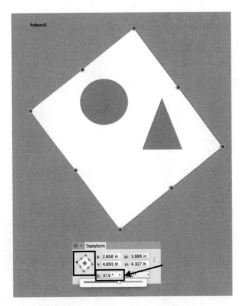

Shearing an Artboard   Rotating an Artboard

Figure 4.11 – Shearing and rotating an Artboard using the Transform panel

However, if you use the **Context Toolbar** icons for **Flip Horizontal**, **Flip Vertical**, **Rotate Clockwise**, and **Rotate Counter Clockwise** not only does the Artboard flip and rotate, but the content on the Artboard flips and rotates as well. See *Figure 4.12*:

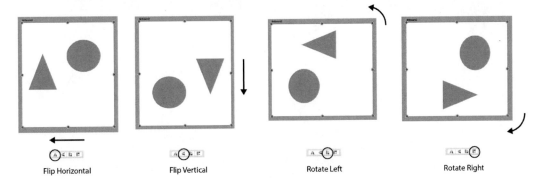

Flip Horizontal   Flip Vertical   Rotate Left   Rotate Right

Figure 4.12 – Flipping and rotating an Artboard using the context toolbar icons

- **Artboard clipping behavior**

  Each Artboard has a clipping behavior where if you drag an element partially outside of the Artboard, it will get clipped. If you drag the element completely off of the Artboard, it will be removed from that artboard and sit on the pasteboard. This will remove it as well from that Artboard's layer stack in the Layers panel and put each element in its own layer. Subsequently, dragging an element from one Artboard to another Artboard will not only move it to the new Artboard but will also move it to the new Artboard's layer stack in the Layers panel. This is called reparenting:

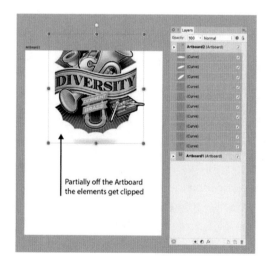
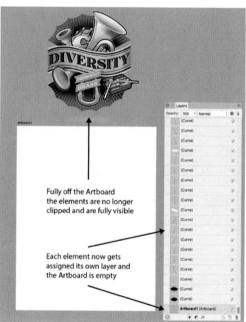

Figure 4.13 – Clipping behavior of Artboards

- **Converting an object into an Artboard**

  In Affinity Designer, a selected object can be converted to an Artboard. To do this, select a suitable object and go to **LAYER | CONVERT OBJECT TO ARTBOARD**. In *Figure 4.14*, I have duplicated an ellipse from Artboard 1 onto the pasteboard and converted it into an Artboard:

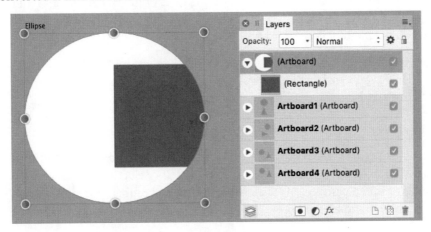

Figure 4.14 – Object converted to an Artboard

Then I drew a rectangle onto the new Artboard. Notice how the rectangle is being clipped as its shape bleeds off the right side of the new Ellipse Artboard. That confirms to me that the Ellipse is indeed an Artboard now. Notice also how the new Artboard's name in the document window is now **Ellipse**, taken from the original shape's name. The Layers panel shows the nested rectangle below the Ellipse Artboard, but the Artboard's new name is not in the Layers panel for some reason. I believe this is an oversight as it should reference the same name as the document window name. For now, it appears that you will need to name any objects you convert into Artboards manually in the Layers panel.

Using grids, rulers, and guides with Artboards

Artboards can have unique rulers, guides, and grids for each Artboard. For example, you can have a custom isometric grid on one Artboard and a normal grid or none at all on another Artboard. This is a great feature that allows you access to different grids for different functions within the same document.

If you have rulers active (**VIEW | SHOW RULERS**) and you click on each Artboard, you will notice each Artboard will have its own 0 to 0 starting location in the upper left-hand corner of the Artboard, no matter where the Artboard is located in your document window.

Guides follow a similar workflow in that you can have different guides for each Artboard.

You must first select the Artboard before adding guides or grids. Affinity Designer needs to know which Artboard to apply the guides or grid to. To add a guide, click and hold inside the ruler area, then drag to position your guide on the chosen Artboard.

When you have different grids, rulers, or guides, clicking on each Artboard will display only that specific Artboard's grids, rulers, and guides and will hide all of the other Artboard's grids, rulers, and guides.

Exporting Artboards – Designer Persona

In the Designer Persona, there are a few different options available for you to export Artboards. You can export individual Artboards, specific selections, or all of your Artboards as one single image. Most of the time, you will probably want to export each Artboard as an individual image.

To export an Artboard, go to **FILE | EXPORT** and choose the file format you need in the upper row of format icons. Then click on the **Area** dropdown and choose from the options listed in the following screenshot. If you have an Artboard selected when you call the Export dialog, that Artboard should be the target of the export and should be already selected in the **Area** dropdown. The options in the upper part of the dialog will change depending on which file format you have chosen. The options list in the **Area** dropdown will be dependent on how many Artboards you have in your document and if you have an active selection. They will all be listed as shown in *Figure 4.15*. For this example, I had **Artboard3** selected in my document window, this would be the result:

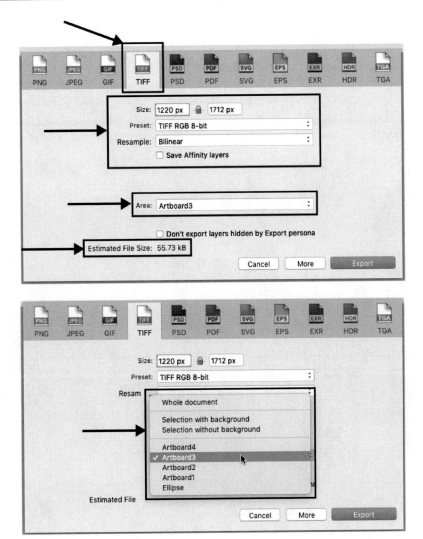

Figure 4.15 – Designer Persona Export dialog showing Artboard options

Exporting Artboards – Export Persona

In the Export Persona as you might expect there are a few more options. The main difference is the ability to export different file formats and resolutions simultaneously. See *Figure 4.16* for an idea of the options available in the Export Persona for exporting artboards. In my example, I have selected **Artboard3**, as in the previous example. For more information on exporting Artboards using the Export Persona, go to **HELP | AFFINITY DESIGNER HELP**, navigate to the **Artboards** flyout, and select **Exporting**:

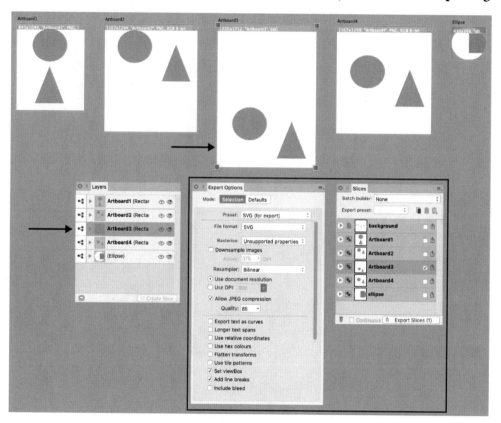

Figure 4.16 – Export Persona Export dialogs showing Artboard options

Printing Artboards

Printing Artboards is pretty straightforward. Go to **FILE | PRINT**, and when the print dialog pops up click on **Show Details**. Check to make sure that the correct printer is selected (if you have more than one) and that the correct paper size is selected for what you need. Ensure **Range and Scale** is visible in the dropdown just below the **Paper Size** dropdown. Then select one of the options presented to you for what you need to print. The options should include the following:

- **Entire Document**: This will print all of your Artboards on one sheet of paper. Use this if you want to see your entire project on one page.

- **Artboards**: This option will print all of your Artboards on separate pages.

- **Artboards List**: This lists each Artboard in your document by name for you to select individual Artboards to print separately.

Review the other settings included in the print dialog before hitting the **Print** button:

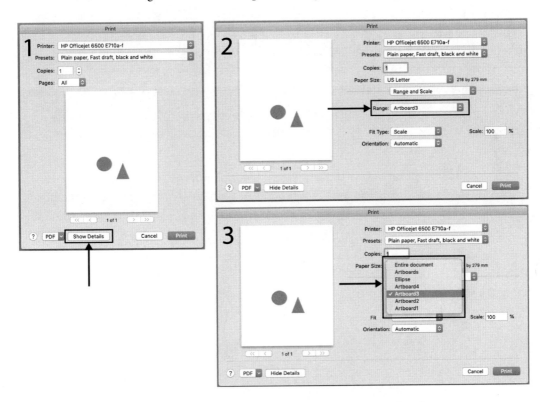

Figure 4.17 – Print dialogs with options for printing artboards

Deleting Artboards

You can delete Artboards from the document window by selecting one or multiple Artboards and pressing the *Delete* key. Similarly, you can delete selected Artboards from the Layers panel by clicking on the tiny trash can in the bottom right-hand corner of the panel or by right-clicking on the selected Artboards and selecting **Delete** from the context menu.

> **A very important difference between these two deleting options!**
>
> When you delete selected Artboards from the document window, you will get a warning asking if you want to keep the selected Artboards' contents or delete it along with the Artboards. However, when deleting Artboards from the Layers panel, the deletion is immediate and you are not given the chance to decide whether or not to keep the deleted Artboards' contents. Use *Cmd* or *Ctrl* + *Z* immediately to restore the Artboard!

Summary

In this chapter, we got started by opening up Affinity Designer for the first time and learning about the registration panel with its quick access links to the Affinity store, your Affinity account, and other online resources. We discovered the Affinity Designer welcome panel with its sample files, links to tutorials, user forums, and social media pages.

We then took a look at setting up a new document and explored some of the various settings and options available to you when you are creating a new document and for editing an existing documents' settings.

Finally, we navigated our way through an extended look into Affinity Designer's powerful Artboard system, exploring the uses and benefits of Artboards and what makes them so well adapted for a flexible daily workflow.

In the next chapter, we are going to continue our closer inspection of Affinity Designer with a more specific look at some of its main studio panels. We will learn which panels play the most important roles in the construction of a successful project and which play more of a supporting role.

5
Main Studio Panels and Managers

Welcome to the fifth chapter of *Up and Running with Affinity Designer*.

In this chapter, we are going to get more familiar with Affinity Designer's main Studio panels and managers. Studio panels allow you to get the most out of Affinity Designer's powerful toolset with options and features for adjusting color and effects, utilizing vector and raster brushes, and applying text and type to your documents. Managers allow you to organize and streamline design aids such as guides, grids, snapping, and other resources.

There are many panels in Affinity Designer. In this chapter, we'll start to focus on the Studio panels that will relate to us the most for the type of work we will be taking on in the three exercise chapters, while other panels will be covered as we need them or come across them.

We'll first look at panel behavior, and then we'll begin exploring the main Studio panels' specific uses and functionality. Finally, we will explore Affinity Designer's managers and how they can aid in rounding out our workflow and productivity.

In this chapter, we'll be looking at the following topics:

- Panel behavior
- The Color panels
- The Effects panel
- The Styles panel
- The Brushes panel
- The Type panels
- Manager panels

Panel behavior

Most, if not all, of the panels in Affinity Designer share the same basic behavior. In *Chapter 1, Getting Familiar with Affinity Designer's Interface*, we were introduced to Studio panels and I laid out a few of them in *Figure 1.47*. In *Chapter 3, How to Customize Your Affinity Designer Workspace*, as part of our discussion of setting up our UI, we talked about moving around, repositioning, docking, and closing Studio panels and I gave an example of my default customized setup in *Figure 3.19*.

In this chapter, we won't repeat what we've already covered, but we will perhaps add a little bit to that knowledge as we take a closer look at specific panels.

Affinity Designer's Studio panels can be found by going to **View** | **Studio**; they are listed alphabetically:

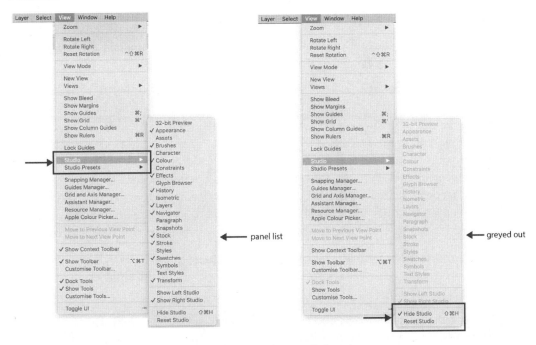

Figure 5.1 – The Studio panels dropdown

When a panel is active or visible in the UI, it will have a checkmark in the menu list indicating that it is onscreen somewhere. If you don't see the panel, that may be because it's nested behind another panel. Just locate and click on its tab to bring it to the front of the stack. If you have pressed the *Tab* key, which hides all of the Studio panels, the list will appear grayed out in the Studio panels dropdown. Pressing *Tab* will toggle the panels back onscreen. If, however, you have pressed *Tab* and the Studio panels do not reappear, you may have **Hide Studio** selected in the Studio panels dropdown and may need to deselect it.

As you can see, there are a number of ways to hide and show the Studio panels and it may be confusing at first, but with time and practice, you will get more accustomed to the behavior, and honestly, once you get set up, there's not usually much call to change it often.

Resizing and hiding Studio panels

In addition to moving, docking, and closing panels as discussed in *Chapter 3, How to Customize Your Affinity Designer Workspace*, you can also resize a panel.

The resizing method depends on whether the panel is docked or floating. To resize a floating panel, hover your cursor above any of the panel's corners or sides until you see either a double-angled arrow or a horizontal single arrow. While all panels can be resized horizontally increasing their width, only some panels' height can be resized vertically. Generally, if you can add new content to a panel such as adding new layers to the Layers panel or a new color swatch to the Swatches panel, then it will be able to be resized vertically to accommodate the additional content. If you do happen to run out of room, the panel will automatically add a scroll bar. Other panels that don't allow content to be added are the Color panel and the Stroke panel, which won't allow any vertical resizing.

If the panels are stacked or docked in a column along either side of the UI, you will be able to widen them by hovering over their sides until a line with a left and right arrow appear. Drag to increase or decrease the column's width.

Now that we learned about the Studio panel's behavior and how we can resize and hide it, let's move on to the main Studio panel and learn about its functionality.

The Color panels

The first three Studio panels we will discuss are what I call the color panels because of their related functionality. These panels are intertwined with each other so much so that they really should be covered as a group. They are the **Color**, **Swatches**, and **Stroke** panels:

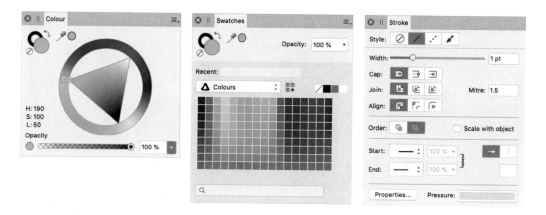

Figure 5.2 – The Color, Swatches, and Stroke panels

> **Fills and strokes**
>
> Vector objects in Affinity Designer consist of either fills or strokes. Think of the fill as the inside of a shape and the stroke as an outline applied to the outside of a shape. A stroke can also just be a line with no fill, referred to as a vector curve or path.

The Color and Swatches panels relate to Color properties for both fills and strokes. The Stroke panel relates to the many options and properties of a stroke. Some of the options in all three of these panels will change depending on the type of object selected or which options on the panel are selected. We will take a closer look at these panels next, starting with the Color panel.

The Color panel

The Color panel is where you choose the color for your selected objects, brushes, or tools. You are given a few different ways to define your colors and there are different color mode options to choose from when deciding on a color. These options generally depend on the type of work you are doing. Different types of work require specific color modes. For example, for work created for online or screen work, you will want to use an **RGB** color mode, whereas work that will be printed usually requires a **CMYK** color mode. You will often need to produce work for multiple forms of output, so knowing when to use the right mode can be crucial. If you are unsure which format to use, it's always a good idea to ask your printer or the person who will be receiving your document before you get too far along with your project.

In *Figure 5.3*, you can see the four different views the Color panel has to define the color options you have. These are **Color Wheel**, **Color Sliders**, **Color Boxes**, and **Color Tint**. In the upper-right corner of the Color panel is a view preference dropdown for access to the other Color panel views. On the Sliders and Boxes views, there are additional drop-down menus in each panel for additional color options. The Color panel views are as follows:

- **Wheel**: In this view of the Color panel, the outer ring defines the hue of the Color while the inner triangle defines the saturation and lightness of the chosen hue.

- **Sliders**: In this view of the Color panel, the additional options are called color modes. This is where you will access those color modes discussed earlier for different types of work. They are **RGB**, **RGB Hex**, **HSL**, **CMYK**, **LAB**, and **Greyscale**.

- **Boxes**: In this view of the Color panel, the additional options are yet another way to adjust the **HSL**, or **Hue, Saturation**, and **Lightness**. This view has a slider above a large Color box area. They both change depending on which value of HSL you are adjusting.

- **Tint**: In this view, there is just a simple slider that controls the amount of a particular hue. Dragging it to the left will lighten the hue. Lightening is different from opacity, which we will discuss when we talk about opacity later:

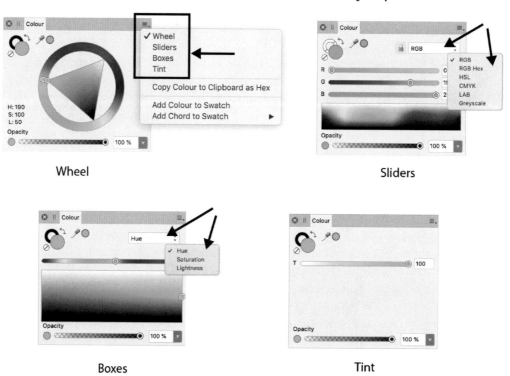

Figure 5.3 – The Color panel – Wheel, Sliders, Boxes, and Tint

In all of these Color panel views, there are some common settings:

- **Fill** and **Stroke**: In the upper left are the **Fill** and **Stroke** (Designer Persona) or **Primary** and **Secondary** color selector (Pixel Persona) icons. By clicking on one of these selectors, you determine where the selected color will be applied. Clicking on one or the other will bring it to the front and make it the active color. For example, if you want to apply a new color to the stroke of a selected object, you first need to click on the stroke circle in the panel to make it active. It will pop in front of the fill circle, indicating that it is the active attribute. The same process goes for the primary and secondary colors in the Pixel Persona.

  To remove a stoke, fill, or primary or secondary color completely from a selected object, click on either the fill, stroke, or primary or secondary color icon to make it active, then click on the tiny circle icon just down to the left with the red line going through it to remove it.

- **Color Picker**: The color picker consists of a small eyedropper icon and color circle shape known as the **picked color swatch**. To use it to "pick" another color from anywhere in your document, including the interface elements, select your object, then select either the fill or stroke selector icon depending on what you want your new color to be applied to, then click and hold on the eyedropper icon and drag across the screen to the desired color. An enlarged magnified circle will follow the cursor and magnify whatever is below it. Letting go will load that picked color into the picker. However, this will not automatically apply your color to the selected object. In order to apply that color, you need to return to the picker in the panel and click the picked color swatch. To me, this is an unnecessary extra step. You would expect the color to be applied instantly after letting go of the cursor but that is currently not the case.

- **Color Chooser**: If you double-click on either the **Fill** or **Stroke Selectors** a **Color Chooser Panel** will pop up allowing you to fine-tune your color decision in a rather large color area to drag around in, or if you prefer, more precise color input fields for HSL, RGB, RGB Hex, and CMYK:

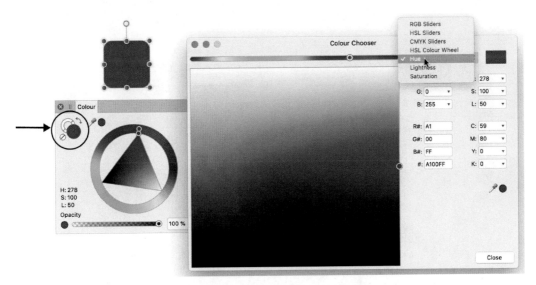

Figure 5.4 – The Color Chooser panel

Using the color picker is universal across the color panels. *Figure 5.5* illustrates the four-part process:

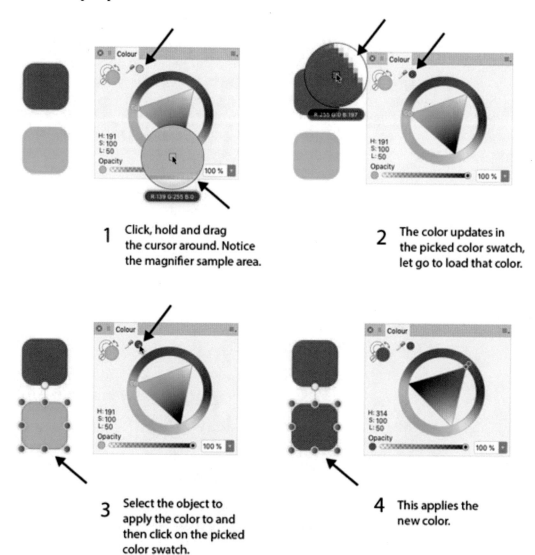

1 Click, hold and drag the cursor around. Notice the magnifier sample area.

2 The color updates in the picked color swatch, let go to load that color.

3 Select the object to apply the color to and then click on the picked color swatch.

4 This applies the new color.

Figure 5.5 – The Color panel – using the color picker

- **Opacity**: Along the bottom of the Color panel is the **Opacity** slider. This controls the selected object's color opacity. Dragging the slider to the left or entering a number less than 100% reduces the color's opacity, making it more transparent. Notice in *Figure 5.6* that although the fill color circle appears lighter, the actual color does not change, as seen in the HSL numbers; just the color's opacity changes:

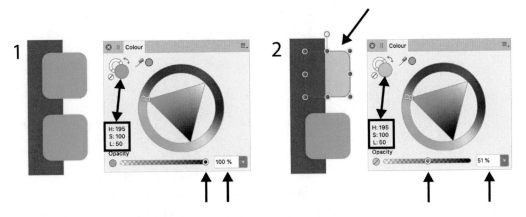

Figure 5.6 – The Color panel – the Opacity slider

- **Noise**: Completely hidden in the Color panel is the ability to add noise to a selected object's fill color. This feature shares the same location in the Color panel as the **Opacity** slider but is hidden until you click on the small round swatch below the word **Opacity**. This changes the word to **Noise** and now the slider will add noise from 0 to 100%, as shown in *Figure 5.7*. If you hover over the swatch for a second or two, the word **Switch** will appear, giving you the only clue that something may happen if you click on the swatch. Clicking the swatch again will revert to the **Opacity** slider:

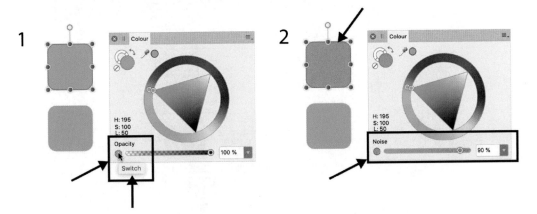

Figure 5.7 – The Color panel – the (hidden) Noise slider

This is a quick and easy way to apply different levels of noise to individual objects in your document (once you know it's there). However, currently only vector fills can have noise added to them with this method, so any strokes or pixel-based elements will need a different method for adding noise. Fortunately, there is an easy way to add noise to your entire document as mentioned at the very end of *Chapter 12, Creating Astronaut Ricky and Sidekick K9.*

In the next section, we'll continue with the Swatches panel, the second of the color panel's group of three.

The Swatches panel

The Swatches panel is where you add, delete, store, and manage your color swatches and palettes for use in your documents. The Swatches panel works in tandem with the Color panel and the context toolbar, giving you three locations to access your fill and stroke color selectors as well as other color-related options. The Swatches panel shares a few options with the Color panel. In the Swatches panel, you have the same fill and stroke (Designer Persona) and primary and secondary (Pixel Persona) color selectors as well as the same color picker eyedropper setup but instead of an **Opacity** slider setup at the bottom, you gain access to the **Opacity** slider by clicking on the **%** number item in the top right of the panel. All of these options perform the same operations as the Color panel.

Let's take a closer look now at some of the more relevant options that the Swatches panel has to offer:

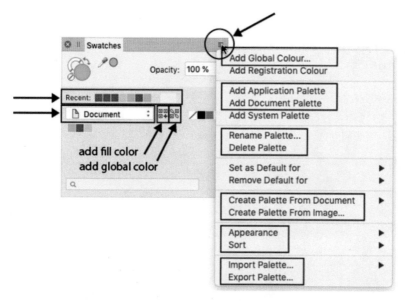

Figure 5.8 – The Swatches panel options and panel preferences

Starting on the left is a row of the most recent colors used in your document. Think of this single row of swatches like a trail of breadcrumbs showing you your most recently used colors. It's very handy to quickly grab a recent color without having to create a palette swatch or resample it with the color picker. Below that is the color palettes dropdown, which is a menu containing various different color palettes. More on the color palettes follows.

Just to the right of the color palettes dropdown are two small icons. This left icon is the add current fill button. Clicking this will add the current fill color as a swatch to the document palette or an application palette. It's recommended to create a document palette before adding the current fill or it will add it to an already created application palette and that may not be your intent. You can only add your current fill to a swatch palette if it is a document palette or an application palette. More on the different types of palettes will be covered when we look closer at the Swatches panel color palettes dropdown.

The second or right-side icon will add the current fill color to the document palette as a global color swatch. In order to add a global color, you must be using a document palette. You can't add global colors to any other kind of palette. In fact, the add global color icon won't be available unless you are using a document palette.

> **Global color**
>
> A global color is a color that allows you to change all occurrences of that color across your whole document by just editing its global color swatch. This is great for making quick global color revisions while you are working or for multiple color versions of a project.

In the upper-right corner are the Swatches panel preferences; see *Figure 5.8*. Starting at the top, we have **Add Global Color…**. This will also add the current fill color as a swatch to the document palette.

Add Application Palette allows you to create a color palette that will be accessible inside of any Affinity Designer file.

Add Document Palette creates a color palette that will only be accessible in the document that it was created in.

Rename Palette… allows you to rename a saved color palette.

Delete Palette will delete the current palette.

Create Palette From Document will create a palette based on all of the colors in your document and give it a name based on the document's name.

Create Palette From Image… will create a palette based on an image you choose from your hard drive and give it a name based on the image's name.

Appearance gives you the option of the size of the palette's color swatches – **small**, **medium**, or **large** – or to show the swatches as a list.

Sort allows viewing of the color swatches either alphabetically or by color.

Import Palette… allows you to import saved or exported Affinity Designer color palettes created and shared by other users in the Serif community. You can even import Adobe Swatch Exchange (.ase) files.

Export Palette… allows you to export palettes to share with other Affinity Designer users or to use in other documents.

Continuing on with the Swatches panel, let's take a closer look at the color palettes drop-down list:

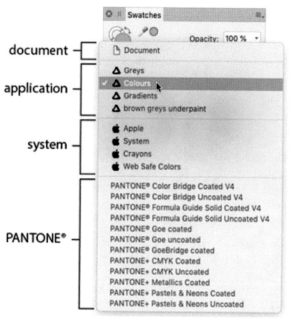

Figure 5.9 – The Swatches panel color palettes drop-down menu

This is where you can choose from the different palettes you have available to you, including the palettes that come with the application and palettes that you create or import. Color palettes in Affinity Designer are categorized into the following categories:

- The **document palette** is the palette for the current document you are working in. Your own fill color or global color swatches that you have created will appear here.

- **Application palettes** are palettes that come shipped with Affinity Designer or palettes that you have created yourself as application palettes from the Swatches panel preferences. You can add your own fill color swatches to these as well.

- **System palettes** are palettes that your operating system has and are also available in other applications.
- **PANTONE® palettes** are based on the worldwide PANTONE® color matching system. It's used mostly for commercial printing or for matching specific PANTONE® colors.

Often working side by side with the Swatches panel is the Stroke panel. It is a good idea to have it accessible when working with or adjusting color for your objects.

The Stroke panel

The Stroke panel is the epicenter for all things stroke- or path-related. The Stroke panel allows you to change the width of a stroke, the color, the line style, end caps, corner joins alignment along a path, the stacking order, arrowheads and tails, dashed lines, properties, and having variable-width strokes with the pressure feature. Here are a few examples:

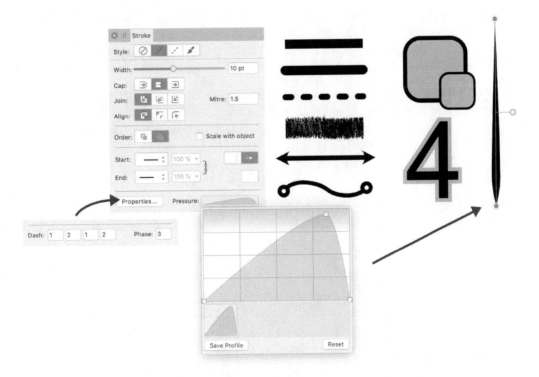

Figure 5.10 – The Stroke panel with some examples

Along with the various examples, let's take a look at what the Stroke panel options have to offer:

- **Style** can be set to **None, Solid, Dashed**, or **Brush** (taken from the Brushes panel).

- **Width** controls the width along the entire length of the path.

- **Cap** sets the end cap style (**Round, Butt**, or **Square**) for an open path.

- **Join** sets the shape of a corner where two paths join (**Round, Bevel**, or **Mitre**).

- **Mitre** sets the sharpness or flatness of the corner join.

- **Order** sets the stacking order of the stroke, either in front of or behind the object it is affecting.

- **Scale with object** allows the stroke width to scale up or down when the object is scaled up or down. If unchecked, the stroke will remain the same width whether scaled or not.

- **Start** and **End**: This refers to adding arrowheads to a path. You can add them to the start or end of the paths and the numbers are for scaling the arrowheads as a percentage. The link icon allows you to scale the arrowheads proportionately to each other. Click this to size each independently of each other.

- **Pressure** allows you to adjust the width of a stroke along its path using a profile graph. You click on the pressure icon and a small pop-up graph will appear for you to add or delete points you drag around to make your custom variable line width. You can save the profile for use on other stroked paths or reset it back to a single-line width stroke by clicking either the **Save Profile** or **Reset** buttons. Any saved profiles will show up with a small thumbnail below the graph. The example in *Figure 5.10* illustrates this feature and shows the saved thumbnail.

- **Properties…**: We click this for a separate pop-up properties panel with even more editing options for your selected path, as shown in the following screenshot:

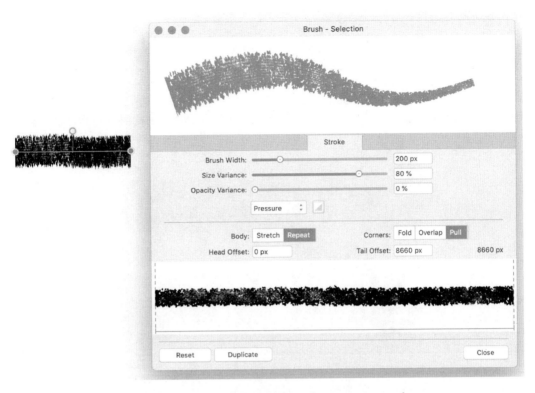

Figure 5.11 – The Stroke panel's stroke properties panel

- **Dash**: When a dashed line is created or selected, this row of options will replace the **Properties** and **Pressure** options at the bottom of the panel and allows you to create dashed lines by inputting numbers that represent dashes and spaces. The **Phase** option adjusts the starting point of the dash.

This brief introduction to the Color, Swatches, and Stroke panels, I hope, has given you a good sense of the amount of creative control these three panel options and features can offer. There is always more to explore, of course, and I encourage you to use the Affinity Designer help menu, visit the Affinity user forums, and watch and read tutorials online for more information.

Let's now move on to explore Affinity Designer's Effects panel and Styles panel.

The Effects panel

The Effects panel in Affinity Designer offers a host of fun options and features when you're ready to experiment or add a bit more control over the appearance of objects and elements in your projects. The Effects panel lets you add blurs, shadows, glows, outlines, 3D, bevel, and emboss effects, as well as color and gradient overlay effects to your work. It's amazing how handy some of these effects can be when you need to add that special something to an object or element. Let's explore what this panel can offer; see *Figure 5.12* for an idea of what type of effects are available:

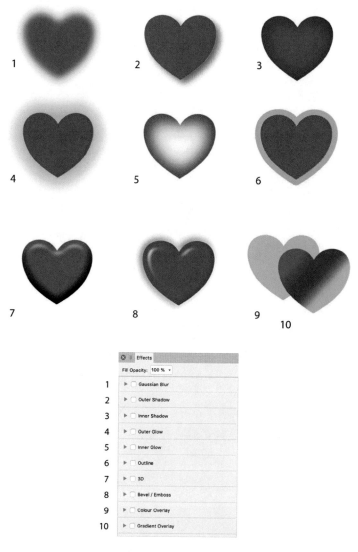

Figure 5.12 – The Effects panel with examples

The Effects panel, as shown by the examples in *Figure 5.12*, can offer you a ton of options for adding effects to your objects. There are too many to mention all of them here but here are some descriptions:

- **Gaussian Blur** adds a blur to the object. The amount of softness of the blur is adjustable.

- **Outer Shadow** is basically a drop shadow. You can change the color, blurriness, intensity, opacity, and position of the shadow.

- **Inner Shadow** adds a shadow inside of the object's shape. You can change the color, blurriness, intensity, opacity, and position of the shadow.

- **Outer Glow** is similar to **Outer Shadow** but with a different blend mode that produces more of a glow than a shadow. You can change the color, blurriness, intensity, opacity, and position of the glow.

- **Inner Glow** is similar to **Outer Glow** but is applied to the inside of the object's shape. You can change the color, blurriness, intensity, opacity, and position of the glow.

- **Outline** applies an outline to the outside of the object. You can adjust the outline width, alignment along the shape's path (inside, outside, middle), and whether the outline is solid, contoured, or a gradient.

- **3D** adds lighting and shading effects to your object, giving it a 3D appearance. You can adjust the light and shadow direction, the ambient color, and the amount and softness of the effect and add multiple lights.

- **Bevel / Emboss** is similar to 3D but has a few more options and controls for dimensional effects.

- **Color Overlay** and **Gradient Overlay** apply a solid color or gradient to the object. These are different from normal solid or gradient fills as they add the color or gradient overlay on top of what is already there, as in the 3D heart example shown in *Figure 5.13*:

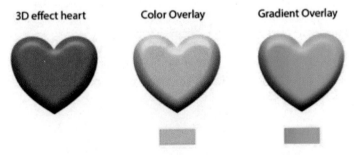

Figure 5.13 – The Effects panel option examples

All of these effects except **Gaussian Blur** are further adjustable with more advanced controls and other options accessible from a pop-up panel called the Layer Effects panel accessed by clicking on the small gray gear icon in the upper-right corner of each of the effect panes (except **Gaussian Blur**). See *Figure 5.14* for an example of the **Bevel / Emboss** effect:

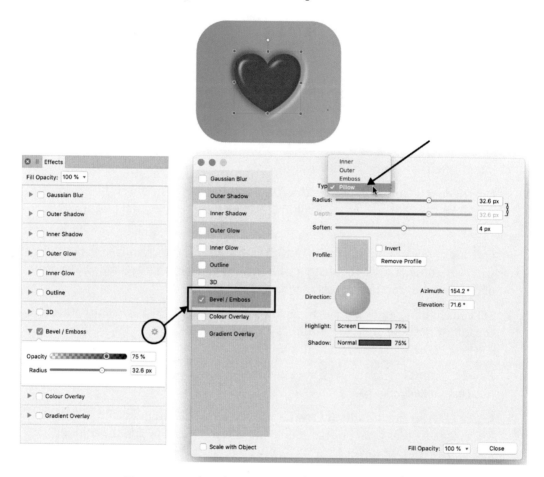

Figure 5.14 – The Effects panel with the Layer Effects panel

We will be covering more of the Effects panel in *Chapters 12, Creating Astronaut Ricky and Sidekick K9 and 13, Rocketing into the Pixel Cosmos,* using a real project example where we will be using several of these effects. In the meantime, let's continue this tour through the Studio panels chapter by taking a look at the Styles panel next.

The Styles panel

When you create or apply effects or certain fill and stroke attributes to objects, sometimes you'll find you will want to apply these same effects to other objects without having to recreate them each time. You can do this easily by creating a style. When you create a style, it gets stored in the Styles panel. You can then apply that style to other objects or strokes or even type or text elements in one click. Styles are a great time-saver for reusing and reapplying certain attributes that you use often. The Styles panel lets you create categories, name your styles, and even search for particular styles in the search field.

Figure 5.15 shows the Styles panel and it uses a gear icon to display each style with its name below it:

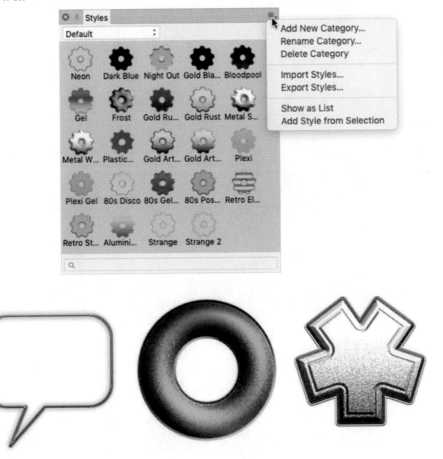

Figure 5.15 – The Styles panel

Above and to the left of the icons there is a category dropdown. This is where you'll find other categories if you have created or imported any. The group of styles in *Figure 5.15* is the **Default** styles that come with Affinity Designer. At the top right are the Style panel preferences. I have clicked on it so we can see what the preferences are for this panel. They are self-explanatory, I think. The last item in the list will let you add a style to the panel from a selected object or element. The bottom three shapes shown in *Figure 5.15* are examples of three of the styles from the panel. It's important to note that the shapes are not part of the style, just the effects, strokes, and fills. We'll create a new style in *Figure 5.16*:

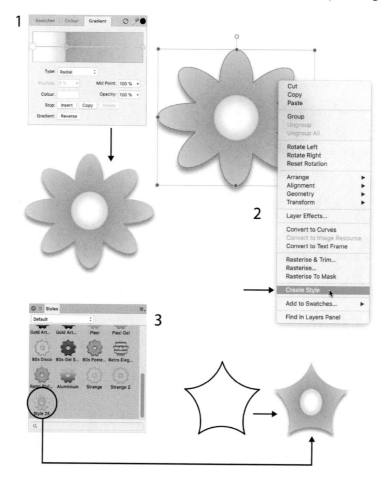

Figure 5.16 – Creating a style

Figure 5.16 shows a three-step process to create a custom style:

- We first created an interesting sun-like **Elliptical Gradient** for the inside of a flower-like shape (**1**) (we'll cover gradients in *Chapter 6, Tools – Designer Persona*).

- Then, we right-clicked or *Ctrl*-clicked on the object and chose **Create Style** from the context drop-down menu (**2**). Once we click a style, it will show up in the Styles panel. We renamed it `Sunflower`.

- Next, we created an entirely different shape and while it was still selected, clicked on the **Sunflower** style to apply it to the new shape (**3**).

Note how it just applies the elliptical gradient and the drop shadow that was part of the style but doesn't change the object to the flower shape.

Depending on the type of work you do, styles can be a real time-saver. Having the ability to apply styles to all kinds of different shapes and objects in your projects can be a game-changer. Along with assets and symbols, covered in *Chapter 10, Workflow: Symbols, Assets, and History*, using styles is a powerful way to speed up your workflow.

The Brushes panel – Designer and Pixel Personas

Brushes are a great way to add character or an organic feel to your work. There are two types of brushes in Affinity Designer, **Designer Persona** brushes and **Pixel Persona** brushes. As you might expect, the Designer Persona brushes are vector-based and the Pixel Persona brushes are pixel-based and the two setups, while similar in appearance, have slightly different working methods.

The Designer Persona brushes rely on vector strokes, curves, and paths. The brushes are applied to the vector curves along the paths. You can draw with a chosen brush from the Brushes panel using the vector brush tool, which allows immediate feedback. Or, you can create curves or shapes with the pen, pencil, or shape tools found in the Tool panel, then choose a brush in the vector brushes panel to apply that brush to the selected curve or shape. The advantage of the vector workflow is that it is a little more of an indestructible workflow than the Pixel workflow. Adjustments are often easier to make because there is an underlying curve that can always be adjusted or repositioned or even added to, and once a brush is chosen, it can be easily replaced by another simply by picking a different brush from the Brushes panel.

The Pixel persona brushes don't rely on vector paths but rather, they are painted freehand using the paint or pixel brush tools from the Pixel Persona Tool panel. While the Pixel workflow is a bit more destructive in nature, not allowing for some of that back and forth adjusting control of the Designer brushes, it does allow for more of a painterly and some might say a more creatively freeing approach. It is basically "digital" painting and depending on the brushes you use, it can be very similar looking to actual painting.

Affinity Designer is technically a vector-based drawing application, but with both the Designer Persona and the Pixel Persona brushes, you'll be able to blur the lines of what a vector application can look and feel like. The two personas work seamlessly together, so the combinations of what you can achieve are virtually limitless and are only confined by your imagination and maybe the processing power of your computer or tablet.

In upcoming chapters, we'll get the chance to try out some of Affinity Designer's brush workflow, but for now, let's take a look at the Designer and Pixel Brushes panels and how they are set up and work.

Figure 5.17 shows the **Designer Persona Brushes** panel with the **Layers** panel and showing the nature of how these vector brushes and how they use vector curves either as open or closed paths. In the Layers panel, each curve gets its own layer, making any adjustments or management of these brushes quite straightforward:

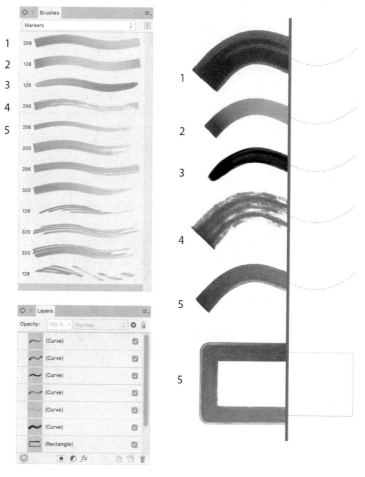

Figure 5.17 – The Designer Persona Brushes and Layers panels with examples

In *Figure 5.18* the **Pixel Persona Brushes** panel with the **Layers** panel shows a slightly different setup as compared to the Designer Persona brush behavior. In the Layers panel, all of the brush marks are placed in the active pixel layer. If you want to separate them into individual pixel layers similar to the Designer Persona behavior, you will need to first add a new pixel layer and then use the brush on that layer and continue to repeat that process for each individual layer:

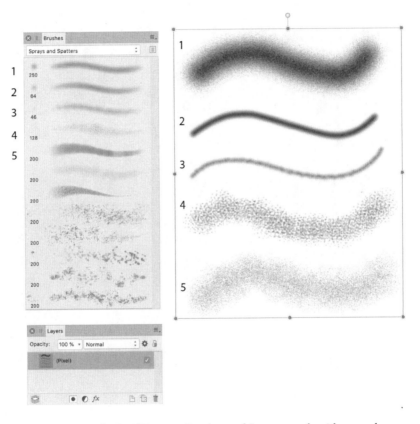

Figure 5.18 – The Pixel Persona Brushes and Layers panels with examples

Figure 5.19 shows the related menus and editing panel for the Designer Persona Brushes panel. The first screenshot shows the additional brushes menu accessed through the dropdown at the top of the panel (**1**). The second screenshot shows the preferences related to categories, importing and exporting, and adding new types of brushes (**2**). The third screenshot shows the brush editing dialog for the fine-tuning of a selected brush (**3**):

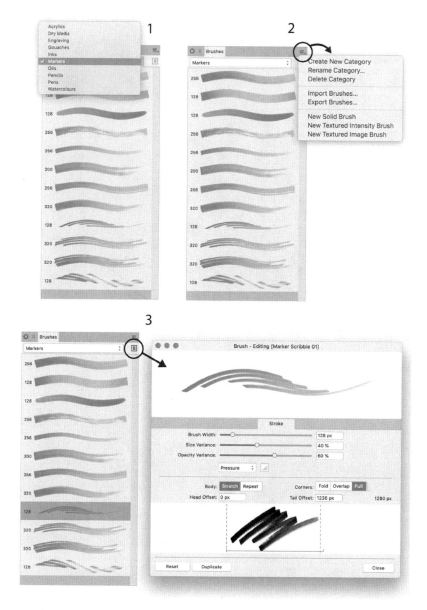

Figure 5.19 – The Designer Persona Brushes panel with supporting menus and panel

Figure 5.20 shows the related menus and editing panel for the **Pixel Persona Brushes** panel. The first screenshot shows the additional brushes menu accessed through the dropdown at the top of the panel (**1**). The second screenshot shows the preferences related to categories, importing and exporting, and adding new types of brushes (**2**). The third screenshot shows the brush editing dialog for the fine-tuning of a selected brush (**3**). Note that there are three more tabs in this dialog than there were in the Designer Brushes editing panel:

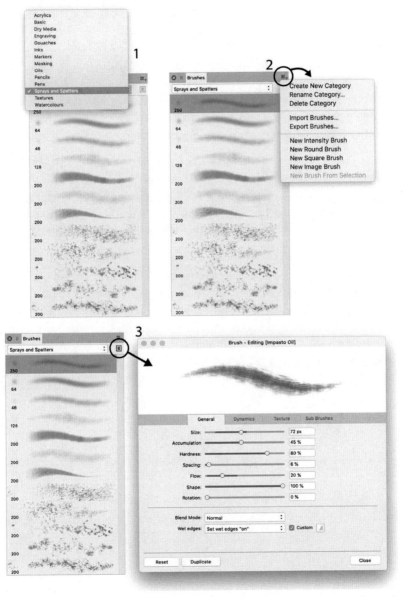

Figure 5.20 – The Pixel Persona Brushes panel with supporting menus and panel

Having the choice in Affinity Designer between the vector and pixel brush workflows will give you ample ways to achieve just about any kind of creative effect you can imagine.

Let's move on now to the next section and explore the many text-related options the application has to offer with its impressive and extensive group of type panels.

The Type panels – Character, Paragraph Typography, and Text Styles

When it comes to type, Affinity Designer has you covered. Admittedly, I don't use a lot of text in the type of illustration work I do with Affinity Designer but when I do, I am amazed at the sheer number of options available. That being said, type and text is a wide topic with a huge array of varieties available, including art text, frame text, path text, and shape text, and within each of these varieties, there are many options that could take a whole book to cover.

For our purposes, we won't be diving into each and every aspect of these varieties. Instead, we will take a look at the related relevant panels, as well as touching a bit further on text in the two exercise chapters. Hopefully, this will be enough to get you started or make you curious to learn more about text on your own. As always, the **Affinity Designer Help** system is an amazing resource to tap into. There is a huge section on text that will most likely answer all of your text-related questions beyond what we will cover in this section.

There is a good chance your introduction to text in Affinity Designer will most likely be the **Character** panel. The Character panel allows you to choose your text's font family, size, weight, style, color, decoration, positioning and transforms (leading, kerning, tracking, baseline, horizontal and vertical scaling, shearing, super and subscript, and letter and word spacing), special typographical ligatures, alternatives, fractions, and languages and optical alignment. All of this is in the Character panel:

Figure 5.21 – The Character panel

The next text-related panel you would likely come across will probably be the Paragraph panel. The Paragraph panel allows control of, you guessed it, paragraphs, as well as "stories," or collections of paragraphs.

Specifically, you can control overall paragraph alignment or justification, spacing including leading, indenting, spacing before, between, and after each paragraph, tab stops, specific justification with word and letter spacing, bullets, and numbering. Again, there's a lot going on in one panel:

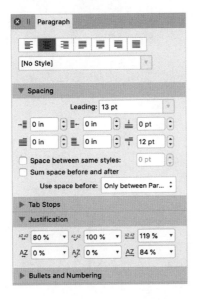

Figure 5.22 – The Paragraph panel

Three more text-related panels you might also come across if you do a lot of work with text are the Text Styles, Glyph Browser, and Typography panels. They are fairly specialized and I personally don't use them very often but they are there if you need them. You can see what they look like in *Figure 5.23*:

Figure 5.23 – The Text Styles, Glyph Browser, and Typography panels

Text Styles allows you to create and save text styles, as well as modifying text styles globally across a document.

Glyphs are a sort of icon or graphic that are included in most typefaces that represent certain ideas or concepts. A dollar sign is a glyph. The Glyph Browser panel is the place to find these types of characters.

The Typography panel is a special panel that allows quick access to many common type-related options such as **Ligatures**, **Figure Position**, and **Capitals**.

All five of these type panels can be found from the **Text** dropdown in the main menu bar.

As I said earlier, there is a lot more type-related information that Affinity Designer has under the hood that we didn't get to discuss here. Although we didn't hit on all of it, we did get an introduction to the main type panels and hopefully I have given you a sense of what to expect when you start investigating or exploring all things type in Affinity Designer.

Manager panels – Guides, Grids, Snapping, and Resources

Let's finish off this long chapter by taking a look at some of Affinity Designer's main manager panels: Guides, Grids, Snapping, and Resources.

Books about creative applications such as Affinity Designer tend to concentrate on the drawing and painting, or basically the "creation," side of things predominantly, and for good reason – it's fun and there is usually a lot to explore. However, often the difference between a good application and a great application is the supporting aspects of the software. Looking only to the creative side of things is really only half of the picture. The other half may not be as engaging at first glance but it's certainly as important. In fact, if done right, it enables you to really concentrate on the creative side all the more.

Guides manager

Let's start with the Guides manager, as shown in *Figure 5.24*:

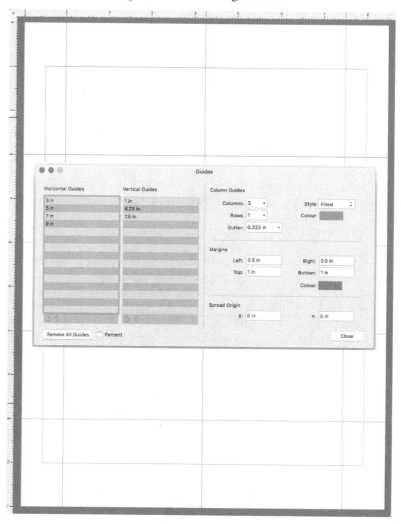

Figure 5.24 – The Guides manager

The Guides manager is the place to manage all of your document guides. To add a guide, you can either drag out a guide from the top- or left-side rulers by clicking inside of a ruler, holding and dragging out into the document approximately where you want your guides to be, or you can click on the new guide icon in the bottom left-hand corners of the horizontal or vertical guide input areas and input exact measurements or a percentage if the **Percent** box is checked. Selecting a guide and then clicking the small trash can icon will remove it. Or, click the **Remove All Guides** button to clear all of your document's guides.

To the right are controls and options for **Column Guides**, **Margins**, and the **Spread Origin**. **Spread Origin** is the location of the origin or start of the 0 (zero) location for the top (*x*) or side (*y*) rulers. Let's look at Grids now.

Grids Manager

Grids can play an important role in your workflow. From laying out page spreads to complicated illustration or logo work, if you are someone who likes to work with grids, then you're going to love Affinity Designer's vast array of grid options.

The Grid and Axis manager controls are wide-ranging and extensive. The following screenshots show just three grid scenarios out of many that are possible in Affinity Designer. The fourth screenshot of the Isometric panel, *Figure 5.27*, isn't really a manager but I thought because of its tight integration with the isometric grid setup it belonged in this chapter.

In its most basic form, *Figure 5.25* shows the Grid and Snapping Axis manager:

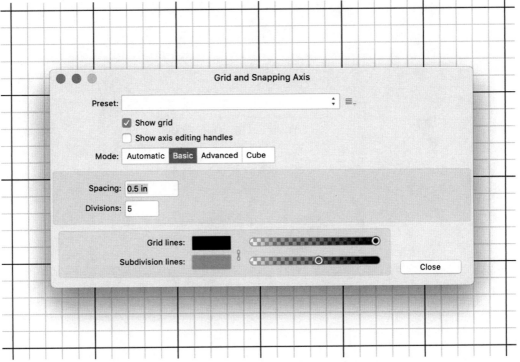

Figure 5.25 – The Grid and Snapping Axis manager with a Basic grid setup

Figure 5.26 shows a couple of different customizable advanced options:

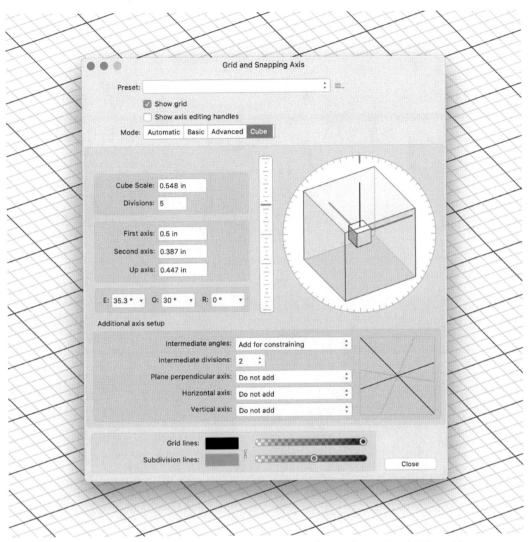

Figure 5.26 – The Grid and Snapping Axis Manager with an Advanced and Cube grid setup

The Isometric panel is a unique, one-of-a-kind, dynamic grid system for snapping and object alignment:

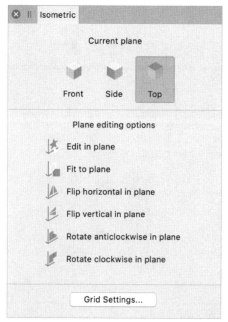

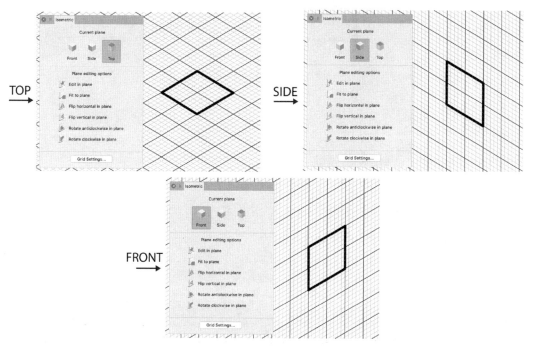

Figure 5.27 – The Isometric panel with examples of isometric grid setups

I do a lot of isometric work in Affinity Designer and having a grid system and a dedicated Isometric panel specifically designed for working with isometric projection is a huge time-saver and makes the work much more enjoyable to create. The ability to edit in plane, fit to plane, flip horizontal or vertical, or rotate clockwise or counterclockwise in plane is invaluable. You can either draw normally and then click the buttons to snap it to the grid plane or you can work in plane so as you draw it adheres to the chosen plane. It's amazing!

Figure 5.28 illustrates how using the isometric grid supports the isometric work I do:

Figure 5.28 – Illustration detail showing the Isometric grid in action

We have just scratched the surface with grids here. Serif has put a lot of work into the grid system of Affinity Designer. I encourage you to dive deeper and explore the full range of possibilities for yourself.

The Snapping manager

Closely related to Guides and Grids is Snapping. Snapping is fairly robust in Affinity Designer and can be set up to work in a variety of ways. Snapping allows you to align with a noticeable snap – objects, images, brush strokes, paths, text objects or text frames to grids, other objects, page guides, margins, artboards, key points on objects, object geometry, and so on. In fact, the options are so extensive that they created a dedicated Snapping manager to address all of the possible scenarios. In addition to the Snapping manager, there is also a Snapping manager dropdown from the toolbar, shown here circled in the upper-right side of the figure; just click on the magnet icon in the toolbar:

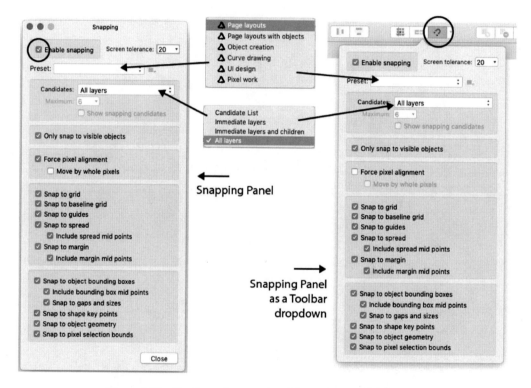

Figure 5.29 – The Snapping panel and Snapping panel dropdown

The options in the Snapping manager dropdown are identical to the floating Snapping manager. On each, there are presets located in the **Preset** dropdown to access. You can create your own presets and access them here as well. Additionally, there are "candidates" that you can target and are located in the **Candidates** dropdown. For a complete rundown of all of the options, please take a look at the Affinity Designer Help menu. There are too many options to mention here, although *Figure 5.29* should give you a good idea of the amount of snapping options you will have access to should you be interested in snapping in Affinity Designer.

Resource Manager

Resource Manager lets you manage the resources you have in your document. At the moment, Affinity Designer allows images and other Affinity Designer documents to be placed as resources in your document. You can place them as **Embedded**, where they are actually a part of the document, or as **Linked**, where they remain as a link outside of the current document:

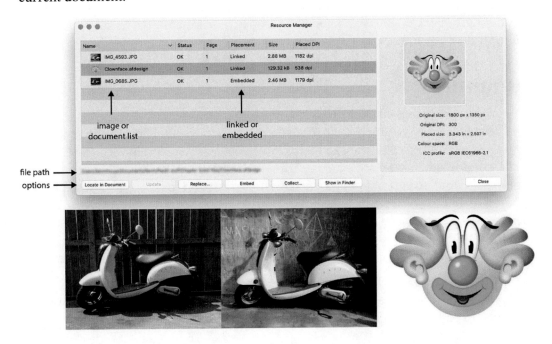

Figure 5.30 – The Resource manager

You can, however, embed or link any resource using the **Embed** or **Linked** buttons at the bottom of the panel. Other options include **Locate in Document**; if your document is large and complex using this to locate a resource may come in handy. **Replace…** will provide a popup to allow you to locate and replace a resource. **Collect…** will collect all of the resources to a desired location and either let you choose or create a folder to put them into. Note that **Collect…** will not collect any fonts. To collect fonts, go to **File | Save as Package**. This will package up your document including resources and fonts. **Show in Finder** will locate the selected resource's location on your computer.

With placed documents (Affinity Designer files), such as the clown face in *Figure 5.30*, one thing to note is that documents are placed as single objects. This means you won't be able to edit the placed document or have access to any of its paths or objects. If you do want to make changes to a placed document, there are two ways of doing this and they depend on whether they are embedded or linked in the current file. If embedded, then you will have to go back to the original file and make your changes to it, save it, and then place it back into your current document. If it's linked, then by double-clicking on it in your current document, Affinity Designer will automatically open it for you in a new window for you to edit it. Once edited and saved, it will automatically update in your current document.

Summary

In this chapter, we explored the myriad of options and features offered by the main Studio panels and managers. We discussed panel behavior and conventions and took a look at not only how the Color, Swatches, and Stroke panels operate but also how closely they are linked to one another. We discovered the Effects and Styles panels' ability to expand the appearance of our objects and design elements in exciting and fun ways, and we explored the Vector and Pixel Brushes panels, learning about their differences and strengths. From there, we looked into the text panels and the very many options that are available to us when working with type. We finally ended this chapter by taking a look at Affinity Designer's managers, which make up a big part of the practical side of this creative application.

In the next chapter, we are going to shift focus and start to look at the tools of the Designer Persona. Getting to know the tools is the next step in getting ourselves closer to being up and running with Affinity Designer.

6

Tools – Designer Persona

Welcome to the sixth chapter of *Up and Running with Affinity Designer*.

Tools are the heart of Affinity Designer. Here, you'll find the design tools, shape tools, text tools, selection tools, retouch tools, and export tools. We'll cover all of these in the next two chapters and lay the groundwork for you to move forward and discover the possibilities Affinity Designer has to offer.

The tools discussed in this chapter pertain to the vector tools in the **Designer Persona**.

In this chapter, we'll cover the following topics:

- Designer Persona tools
- Shape tools
- Text tools
- The Color Picker tool
- The View tool
- The Zoom tool

Note

Rather than listing every single option that is available for each tool, which might indeed double the thickness of this book, I am going to concentrate on the options most likely to benefit us in getting up to speed with Affinity Designer. I encourage you to visit the Help System for a complete and up-to-date rundown of all of the available options and settings offered for each tool. Go to **HELP | AFFINITY DESIGNER HELP | TOOLS** to see this information.

We will look at each of the Design, Shape, and Text tools, what they do, and certain specific options or settings that are available in the Context Toolbar when they are selected. While some tools may share the same options, others will have their own unique options. You can see an overview of the tools in the following screenshot:

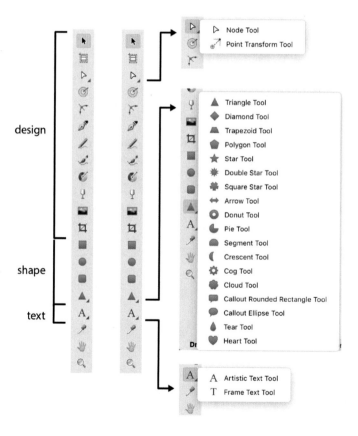

Figure 6.1 – The Designer Persona Tools panel with flyouts

Later, in the practical exercise chapters— *Chapter 11, Creating a Professional Logo, Chapter 12, Creating Astronaut Ricky and Sidekick K9, and Chapter 13, Rocketing into the Pixel Cosmos*—we will cover how to use some of these tools (in particular, the drawing tools) as and when we need them for the exercises. This is the best way to really explore how to use the tools by actually tackling a real project, creating objects and elements. For now, let's just get acquainted with the tools and which options they have available.

Designer Persona tools

In covering our tools chapters, we will be discussing the tools in the order that they appear in the Tools panel, from top to bottom. For this chapter on the Designer Persona tools, we'll start with the Move Tool and finish up with the Zoom Tool.

The Move Tool

The **Move Tool** (shortcut *v*) is the main selection tool. The icon for this tool is shown here:

Figure 6.2 – The Move Tool

Affinity Designer refers to it as the Move Tool, but in other similar applications, it might be called the Selection Tool. The Move Tool is used to make selections of objects or groups of objects. Once selected, these objects can be moved, rotated, scaled to different sizes, or have their properties changed.

Selecting is as simple as clicking on an object with the Move Tool. Before you can modify or move any object or group of objects, you must first select it. In order to select or edit objects on multiple layers or a layer other than the one you are working on, you must have the **Edit All Layers** button selected. This is located in the bottom-left corner of the Layers panel. With the **Edit All Layers** button, you can either deselect it to lock the current layer so that it is the only layer that is editable or select it, unlocking and allowing all layers to be editable, as illustrated in the following screenshot:

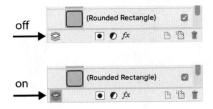

Figure 6.3 – The Edit All Layers toggle in the Layers panel

I like the ability to be able to select anything I want on any layer, so I have **Edit All Layers** selected 95% of the time.

To select multiple objects, you can either hold the *Shift* key down while clicking on multiple elements with the Move Tool or click, hold, and drag out a marquee selection around the objects with the Move Tool.

Depending on what is selected with the Move Tool, different options will be available in the **Context Toolbar**—for example, a **Shape Object**, a **Stroke Object**, or a **Text Object** will present different options for each. Let's take a look at each type of object in the following screenshots and break down what some of these options allow us to do for each when the Move Tool is selected.

When the Move Tool is active and nothing is selected in the document, the Context Toolbar will only display the **Document Setup** and **Preferences** buttons.

These are the three types of objects available: Shape, Text, and Stroke or Curve, as illustrated in the following screenshot:

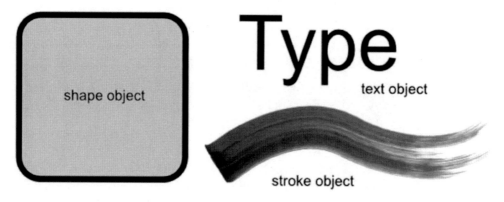

Figure 6.4 – Three types of objects

When a **Shape** object is selected with the **Move Tool**, the following options are available in the Context Toolbar:

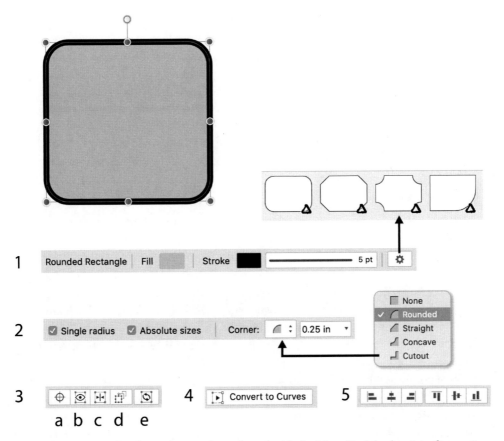

Figure 6.5 – Options for Shape objects when selected with the Move Tool, broken into five sections

In order to get the Context Toolbar larger for better readability, in *Figure 6.5* I have separated the horizontal Context Toolbar into five sections, starting on the left-hand side and continuing to the right, outlined as follows:

- *Section 1*—This starts with the selected object's name. In our case, it's a **Rounded Rectangle**. Next are the **Fill** and **Stroke** colors: a gray fill and a black stroke. This is followed by the style and width of the stroke in points.

> **Note**
> If you click on the thumbnail of a line or a line-width number, a dropdown identical to the **Stroke panel** discussed in *Chapter 5, Main Studio Panels and Managers* will appear.

The last option in *Section 1* is the gear icon with the **Preset** button. Clicking this will pop up a panel of thumbnails with presets to choose from.

- *Section 2*—This section of the Context Toolbar presents options for the corners of the selected shape—specifically, the corner style. **Single radius** means a single type or style of corner for all of the shape's corners. If you want different corner styles for each corner, uncheck this. **Absolute sizes** will allow for a decimal number; unchecking it will calculate the size by a percentage. The **Corner** option is a dropdown of different styles of corner options. If **Single radius** is selected, all of the corners will be the same style. If **Single radius** is unchecked, you may have four different styles, one for each corner. The last option of *Section 2* controls the size of the corners with a drop-down slider.

- *Section 3*—These five icons represent a few handy options that enable certain transforms or design aids for the selected object. Icon **a** is to enable the movable **Transform Origin**. This allows you to set an origin to rotate or scale the selected object around—for example, dragging the transform origin to the upper-left corner of a selected object will allow you to rotate the object around its upper-left corner. The transform origin can also be positioned outside of your shape; basically, it can be moved anywhere in your document to affect the rotation or scaling of your selected object. Icon **b** is a toggle that allows you to **Hide Selection while Dragging**. This behavior will affect every object selected until it is turned off again. Icon **c** allows you to switch on **Alignment Handles**, which will let you align two or more selected objects quickly. Icon **d** allows you to **Transform Objects Separately** or independently of one another rather than as a group. Icon **e** allows you to toggle a **Cycle Selection Box** on the bounds after you have transformed the selected object, as illustrated in the following screenshot:

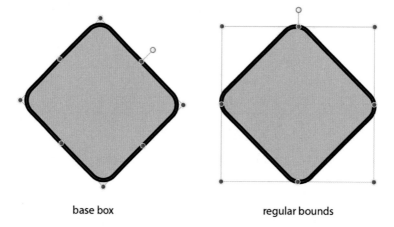

base box   regular bounds

Figure 6.6 – Icon e: Cycle Selection Box toggle

- *Section 4*—This section's option will **Convert to Curves**, essentially removing the dynamic parametric options from the shapes and turning them into basic Bezier curves and nodes. This is useful when you want to edit a shape, to create new shapes that are beyond its default parametric property options.

- *Section 5*—This section contains quick alignment options of two or more selected objects.

When a **Text Object** is selected with the **Move Tool**, the following options are available in the Context Toolbar:

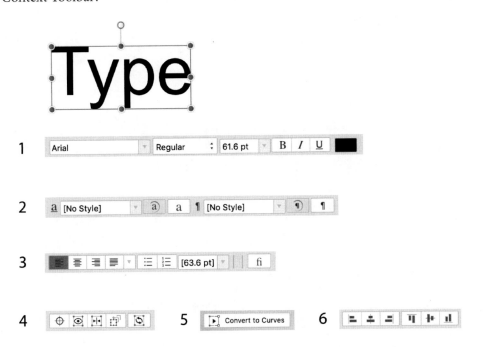

Figure 6.7 – Options for Text Objects when selected with the Move Tool, broken into five sections

- *Section 1*—This shows the first two dropdowns in the Context Toolbar for the Font Family and the Font Weight of the selected text object. Clicking on the first dropdown will give you access to all of the fonts you have accessible on your computer. The second dropdown will give you access to the selected font's weights available for that particular font. To the right are the font properties for size, bold, italic, and underline. The last option in *Section 1* is for the font color. Clicking on this will display the color panel to edit the font's color.

- *Section 2*—This section has two dropdowns to access the Character Styles and the Paragraph Styles as well as the Character panel and the Paragraph panel.

- *Section 3*—This section's text options include **Left**, **Center**, **Right**, and **Left Justified** text alignments, with a small dropdown to the right of the **Left Justified** option for other **Justified** options. Further to the right are options for **Bullets** and **Numbering** text, with the final option in this section being for adjusting the **Paragraph Leading** or the space between text baselines.

- *Sections 4-6*—These are essentially the same as the options for the Shape object. One thing to note for the **Convert to Curves** option: as with the Shape object, once a Text Object is converted to curves, the ability to change the font becomes unavailable. Converting text to curves converts it to regular Bezier curves and nodes.

When a **Stroke Object** is selected with the **Move Tool**, the following options are available in the Context Toolbar:

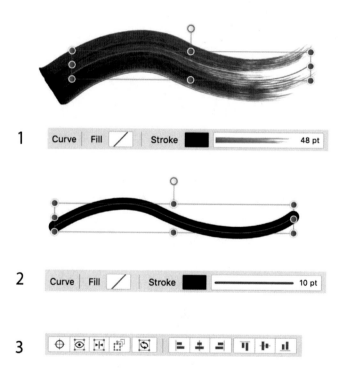

Figure 6.8 – Options for Stroke Objects when selected with the Move Tool, broken into three sections

- *Sections 1-2*—These present options for a curve's **Fill** and **Stroke** color. *Section 1* shows a thumbnail for a **48**-point **Textured Line** style, and *Section 2* shows a thumbnail for a **10**-point **Solid Line** style.

- *Section 3*—This shows the same options available for the **Stroke** as the previous two *Figure 6.7* and *Figure 6.8* options for selected **Shape** and **Text Objects**.

The Artboard Tool

The **Artboard Tool** lets you add, resize, and move artboards in your document. The icon for this tool is shown here:

Figure 6.9 – The Artboard Tool

For more on artboards, see the *Using Artboards* section of *Chapter 4, Document Setup and Modification*.

With the Artboard Tool selected, the following options are available in the Context Toolbar:

Figure 6.10 – The Artboard Tool options

There are two options available in the Context Toolbar for the Artboard Tool. The **Document** dropdown offers a few common preset sizes—this list is for popular **iPhone OS (iOS)** devices and tablets. This will add an artboard at one of those specific sizes. The second option is the **Insert Artboard** button, which will add a new artboard to your document at the same size as the last created artboard. If you have no artboards currently in your document, it will convert your single page into an artboard.

The Node Tool

The **Node Tool** (shortcut *a*) is used to add or remove nodes, remove sections, or edit or transform existing nodes. The icon for this tool is shown here:

Figure 6.11 – The Node Tool

The Node Tool can also be used to adjust **Shape** object parameters and transform **Text Objects** after they have been converted to curves, as illustrated in the following screenshot:

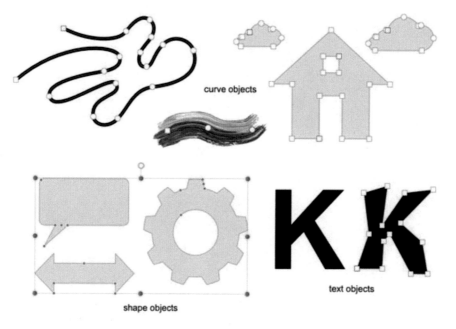

Figure 6.12 – Three types of objects: Curve, Shape, and Text

Affinity Designer's Bezier vector paths have points along the path called nodes where the path changes direction or curves to form the shape of an object. You won't be able to see or edit these nodes unless you have the Node Tool active. You can select the Node Tool in the Tools panel, use the Node Tool shortcut (*a*), or if you have the Move Tool active, double-click on a curve or shape object to activate the Node Tool, allowing you to edit the nodes. If it is a Shape object, the Node Tool will allow you to transform the red editing handles. Double-clicking on the red handles will reset any moved or edited handles to their default positions.

When a **Curve** or **Stroke Object** is selected with the **Node Tool**, the following options are available in the Context Toolbar:

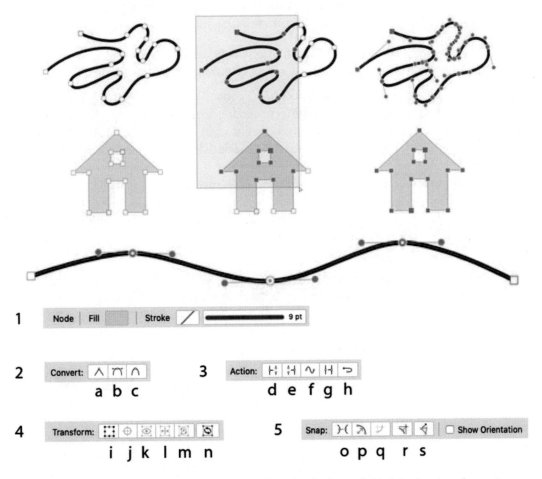

Figure 6.13 – Options for Curve Objects when selected with the Node Tool, broken into five sections

In *Figure 6.13*, I am showing two typical types of objects comprised of curves—a couple of open-ended **Paths** with a black **Stroke** applied to them and a simple **Vector** house-shaped object drawn with a curve and filled in with a gray color. The objects in the first column are initially selected with the Node Tool by clicking once on each of them. In the center of *Figure 6.13*, I am showing a second selection made by Marquee selecting a rectangle around both objects by clicking and dragging the Node Tool around all of the nodes. Notice in the third column the nodes are now solid, and the nodes of the open path curve are showing their Bezier adjustment handles, which can also be adjusted with the Node Tool.

There are some fairly subtle differences between some of these **Convert**, **Action**, and **Snap** options, and I encourage you to go through them one at a time to really see how they can work for your workflow. Let's look at the options in detail, as follows:

- *Section 1*—The **Fill** and **Stroke** options, as well as the **Stroke Weight** and **Style** dropdown that will open the Stroke panel, were covered earlier with the Move Tool.

- *Section 2* **a**, **b**, and **c**—These three icons will convert any selected nodes into **a** —**Sharp Node**, which creates a sharp corner, **b**—**Smooth Node**, which creates a smooth rounded corner or change in direction, and **c**—**Smart Node**, which tries to smooth out the path in a sort of automatic mode, which may or may not be suitable for all circumstances. Any node can be converted into any of the other two nodes by selecting the node you want to change and clicking on one of the icons. Sharp nodes are displayed as small squares or boxes, smooth nodes display as hollow circles, and smart nodes display as circles with dots inside them, as seen in the bottom wavy path just below the house objects.

- *Section 3* **d**, **e**, **f**, **g**, and **h**—These are node actions that control behaviors between the nodes and curves. The first action, **d**—**Break Curve**, will break a curve, splitting the path where the node is located. **e**—**Close Curve** will close the curve if it's an open curve. If it's a closed curve, this option will be unavailable. **f**—**Smooth Curve** will add smooth nodes along the path in order to try to smooth the curve, while **g**— **Join Curves** will join two selected separate curves. For the expected results, initially select the two nodes where you want the join to occur, otherwise Affinity Designer may join two unwanted nodes. **h**—**Reverse Curve** reverses the direction of the curve; this can be handy when you place an arrowhead at the end of a curve in the Stroke panel and need to quickly switch ends of the curve.

- *Section 4* **i, j, k, l, m**, and **n**—These will transform nodes that have been selected with the Node Tool. The first transform, **i—Transform Mode**, will add a transform bounding box around the selected nodes, which can then be scaled, rotated, skewed, or repositioned as a group. Icons **j** through **m** only become available once the Transform Mode icon (**i**) is selected, and icons **j** through **l** behave in the same way as they did with the Move Tool. They are **j—Enable Transform Origin, k— Hide Selection while Dragging**, and **l—Show Alignment Handles**. **m—Selection Box from Curves** puts a selection box around the entire selection, similar to the Transform Mode bounding box (**i**). **n —Cycle Selection Box** is identical to the explanation provided for *Figure 6.5*.

- *Section 5* **o, p, q, r**, and **s** icons are **Snap** options for nodes that have been selected with the Node Tool. The first **Snap** option, **o—Align to Nodes of Selected Curve**, will align a selected node with other nodes of the same or other selected curves as you click and drag the node around with the Node Tool; **p—Snap to Geometry of Selected Curve** will snap to the actual curve geometry of any selected path; **q— Snap All Selected Nodes when Dragging** is only available if the **p** icon is selected. It adds the ability to snap all of the selected nodes to another node or path, either on its own curve or another selected curve. These are some subtle snapping differences, no doubt, but they can come in handy if you need them. The **r** icon will **Align Handle Positions Using Snapping Options** that you have set up in the **Snapping Manager**—that is, snap to grids, guides, geometry, key points, spread, and margins. **s – Perform Construction Snapping** is independent of the **Snapping Manager** and affects only the node's control-handle behavior, as the select handle reacts with adjacent handles in various ways. It's best to experiment with this one to get familiar with its options. Consult the Help System via **HELP | AFFINITY DESIGNER HELP | TOOLS | DESIGN TOOLS | NODE TOOL** for more information. **Show Orientation** will show the orientation or direction of a selected closed curve with a small black outline, as illustrated in the following screenshot:

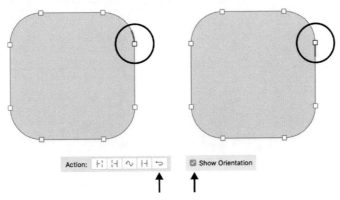

Figure 6.14 – Show Orientation toggled with the reverse curve action option

The Point Transform Tool

Found in the flyout of the Node Tool, the **Point Transform Tool** (shortcut *s*) is a powerful node-based **rotation**, **scaling**, and **repositioning** tool. The icon for this tool is shown here:

Figure 6.15 – The Point Transform Tool

In its basic form, simply clicking and dragging on a node of a selected object will freely rotate and scale the whole object simultaneously, based on the location of the **Transform Origin**, which automatically appears once a tool is selected from the Tools panel. This transform origin can be moved anywhere in the document to affect the selected object's point of transformation. Also, a quick click on a node will relocate the transform origin to that node.

Additional controls are enabled with the *Shift* and *Command* keys, as shown in the following screenshot:

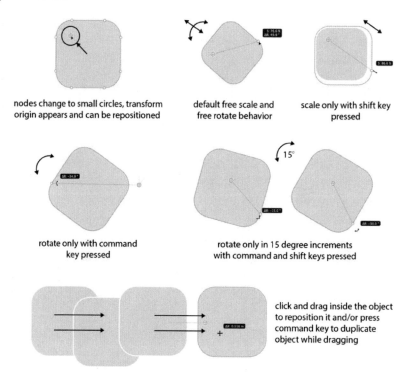

Figure 6.16 – The Point Transform Tool

When a **Curve**, **Shape**, or **Text Object** is selected with the **Point Transform Tool**, the following options are available in the Context Toolbar:

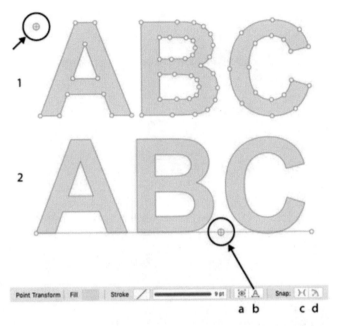

Figure 6.17 – Options for Curve, Shape, and Text objects with the Point Transform Tool

The **Fill** and **Stroke** options, as well as the **Stroke Weight** and **Style** dropdown, are the same as covered earlier with the Move Tool. Icon **a—Hide Selection while Dragging** will hide the selection bounds when an object is moved using the Point Transformation Tool, icon **b—Text Baseline Mode** hides the text nodes (**1**) and displays a text baseline (**2**) to snap the transform origin to for transformations using the baseline, icon **c—Align to Nodes of Selected Curve** allows alignment of the transform origin to nodes of selected objects, and icon **d** allows the transform origin to **Snap to Geometry of Selected Curves**.

The Contour Tool

The **Contour Tool** adds an offset (or inset) outline to a shape, vector, or stroke object, adding or reducing the original object's outline. The icon for this tool is shown here:

Figure 6.18 – The Contour Tool

A contour, as shown in the following screenshot, can be created on the outside or inside of the original object:

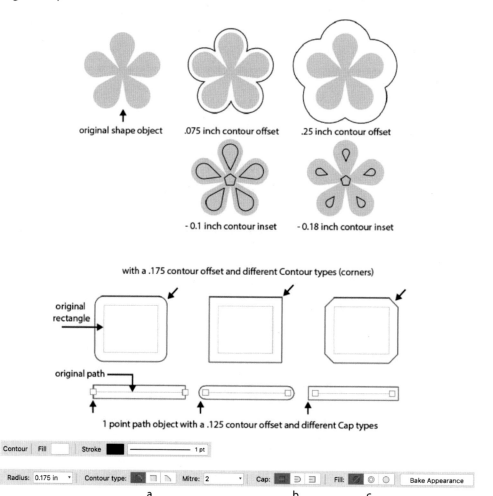

Figure 6.19 – The Contour Tool Offset and Inset options plus Cap types for open paths

When a **Curve**, **Shape**, or **Text Object** is selected, the **Contour Tool** has the following options in the Context Toolbar:

- *Section 1*—The **Fill** and **Stroke** options, as well as the **Stroke Weight** and **Style** dropdown, are again the same as covered earlier with the Move Tool.

- *Section 2*, from left to right, starts with the **Radius** amount. This can be entered numerically, with the slider or with the Contour Tool selected, and clicking and dragging will increase or decrease this amount. Next is the **Contour Type** icon group **a**, which controls the type of corners applied to the original shape. Your choices are **Round**, **Mitre**, or **Bevel**. Then, we have a **Mitre** dropdown, which allows you to apply a custom mitre amount to the **Mitre** option. Next is the **Cap** options icon group **b** for open paths, as shown again in *Figure 6.19*. The choices here are **No Cap**, **Round Cap**, or **Square Cap**. Next is the **Fill** behavior options icon group **c** for the shape. Choose from **Auto Closed**, **Force Open**, or **Force Closed**. This alters the fill type of the shape, making it hollow or filled in. If unsure of what these options do, it's best to experiment with your own shapes to find out what works best for you and your particular needs. The final option is the ability to **Bake Appearance**. This is simply another way of applying a contour effect or converting your shape to curves.

Note

Once baked, a contour will no longer be editable.

The Corner Tool

The **Corner Tool** adjusts corners on **Shape** objects, **Paths**, or **Objects** created with the **Pen Tool**. The icon for this tool is shown here:

Figure 6.20 – The Corner Tool

With a corner node or group of nodes selected, simply click and drag with the Corner Tool to apply the adjustment, as illustrated in the following screenshot:

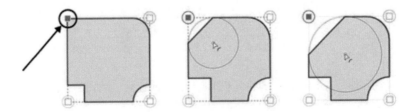

Figure 6.21 – Using the Corner Tool

You can edit all of the corners of a selected object at once if they are all selected, or you can edit each corner independently by selecting each corner separately before adjusting. The corners can also be of different corner types, as shown in *Figure 6.21* and the following screenshot, allowing for some pretty unique shapes to be created by just adjusting the corners. Numerical **Radius** amounts can also be applied for exact sizes:

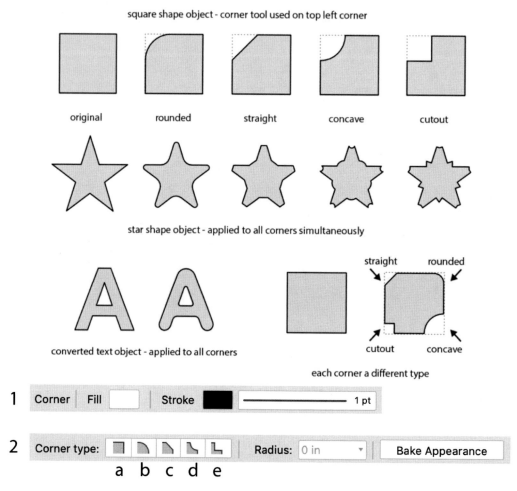

Figure 6.22 – The Corner Tool options and examples

When a **Curve**, **Shape**, or converted **Text Object** corner is selected, the **Corner Tool** has the following options in the Context Toolbar:

- *Section 1*—The **Fill** and **Stroke** options, as well as the **Stroke Weight** and **Style** dropdown, are again the same as covered earlier with the Move Tool.

- *Section 2—***Corner Type** icons, as shown in the top row of *Figure 6.22*, are **a** – **None**, **b**—**Rounded**, **c**—**Straight**, **d**—**Concave**, and **e**—**Cutout**. The **Corner Type** icons are followed by a numerical **Radius** field or slider for inputting specific sizes of your corner adjustments. **Bake Appearance** will convert the selected corner type into a curve.

> **Note**
> Once baked, a corner will no longer be editable.

The Pen Tool

The **Pen Tool** (shortcut *p*) is likely one of the most used tools in the Designer Persona toolset. The icon for this tool is shown here:

Figure 6.23 – The Pen Tool

This tool is very adept at drawing straight, curved, closed, and open shapes in a very controlled and precise manner. Often, you will find yourself needing to create a shape that just can't be accomplished with one of Affinity Designer's shape objects, enter the mighty Pen Tool. At first, it may seem intimidating, and yes—it can take a bit of time to get the hang of, but with practice, you will soon find it to be one of the most versatile tools for creating just about anything.

Creating and combining a few simple line and curve shapes, you can create any sort of object, as illustrated in the following screenshot:

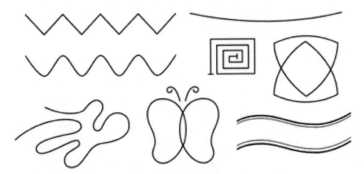

Figure 6.24 – Objects created with the Pen Tool

The Pen Tool—in combination with edits and transforms using the Node, Point Transform, or Move Tool—can really get you started on making simple to complex objects that in *Figure 6.25* are taking the form of a cute stegosaurus and a slightly mad clown:

Figure 6.25 – Combining simple Pen Tool shapes to create more complex-looking objects

With the addition of subtle shading and effects, your Pen Tool-drawn shapes will begin—at least in this case—to take on a bit of character and life.

With the **Pen Tool** selected, the following options are available in the Context Toolbar:

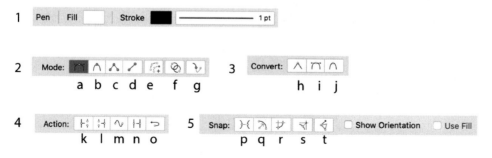

Figure 6.26 – Pen Tool options in the Context Toolbar

- *Section 1*—The **Fill** and **Stroke** color options, as well as the **Stroke Weight** and **Style** dropdown, are the same as discussed previously, but it's worth mentioning again that the **Size** and **Line Styles** dropdown is essentially the **Stroke panel**, which can be useful when working with the Pen Tool.

- *Section 2*—This shows the Pen Tool **Mode**. Icon **a**—**Pen Mode** is the most precise of all of the modes. Smooth curves and sharp corners are all possible with Pen Mode. Icon **b**—**Smart Mode** automatically creates smooth curves by simple one-click node placement. It's a fast and easy way to create smooth curves. Icon **c**—**Polygon Mode** draws continuous straight lines. Curvy or wavy paths are not possible with this mode. This same behavior can be achieved with the Pen Mode by the same one-click node placement to create your path, which is the reason I don't see the need to use this mode very much. Icon **d**—**Line Mode** is used to create single-segment lines. Two clicks will make a single-line segment. Icon **e**—**Preserve Selection when Creating New Curves** works with all Pen Tool modes and allows you to draw a shape and keep it selected as you draw a new shape. The standard behavior is to deselect the previous shape when a new shape is created. Icon **f**—**Add New Curve to Selected Curves Object** works with all Pen Tool modes and allows any newly created curve object to be added to the previously selected object and layer, essentially placing the new object on the same layer as the previously created object in the Layers panel. It's similar to **Grouping**, where selecting two or more objects and grouping them creates a folder in the Layers panel. This doesn't create a folder—it just places all objects on the same layer as the previously created object in the Layers panel. Icon **g**—**Rubber Band Mode** provides a preview of the path you are creating before you click to create each new node. This can be helpful for users who want to see the path before they click and confirm the placement of the nodes.

- *Section 3*—This shows the **Convert** icons. These are grayed out with the Pen Tool selected until you start creating a path. Once they are available and a node is selected, choose one of these **Convert** options to convert the node to either **h**—a **Sharp** node, **i**—a **Smooth** node, or **j**—a **Smart** node. For more description of these **Convert** options, see the *Section 2—a, b, and c* part of the *The Node Tool* section of this chapter.

- *Section 4*—This **Action** section was also discussed earlier in the *Section 3— d, e, f, g, and h* part of the *The Node Tool* section of this chapter.

- *Section 5*—The **Snap** section and the **Show Orientation** option were also discussed earlier in the *Section 5—o, p, q, r, and s* part of the *The Node Tool* section of this chapter. The **Use Fill** option for the Pen Tool, when selected, will show the current fill as you create an object.

The Pencil Tool

The **Pencil Tool** (shortcut *n*) allows you to draw freely hand-drawn paths by clicking and dragging with the Pencil Tool. The icon for this tool is shown here:

Figure 6.27 – The Pencil Tool

This way of working may be preferred by users who would rather create objects more organically than using the Pen Tool or using Affinity Designer's Shape objects. A couple of ways to control or adjust the appearance of these hand-drawn paths are with the **Stabilizer** and **Pressure** options.

As shown in the following screenshot, the characteristic hand-drawn qualities of the Pencil Tool create a different kind of expression that is more organic than some of the methods we've discussed so far:

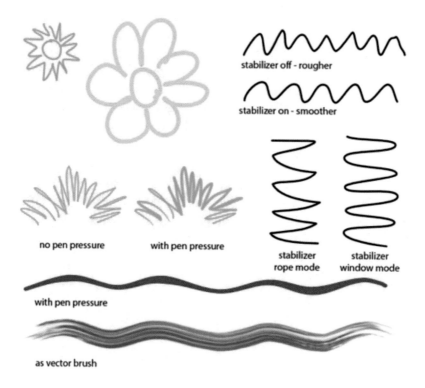

Figure 6.28 – Pencil Tool examples

With the **Pencil Tool** selected, the following options are available in the Context Toolbar:

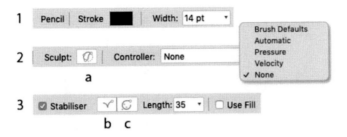

Figure 6.29 – Pencil Tool options

- *Section 1* shows the **Stroke** color option, as well as the **Stroke Weight**.

- *Section 2* shows the **Sculpt** option, denoted by icon **a**. When selected, this option allows you to reshape the currently selected pencil stroke or to continue the currently selected pencil stroke. Reshaping is achieved by running the **Pencil Tool** along the currently selected pencil stroke to smooth or reshape it. Extending or continuing the pencil stroke is achieved by clicking and dragging from either the beginning of the pencil stroke or the end of it. The next option in this section is the **Controller** option. This drop-down menu contains ways of controlling the pencil stroke's sensitivity to pressure or velocity when using the Pencil Tool. Use **Pressure** if you have access to a drawing tablet and want your tablet pen pressure to control the look of your linework. **Velocity** will take into account the speed of your mouse or your pen tablet's movement while drawing. **None** will not take any pressure or speed into account. **Brush Defaults** and **Automatic** will take into account the settings from the brush or the pen tablet settings you are using, if applicable. Results may vary.

- *Section 3* shows the **Stabilizer** option. This option will stabilize and smooth out the Pencil Tool as you draw with it. It attempts to average out your hand movement to produce smoother paths that contain fewer nodes along the path. The **Stabilizer** option has two different modes, icon **b—Rope Mode** and icon **c—Window Mode**. Both of these **Stabilizer** modes are shown in *Figure 6.28*. Rope Mode produces sharper corners than Window Mode. The **Length** or amount of stabilization affects how strong the stabilization effect is. The higher the number, the stronger the effect. This can be input numerically or, when the small arrow to the right of the number is pressed, a slider is presented for you to choose an amount along the slider. As with a lot of the options for these tools, it's best to experiment with each to see for yourself what the differences are between the two and which you prefer. The **Use Fill** option will show the current fill as you create an object.

The Vector Brush Tool

The **Vector Brush Tool** (shortcut *b*) is used to take advantage of the vector brushes to create painted brush strokes. You can see the icon for this tool here:

Figure 6.30 – The Vector Brush Tool

These painted brush strokes can appear like actually painted strokes, depending on the brush you choose from the Designer Persona Brush panel. As covered in *Chapter 5, Main Studio Panels and Managers*, vector brushes work by attaching or stretching an image along the length of a vector curve. This means they can be edited much like any other vector path with nodes along the path, by repositioning or scaling for any desired effect, including changing the width of the path or brush stroke. The Vector Brush Tool is similar to the Pencil Tool in that you click and drag to create your path, as opposed to the multiple-click method of the Pen Tool.

As the following screenshot illustrates, the Vector Brush Tool strokes are built on vector paths—hence the name:

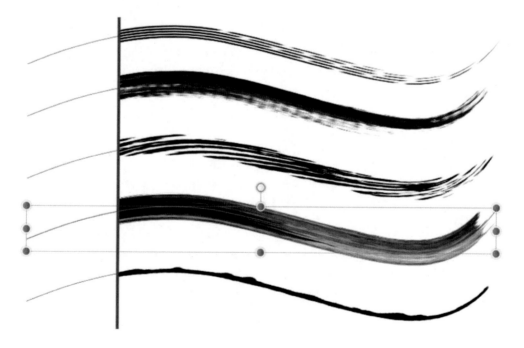

Figure 6.31 – Vector Brush Tool examples

The advantage of these strokes over their Pixel Brush counterparts is the nondestructive editable nature of vector strokes. They can easily be manipulated, adjusted, added to or even changed to a different brush after they have been laid down, for lots of flexibility while creating.

With the **Vector Brush Tool** selected, the following options are available in the Context Toolbar:

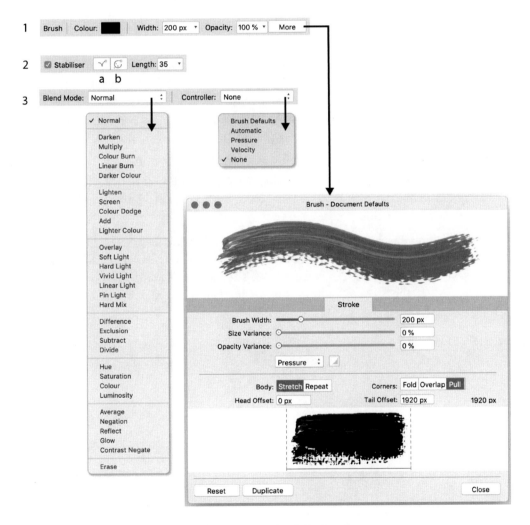

Figure 6.32 – Vector Brush Tool options

- *Section 1* shows the **Stroke** color option, as well as the **Stroke Weight**—in this case, measured in pixels and not points. The **Opacity** option is controlled with a numerical input as well as a slider.

> **Note**
>
> Choose your opacity before you create your brush stroke as you can't change the opacity of a stroke with the Vector Brush Tool after you've made it. You can change it in the **Layers panel** after you've created it, but not in the Vector Brush **Tools Context Toolbar Opacity** option, which I find odd.

After **Opacity**, there is the **More** button. Pressing it will open the **Brush Dialog**, with advanced settings that allow you to change the look of the currently selected brush. These options include additional **Width**, **Size Variance**, and **Opacity** settings, and some advanced options for **Pressure** and **Velocity** responsiveness similar to the Pencil Tool settings, as well as **Stretch**, **Repeat**, and other settings that affect how the stroke image is styled and previewed on the stroke.

- *Section 2* shows the **Stabilizer Rope** and **Window** modes, as well as the **Length** amount options, as described earlier in the *Section 3* options in the *The Pencil Tool* section.

- *Section 3* options include **Blend Mode** control of how the brush's color interacts with other colors in the document. Experimenting with these may lead you to achieve some unexpected creative results. The **Controller** options were discussed previously in the *Section 2* options for the *The Pencil Tool* section.

The Fill Tool

The **Fill Tool** (shortcut *g*) controls the **Fill** and **Stroke** color adjustments for your selected **Vector** or **Text Objects**. The icon for this tool is shown here:

Figure 6.33 – The Fill Tool

This includes what I consider to be the true strength of this tool—the ability to work with gradients for both fills or strokes. In fact, I think this tool should be called the Gradient Tool as it deals predominantly with the application and modification of gradients. Gradients are graduations of tone or color that can be one color, from light to dark, or many colors blending from one to another:

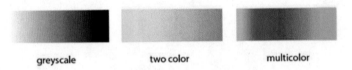

Figure 6.34 – The Fill Tool: simple linear gradient fill examples

I use a combination workflow of pixel painting in Pixel Persona with gradient fills in Designer Persona to shade and light objects in my own work to add a three-dimensional quality. *Figure 6.35* shows a small airplane detail from a larger illustration. The Fill Tool's gradient feature was used almost exclusively for shading all over the airplane. By using subtle gradients of color strategically placed for shading and highlights, you can very quickly add a sense of dimensionality to your work.

With the **Fill Tool** selected, the following options are available in the Context Toolbar:

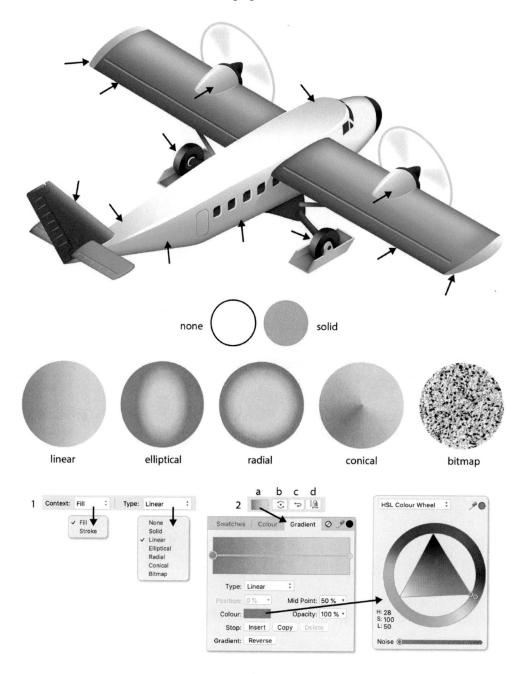

Figure 6.35 – The Fill Tool: gradient fill practical example with options

- *Section 1*—Choose the **Context** (**Fill** or **Stroke**) to apply to your fill or gradient. In Affinity Designer, you can apply a gradient to a stroke. In the next option to the right in the drop-down menu, you have seven different types of fills—**None**, **Solid**, **Linear**, **Elliptical**, **Radial**, **Conical**, or **Bitmap**. These options are illustrated in *Figure 6.35*. Four of these fills are gradient fills, and one is a bitmap fill. The **Bitmap** fill option, once selected, will open up a dialog for you to locate an image. That image will then occupy the fill for your object, with control handles to size or rotate the image. The image will automatically be tiled, making it ideal for the use of textures, as seen in the example screenshot. To change the bitmap fill, simply click on it again in the drop-down menu, and the pop-up dialog will reappear.

- *Section 2*—This shows icon **a**—**Color Panel** swatch button. Clicking this will open a Color Panel, presenting either the current **Swatches panel**, the **Color Panel**, or a **Gradient Color Editor panel**. The **Gradient Color Editor** is where you will spend your time when working with gradients. In this editor, you will find a color preview area to view your gradient, where you can also drag the color stops to any position along the gradient. There is an option to assign the gradient **Type**, as just discussed in *Section 1*, and options for adjusting the **Mid Point** and **Opacity** settings using numerical inputs or sliders, **Mid Point** being the space between the selected color stop and its nearest color stop, and **Opacity** being the selected color stop's opacity. The ability to control the opacity of individual color stops along a gradient opens up some interesting creative possibilities.

The **Color** option displays the currently selected **Color Stop** color. Clicking on the color swatch will pop up another Color panel where you can choose a new color from a number of color sources, including your document's color Swatch Panel. The new color will replace the currently selected color stop. To add, copy, or remove a color stop, click the **Stop: Insert**, **Copy**, or **Delete** buttons.

> **Note**
>
> A gradient has to have at least two color stops, so until there are at least three color stops, the **Delete** button will be grayed out. Also, you cannot remove the first and last color stops.

Gradient—**Reverse** will reverse or flip the gradient. Icon **b** is the **Rotate Gradient** option, which will rotate the gradient 90°. Icon **c** will reverse the gradient, and icon **d** will maintain the **Fill Aspect Ratio** when editing **Elliptical** and **Bitmap** fills. This option is **Off** by default.

The Transparency Tool

The **Transparency Tool** (shortcut *y*) allows you to add transparency gradients to vector and text objects. The icon for this tool is shown here:

Figure 6.36 – The Transparency Tool

This is one of the most used tools in the toolkit for the type of work I do. Simply select the tool, and click and drag it across a selected vector or type object to apply a transparency effect. It's quick and easy, and the options allow for some great flexibility.

With the **Transparency Tool** selected, the following options are available in the Context Toolbar:

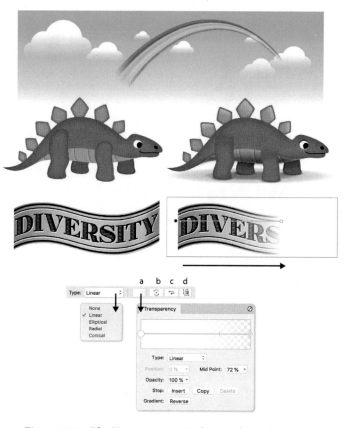

Figure 6.37 – The Transparency Tool examples and options

The **Type** of transparency gradient is presented in a familiar drop-down menu. Here, you have **None**, **Linear**, **Elliptical**, **Radial**, or **Conical** to choose from. These options are similar to the Fill Tool gradient types and behave much the same, only they don't apply color—they apply a gradient of transparency to the selected objects. *Figure 6.37* illustrates this in a few different ways. At the top, the blue sky fades to transparent, as well as the clouds and the rainbow's two ends. Below, the **Diversity** banner has a straight horizontal transparent gradient applied to it, showing that you can apply this effect to groups of objects as well as individual objects. The middle section illustrates the advantages of using transparency gradients to add further enhancement and dimension to the dinosaur object. The left example has a flatter appearance, with a minimal amount of shading. On the right example, I have added a few transparency gradients to add further shading and highlighting, including a ground shadow with the Transparency tool.

Continuing along the Context Toolbar, we have icon **a**—the **Transparency Swatch**. Clicking this will open the **Transparency panel**. This panel is very similar to the Fill Tool Gradient panel and the behavior is much the same, only it deals with transparency instead of color. Icon **b** is the **Rotate Transparency Gradient**, which will rotate the gradient 90°. Icon **c** will reverse the Transparency Gradient, and icon **d** will maintain the **Fill Aspect Ratio** when editing elliptical transparency gradients. This option is **Off** by default. I used elliptical transparency gradients for the ground shadows underneath the dinosaur on the right-hand side.

The Place Image Tool

This **Place Image Tool** has one job: to locate and place an image or an Affinity Designer document into your document. The icon for this tool is shown here:

Figure 6.38 – The Place Image Tool

Upon clicking on the Place Image Tool in the Tools panel, it will immediately open a dialog dropdown for you to navigate and find the location of the image you'd like to place into the current document. The image will then be placed at its default size below the cursor click. I use this predominantly to place a sketch of the piece I am going to work on or to add an image texture to work with in my documents:

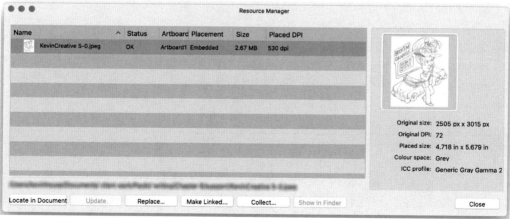

Figure 6.39 – The placed image and the Resource Manager for that image

Once an image is placed in your document, there are no options specifically available for the **Place Image Tool**. In fact, after you have placed the image, the image becomes selected and the Move tool becomes active in the Tools panel. The closest thing to options for the Place Image Tool is the options available in the Resource Manager, as shown in *Figure 6.39*. Please refer to the **Move Tool** information earlier in this chapter and the **Resource Manager** information discussed in *Chapter 5, Main Studio Panels and Managers*.

The Vector Crop Tool

The **Vector Crop Tool** allows you to crop or mask objects or images in your document nondestructively. The icon for this tool is shown here:

Figure 6.40 – The Vector Crop Tool

As of this writing, the Vector Crop Tool is limited to rectilinear crop shapes, as in *Figure 6.41*:

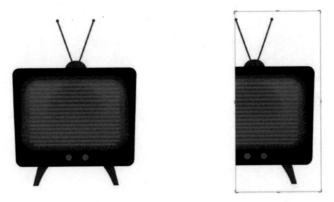

Figure 6.41 – Vector Crop Tool example

There are no Context Toolbar options for the **Vector Crop Tool**.

Let's now take a look at the Designer Persona's basic Shape Tool offerings. Unlike some other comparable applications out there, Affinity Designer furnishes a robust offering of basic vector shapes, with many customizable options that will enhance your workflow.

Shape tools

Basic shapes are undoubtedly some of the most important objects in the history of art and design. Many a masterpiece began as a collection of simple shapes. Affinity Designer has a long list of basic and customizable **Shape Tools** to get you started in your projects. The following screenshots show the Shape Tools currently available, with examples of their adjustable shape options. The blue shape is the default, while the gray shapes are the configurable options available. I encourage you to experiment with each of these Shape Tools to get familiar with the possibilities each has to offer. The shape tools will remain adjustable until you convert them to curves. The red dots are the edit handles:

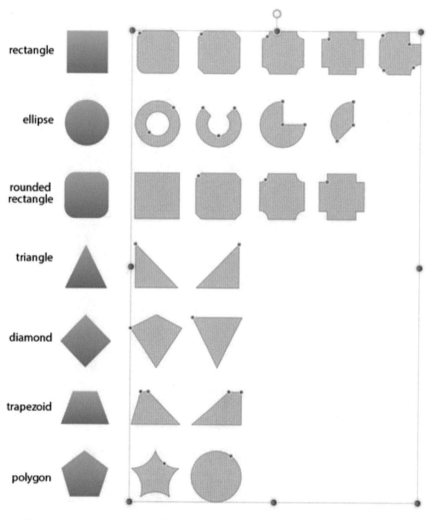

Figure 6.42 – Shape Tools defaults (blue) and option examples (gray): group 1

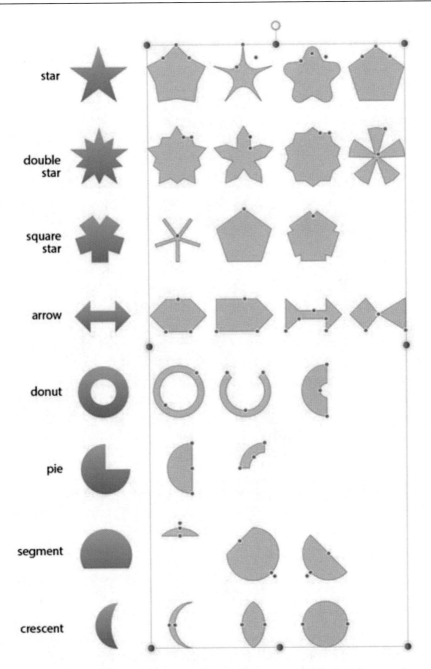

Figure 6.43 – Shape Tools defaults (blue) and option examples (gray): group 2

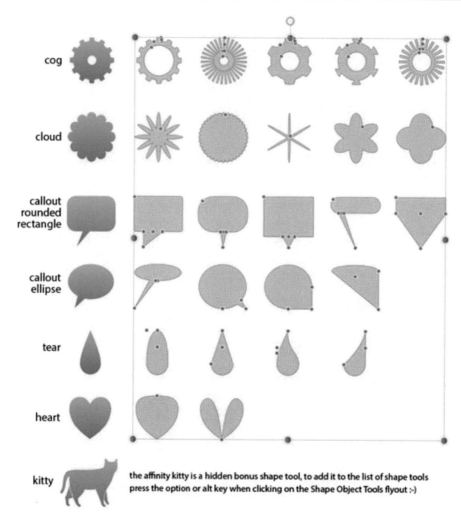

cog

cloud

callout
rounded
rectangle

callout
ellipse

tear

heart

kitty   the affinity kitty is a hidden bonus shape tool, to add it to the list of shape tools
press the option or alt key when clicking on the Shape Object Tools flyout :-)

Figure 6.44 – Shape Tools defaults (blue) and option examples (gray): group 3

As you can see, there are certainly a few options for you to take advantage of, and many unique shapes you'll be able to make right out of the box. These are not all of the possible combinations of what you can make but are hopefully a good indication of the potential that the Shape Tools have to offer. Go ahead and start exploring.

We're getting close to the end of our look at the Designer Persona Tools—just a few more left to explore. It's now time to move away from the vector creation tools and take a look at the Text Tool options. The first of two Text Tools is the Artistic Text Tool.

Text tools

The Text Tools allow you to add text to your documents. The Text options depend on whether you are using Artistic text or Frame text.

The Artistic Text Tool

The **Artistic Text Tool** (shortcut *t*) is designed and best used for smaller amounts of text (just a few words) or decorative text for short headlines or titles. The icon for this tool is shown here:

Figure 6.45 – The Artistic Text Tool

If you want to apply text to a curve, the **Path Text** tool is the one to use.

With the **Artistic Text Tool** selected, the following options are available in the Context Toolbar:

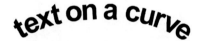

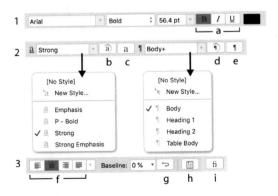

Figure 6.46 – The Artistic Text Tool examples with options

- *Section 1* starts out with the **Font Name** dropdown. This will list all of the fonts you have available to access. Next, we have the **Font Weight** dropdown and a numerical **Size** input with a drop-down slider. Icon group **a** is **Bold**, **Italic**, and **Underline** options, followed by a color swatch that will open the **Color Panel**.

- *Section 2* shows a **Character Style** dropdown, including an option to add a new character style. Icon **b** is the **Update Character Style** button, while icon **c** is a button that will open the **Character panel**. Next, we have the **Paragraph Style** dropdown, with an option to add a new paragraph style. Then, we have icon **d**—the **Update Paragraph Style** button, and finally, icon **e** will open the **Paragraph panel**. The Character panel and the Paragraph panel were discussed in *Chapter 5*, *Main Studio Panels and Managers*.

- *Section 3* shows icon group **f**—the **Text Alignment** and **Justification** options. Next, we have the text **Baseline Adjustment** numerical input and slider. This is only applicable to **Path Text**. This adjusts where the baseline or the type sits on the curve as it runs through the type. Adjusting this will affect the location of the type and the appearance of the letter spacing between the individual characters, depending on how much of a curve they are sitting on or how much distance is applied. See the following example screenshot:

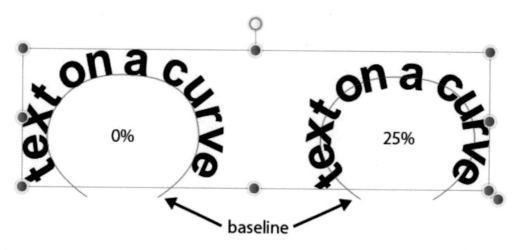

Figure 6.47 – Artistic text baseline adjustment

Icon **g** is the **Reverse Path** button. This will essentially flip the text to the other side of the path, making it appear upside down. Again, this option is only applicable to **Path Text**. Icon **h** will pop up the **Text Frame Panel**, and icon **i** will pop up the **Typography Panel**, a panel with options for **Ligatures**, **Figure Positions**, and **Capitals**, as seen in *Chapter 5*, *Main Studio Panels and Managers*.

The Frame Text Tool

The **Frame Text Tool** creates frames to accommodate text for short paragraphs of copy or titles and headlines. The icon for this tool is shown here:

Figure 6.48 – The Frame Text Tool

To use the Frame Text Tool, select it from the **Artistic Text Tool** flyout, and click and drag to create a frame. Clicking inside the frame and typing will fill the frame with text. You can also copy text from another file or text frame and paste it into a new frame. To paste the new copy without its original formatting, go to **Edit | Paste Without Format**. You can also place text from an external file by going to **File | Place** and navigating to the external text file to place it into a frame.

> **Note**
> The **Place Image Tool** will not work for placing text into a text frame.

Text frames can also be created from closed vector curve shapes, either by clicking inside of the shape with the Frame Text Tool and typing or by pasting copy from the clipboard, as illustrated in the following screenshot:

Figure 6.49 – The Frame Text Tool examples and Text Frame panel

Once you have your copy in the frame, there are a number of options to adjust the text.

The Color Picker Tool

The **Color Picker Tool** (shortcut *i*) samples colors from your document or anywhere on your screen and stores them in the swatch next to the Color Picker icon, either on the various Color or Swatch panels. The icon for this tool is shown here:

Figure 6.50 – The Color Picker Tool

With the **Color Picker Tool** selected, the following options are available in the Context Toolbar:

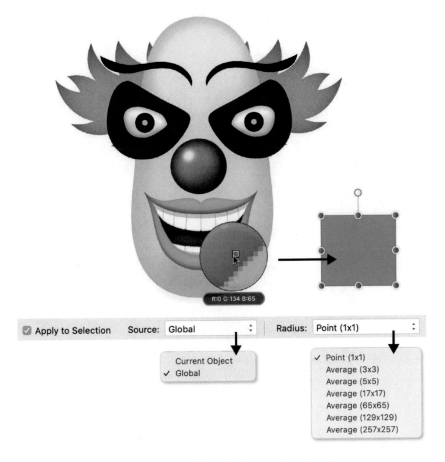

Figure 6.51 – Color Picker Tool example and options

The **Apply to Selection** option will immediately apply your sampled color to the selected object. This is the default behavior. **Source** controls where the sample is picked from. **Current Object** restricts the sample to the current object only, while **Global** will sample from all objects or layers. **Radius** determines how wide your sample is collected from, based on the cursor location when clicked. It starts with a single **Point** sample of 1 pixel in size and goes up from there. **Average** averages the color sample as the size increases. **Point** is the most accurate and is the default.

The View Tool

The **View Tool** (shortcut *h*) is used to pan or move the view of your document. The icon for this tool is shown here:

Figure 6.52 – The View Tool

The *spacebar* can be used as a View tool toggle to quickly move the view around without leaving the current tool. Press the *spacebar* to move the view, then release it.

With the **View Tool** selected, the following options are available in the Context Toolbar:

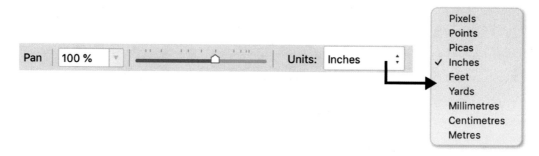

Figure 6.53 – The View Tool options

The **Pan** percentage is your current document zoom level. You can either input it numerically or adjust the slider. **Units** are the current measurement system units of your document.

The Zoom Tool

The Zoom Tool (shortcut *z*) is used to zoom in or out in your document. The icon for this tool is shown here:

Figure 6.54 – The Zoom Tool

When the tool is selected, the zoom default is set to zoom in. In order to switch that to zoom out, press and hold the *Option* or *Alt* key; letting go resumes to the default zoom-out function. I rarely ever use the actual Zoom Tool to zoom in or out as there are many other quicker ways to achieve this, as covered in *Chapter 1, Getting Familiar with Affinity Designer's Interface*.

With the **Zoom Tool** selected, the following options are available in the Context Toolbar:

Figure 6.55 – The Zoom Tool options

These options, incidentally, are identical to the View Tool. The **Zoom** percentage is your current document zoom level. You can either input this numerically or adjust the slider. **Units** are the current measurement system units of your document.

Summary

In this chapter, we have taken a fairly in-depth look at the Designer Persona toolset. We covered the Artboard tool, the selection tools, the vector creation, adjustment, and transform tools, the color tools, the shape tools, and the navigation tools. That's a lot of tools to cover, and it's roughly only half of what Affinity Designer has to offer.

I encourage you to go back and explore some of the features and options we covered in this chapter, and when you're ready, we'll continue our look at Affinity Designer's tools in our next chapter, exploring the Pixel Persona toolset. The pixel-based tools are just as varied as the vector tools and are the perfect companion for them in this well-rounded application. Let's now dive into Affinity Designer's Pixel Persona toolset!

7
Tools – Pixel Persona

Welcome to the seventh chapter of *Up and Running with Affinity Designer*.

Affinity Designer's Pixel Persona tools are the perfect complement to the Designer Persona tools. Here you'll find the pixel selection tools, as well as the powerful paint and retouch tools. We'll cover all of these in this chapter and hopefully, give you a good sense of how the Pixel Persona tools can add another dimension of creativity to your workflow.

The tools discussed in this chapter pertain to the pixel tools in the **Pixel Persona**.

> **Note**
> As with the Designer Persona, rather than listing every single option that is available for each tool, which might indeed double the thickness of this book, I am going to concentrate on the options most likely to benefit us in getting up to speed with Affinity Designer. I again encourage you to visit the Help System for a complete and up-to-date rundown of all of the available options and settings offered for each tool. Go to **HELP | AFFINITY DESIGNER HELP | TOOLS**.

We will look at each of the Selection, Paint, and Retouch tools, what they do, and certain specific options or settings that are available in the context toolbar when they are selected. While some tools may share the same options, others will have their own unique options.

The specific tools we will be discussing in this chapter are:

- **Selection Tools** – Move Tool, Marquee Selection Tools, Freehand Selection Tool, Selection Brush Tool, and Flood Selection Tool (with a brief discussion on the different setup behavior of the Pixel Persona as compared to the Designer Persona)

- **Painting Tools** – Pixel Tool, Paint Brush Tool, Eraser Brush Tool, and Flood Fill Tool

- **Retouching Tools** – Dodge Brush Tool, Burn Brush Tool, Smudge Brush Tool, Blur Brush Tool, and Sharpen Brush Tool

- **Additional Tools** – Color Picker Tool, View Tool, and Zoom Tool

---

Repetition

A few of the tools in this chapter share the same options or features. Rather than adding pages of duplicated information, I will make a note of where any information has already been covered and direct you to where you can find that information. Any unique options or slight deviations of a feature will be covered individually where they occur.

Later in the practical exercise chapters, *Chapter 11, Creating a Professional Logo, Chapter 12, Creating Astronaut Ricky and Sidekick K9, and Chapter 13, Rocketing into the Pixel Cosmos,* we will cover how to use some of these tools, in particular the painting tools, as and when we need them for the exercises. This is the best way to explore how to use the tools, by actually tackling a real project, creating objects and elements. For now, let's just get acquainted with the tools and what options they have available.

Pixel Persona tools

As with the Designer Persona tools, we will be discussing the Pixel Persona tools in the order that they appear in the tools panel from top to bottom. For this chapter, we'll start with the Move tool and finish up with the Zoom tool:

Figure 7.1 – The Pixel Persona tool panel

Some of these tools are basically the same as in the Designer Persona but I think they are worth repeating to really let them sink in.

The Move tool

The **Move** tool (shortcut *v*) is the main selection tool:

Figure 7.2 – The Move tool

The Move tool in the Pixel Persona is used to select and move pixel layers or pixel selections around. Once selected, these layers or selections can be moved, rotated, and scaled to different sizes or have their properties changed.

Selecting is as simple as clicking on the layer or selecting it with the Move tool. Before you can modify or move any object or group of objects, you must first select them. In order to select or edit objects on multiple layers or another layer other than the one you are working on, you must have the **Edit All Layers** button selected. It is located in the bottom-left corner of the **Layers** panel. With the **Edit All Layers** button, you can either deselect it to lock the current layer so that it is the only layer that is editable, or select it, unlocking and allowing all layers to be editable. I like the ability to be able to select anything I want on any layer so I have **Edit All Layers** selected 95% of the time.

To select multiple objects, you can either hold the *Shift* key down while clicking on multiple elements with the Move tool or click, hold, and drag out a marquee selection around the objects with the Move tool. Or, select multiple layers in the **Layers** panel:

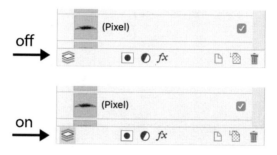

Figure 7.3 – The Edit All Layers toggle in the Layers panel

Before we get too far into this Pixel Persona tools chapter, let's take a quick look at some of the behaviors and workflows you may encounter that are a little different and unique to working with pixels when compared to the vector workflow of the Designer Persona.

Painting, layer behavior, and the Assistant Manager

To start with, all painting in the Pixel Persona takes place on Pixel Layers. When you paint on a pixel layer and put down your strokes, you normally pause and start as you paint, essentially releasing and activating your Brush tool. Each time you pause and start, the painted marks are put down on the same layer. This is the Pixel Persona default and is generally the expected behavior of painting. This works because the current layer you are painting on is still active or selected. In other words, Affinity Designer doesn't create a new layer every time you paint a new stroke. However, if the layer gets deactivated or unselected (because you perform some other operation or select a different tool), when you start painting again you might expect that you would be painting on the same layer, but this may not be the case.

Two possible scenarios will occur. You will either start painting again but on a completely new layer or you may start to paint and nothing happens. This is because Affinity Designer requires an active Pixel Layer to paint on and because none of your pixel layers are active, it doesn't know where to put the paint pixels.

That new layer gets created and selected because of a default behavior setting called **Painting with no layer selected** that is controlled by a manager called the Assistant Manager. Depending on whether your Assistant Manager is set to default behavior or not will determine whether you get a newly selected pixel layer to paint on or not.

If the default behavior is on in the Assistant Manager and you start painting on a new layer, you may not be aware it's a different layer and this could cause some issues for you depending on what you're trying to accomplish. Fortunately, the Assistant Manager has an option to alert you when you are painting on a new layer and it will pop up in the upper right-hand corner of the document UI telling you that you are now painting on a new pixel layer. In short, the Assistant Manager will create a new layer for you if you have the option turned on and alert you when it's created. If you don't have the option or alert on it will do nothing. The fact that nothing is happening will remind you to either create a new layer manually using the **Add Pixel Layer** button in the **Layers** panel (see *Figure 7.4*) or reselect an existing pixel layer to continue painting on.

That was a bit of a long-winded description but one I find important for new users to be aware of if you find yourself getting confused or frustrated about how the pixel layers workflow is set up.

Figure 7.4 shows the **Assistant alert popup – 1**, the **Assistant Manager panel – 2**, and the **Painting with no layer selected – 3** option dropdown. In order for the **Add new pixel layer and paint** option to be activated and for the **Assistant alert** to be called when a new layer is created, the **Enable assistant** and **Alert when assistant takes an action** options need to be checked. Notice as well, on the Alert popup, that there is a button to call the **Assistant** Manager if you need to. Also, notice on the **Assistant** Manager panel, that there are six other unrelated options available for you to get alerts for that are not limited to painting:

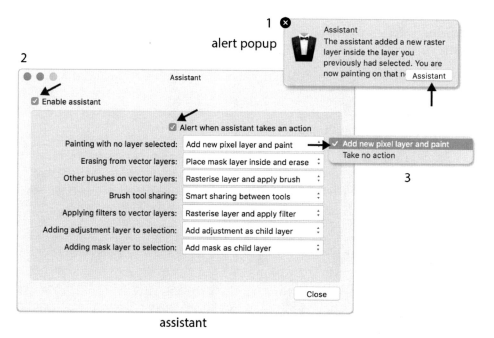

Figure 7.4 – The Assistant Manager and Alert popup

Let's take a look at the difference between single and separate layers and why to use them.

Single or separate layers

If you want to be able to have separate painting areas that you wish to either move around or transform independently, you'll want to create a new layer for that painting area in the **Layers** panel. This is achieved by clicking on the **Add Pixel Layer** button located at the bottom of the Layers panel. If for some reason, you have everything on one layer and you realize that you now need to have things separate, you can of course use the selection tools to select the areas you want to be separated and then, to separate them, either move them to another area of the same layer or copy and paste them to a new layer. We will cover the selection tools of the Pixel Persona in the next section of this chapter.

> **Note**
>
> This will work as long as the areas you need to select are easily separated or selectable. Sometimes it may be difficult or impossible to select what you need without erasing or destroying parts of the layer, so planning ahead here is the best way to ensure success.

Figure 7.5 shows the Layers panel in both a single layer and a separate layer scenario. For ultimate control over how you create your pixel work, get used to planning ahead and taking full advantage of the Layer panel's flexibility. It will enable you to transform or reposition elements more easily or hide layers when you need to:

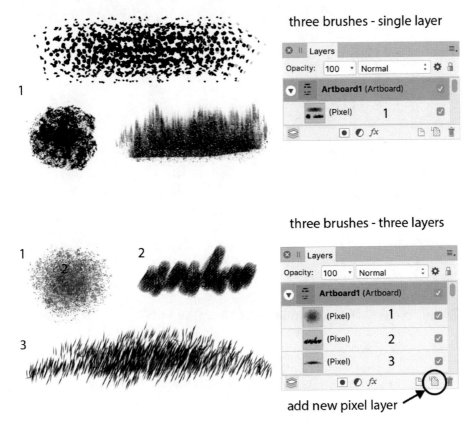

Figure 7.5 – Single or separate layers

When the Move tool is selected and nothing is selected in the document, the context toolbar will only display the **Document Setup** and **Preferences** buttons.

When a **Pixel Object** or **Layer** is selected with the **Move** tool, the following options are available in the context toolbar:

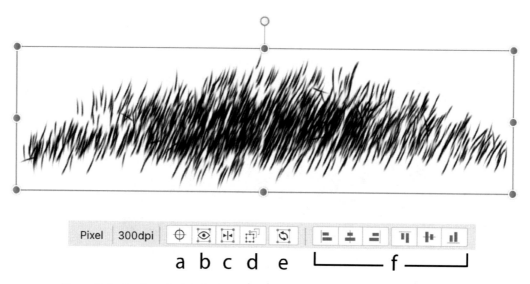

Figure 7.6 – Options for Pixel Objects or Layers when selected with the Move tool

- The first five icons **a** to **e** represent a few handy options that enable certain transforms or design aids for the selected object. Icon **a** is to enable the movable **Transform Origin**. This allows you to set an origin to rotate or scale the selected object around. For example, dragging the transform origin to the upper-left corner of the selected object bounds will allow you to rotate the object around its upper-left corner. The transform origin can also be positioned outside of the selected object or anywhere on the layer. Basically, it can be moved anywhere in your document to affect the rotation or scaling of your selected object. Icon **b** is a toggle that allows you to **Hide Selection while Dragging**. This behavior will affect every object selected until it is turned off again. Icon **c** allows you to switch on **Alignment Handles** that will let you align two or more selected objects quickly. Icon **d** allows you to **Transform Objects Separately** or independently of one another rather than as a group. Icon **e** allows you to **Cycle Selection Box** or the bounds after you have transformed the selected object, essentially meaning that after you transform your selection, clicking this icon will toggle or 'cycle' the new translated selection bounds with the original selection bounds, as shown in *Figure 7.7*:

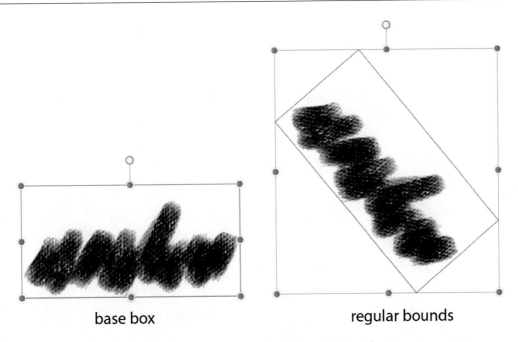

base box   regular bounds

Figure 7.7 – Icon e – Cycle Selection Box toggle

The section **f** group of icons contains quick alignment options for two or more selected pixel objects.

Selection Tools

In order to edit existing pixels in your document you first need to make selections. Next up we will cover the various Selection Tools the Pixel Persona has to offer.

The Marquee Selection tools

The **Marquee Selection** tools (shortcut *m*) are various shape selection tools:

Figure 7.8 – The Marquee Selection tools

The **Marquee Selection** tools come in four shapes: Rectangular, Elliptical, Row Marquee, and Column Marquee. They allow you to click and drag out a pixel selection border. You may notice these four tools all have the same shortcut. By repeatedly pressing *m* you can cycle through each of these tools until you find the one you need. Alternatively, you can reassign them new shortcuts by going to **PREFERENCES | KEYBOARD SHORTCUTS**.

With any of the Marquee Selection tools selected, the following options are available in the context toolbar. As they behave so similar to one another, I am presenting them here as a group of four, which also makes it easier to compare them:

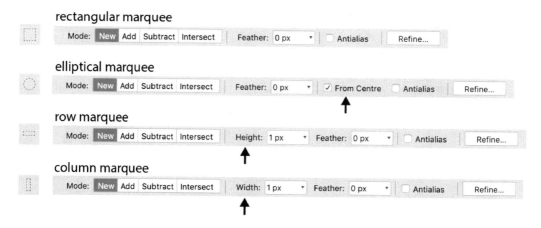

Figure 7.9 – The Marquee Selection tool options

Looking at *Figure 7.9*, you will notice that the settings for these tools are almost identical. The arrows mark the three options that are different.

The first four options are the selection modes available for each of the Marquee Selection tools: **New**, which will create a new selection; **Add**, which will add more of a selection area to a current selection; **Subtract**, which will remove or subtract from a current selection; and **Intersect**, which will create a new selection where it intersects with the current selection as you drag it out. Play around with this one to see what it does.

For the **Rectangular** and **Elliptical** Marquee selections, next up is a **Feather** option with a numerical input and a slider dropdown to add a feathering amount to soften the section edge.

For the **Row Marquee** and **Column Marquee**, the next options are **Height** for the row and **Width** for the column. Here you can enter a number for **Height** or **Width** in pixels or click for the slider dropdown. This is followed by the **Feather** option for both.

The **Elliptical Marquee** has an exclusive option to draw the shape **From Centre**.

All of the Marquee Selection tools have the **Antialias** option, which, if checked, will smoothen the selection border.

With all of the Marquee Selection options listed above there is a **Refine Selection** option. This is a powerful group of settings that enables you to fine-tune or refine your selection in a variety of ways. *Figure 7.10* shows the **Refine Selection** pop-up dialog that displays when you have an active selection and the **Refine...** button is pressed.

I don't use this for my work so I am not familiar with all of these settings but in its basic form, you have the option of painting around the edges of a selection area to refine it using different types of overlays and settings sliders to fine-tune your selection:

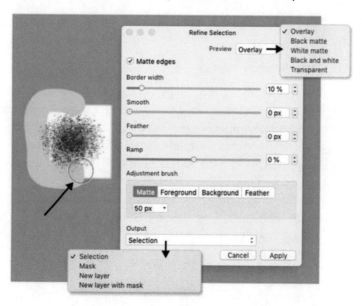

Figure 7.10 – The Refine Selection popup

Now that we've covered the four Marquee Selection tools, let's take a look at the three remaining selection tools, starting with the Freehand Selection tool.

The next three selection methods allow a little more flexibility than the shape-based Marquee Selection methods. They are the Freehand Selection Tool, the Selection Brush and the Flood Select Tool.

The Freehand Selection tool

The **Freehand Selection** tool (shortcut *l*) is used to create freehand pixel selections:

Figure 7.11 – The Freehand Selection tool

When the **Freehand Selection** tool is selected, the following options are available in the context toolbar:

Figure 7.12 – The Freehand Selection tool options

The **Freehand Selection** tool has three modes: firstly, icon **a** – **Freehand**, where you click and drag to draw a freehand shape selection. Letting go will close the selection with a straight line. Next is icon **b** – **Polygonal**, where you click, click, and click, creating straight lines between the clicks (nodes) to create straight-sided polygonal selections. Double-clicking the second last node will close the selection shape. The final mode is icon **c** – **Magnetic**. This mode lays down nodes that snap to edges that follow the cursor. I have to admit this mode is a bit of a mystery to me. I had a hard time controlling it. Double-clicking the second last node will also close the selection shape. All of the Freehand selection modes options for **Feather**, **Antialias**, and **Refine** are identical to the Marquee Selection tools, which we have covered in the previous section. Please refer to that section for information on these options.

Sometimes a more organic or painterly way of selecting is just what's needed. This is where the Selection Brush comes in handy.

The Selection Brush tool

The **Selection Brush** tool (shortcut *w*) is used to create pixel selections by painting:

Figure 7.13 – The Selection Brush tool

When the **Selection Brush** tool is selected, the following options are available in the context toolbar:

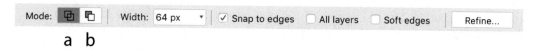

Figure 7.14 – The Selection Brush tool options

The **Selection Brush** tool has two modes: icon **a** – **Add**, where you click and drag to paint a freehand shape selection, and icon **b** – **Subtract**, which will remove or subtract from a current selection. *Interestingly, there is no* **New** *or* **Intersect** *mode as in the other selection tools, and the modes are presented as icons here as opposed to words.* **Width** is the tool's brush width in pixels, controlled either by numerical input or by a drop-down slider. **Snap to edges** will expand the selection as you paint to any edges of objects that are within snapping distance of the cursor. **All layers**, unchecked by default, will apply your brush selection to all layers if checked. When unchecked, it will only apply to the current layer. **Soft edges** adds a soft edge around the outer edge of your selection, somewhat like antialiasing but softer. With this option unchecked, the outer edge will be hard. **Refine…** has been covered in the Marquee Selection tools and was shown in *Figure 7.10*.

When you need to make a selection based on a specific color, the Flood Select Tool is the tool for the job.

The Flood Select tool

The **Flood Select** tool (no default shortcut) is used to create pixel selections of a similar color:

Figure 7.15 – The Flood Select tool

When the **Flood Select** tool is selected, the following options are available in the context toolbar.

Figure 7.16 – The Flood Select tool options

The **Flood Select** tool options include the four familiar selection modes: icon **a** – **New**, which will create a new flood selection; icon **b** – **Add**, which will add more of a selection area to a current flood selection; icon **c** – **Subtract**, which will remove or subtract from a current flood selection; and icon **d** – **Intersect**, which will create a new selection where it intersects with the current flood selection as you drag it out. Next up is the **Source** dropdown, allowing for the flood fill to affect either the **Current Layer** or **All Layers**.

Again, here you may note some inconsistencies with the handling of the options iconography and/or wording. We're back to four selection modes this time with four icons as opposed to the four 'New, Add, Subtract, and Intersect' words and instead of an on/off checkbox option for All Layers, we have a dropdown and a 'Source' option.

Tolerance uses a percentage to control the number of pixels that are selected based on the color of the pixel that is clicked on. A lower number will select pixels closer to the color and a higher number will broaden the selection range to include colors that vary more from the source pixel. **Contiguous**, if unchecked, will select pixels in a similar tonal range and color as the pixel clicked on no matter where in the document or current layer they are. When this option is checked, it will only select pixels of a similar tonal range and color within the same area. **Refine** is again the same as previously covered in the *Marquee Selection tools* section and as shown in *Figure 7.10*.

Let's move on now to the Pixel Persona painting tools. This is where you will be spending most of your time while painting in the Pixel Persona. These tools, combined with the vast assortment of different brushes and brush options, provide ample opportunities to express just about any creative direction you want to go in.

Painting Tools

Perhaps the most time you will spend in the Pixel Persona is when you are painting. The Paint Tools come in two varieties, the Pixel Tool and the Paint Brush Tool.

The Pixel tool

The **Pixel** tool (shortcut *b*) is used to paint aliased or pixel-aligned paint strokes:

Figure 7.17 – The Pixel tool

The **Pixel** tool behavior is very similar to the Paint Brush tool (discussed next) but it lays down brushstrokes that appear harder or sharper because it doesn't apply any antialiasing or smoothing to the pixels as it paints and the pixels are pixel-aligned so there is no blurring. This look can be favored in certain instances. The shortcut of this tool (*b*) is the same as the Paint Brush tool. Clicking it repeatedly will toggle between the two tools:

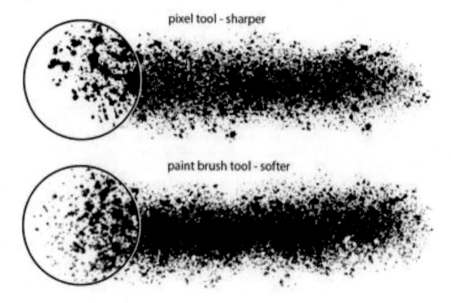

Figure 7.18 – Comparison between the Pixel tool and the Paintbrush tool using the same brush

When the **Pixel** tool is selected, the following options are available in the context toolbar:

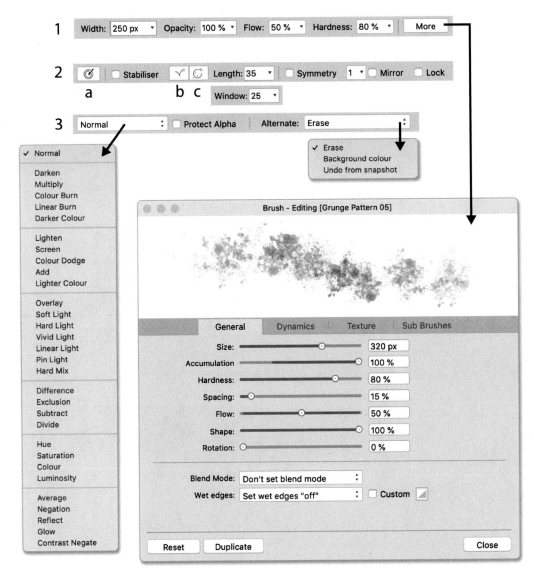

Figure 7.19 – The Pixel tool options

- **Section 1** – Starts off with the **Width** of the brush in pixels using a numerical input as well as a drop-down slider. This is followed by an **Opacity** numerical input and slider dropdown. This adjusts the opacity of the brush from 0% to 100% opacity.

> **Quick Pixel or Paint Brush tool shortcut – Opacity**
>
> To quickly change your brush opacity in 10% increments, use the 1-0 number keys. 1 represents 10% opacity, 2 is 20%, 3 is 30%, and so on, with 0 representing 100%.

Flow controls the flow or speed at which the brush effect is applied. 100% is full speed and 1% is the slowest speed. **Hardness** controls the amount of edge sharpness the brush has, although I didn't notice any difference in this setting using the Pixel tool on a variety of different brushes. The **More** button, when clicked, will present you with the brush defaults popup and a host of advanced brush settings, which I will leave to you to explore further. Use this to adjust the selected brush's behavior.

> **Quick Pixel tool shortcut – erase**
>
> Pressing the *cmd* key on Mac or *Ctrl* key on PC will temporarily switch the current Pixel tool brush to the Eraser tool. Releasing it will bring back your brush. This is chosen in the Alternate setting in the Pixel tool context toolbar.

- **Section 2** – Icon **a** is the **Force Pressure** button. When pressed, it will override the current brush behavior control to allow a pressure-sensitive device (tablet) to control the brush stroke size with pen pressure.

> **Quick Pixel or Paint Brush tool shortcut – brush size and hardness**
>
> Pressing the *ctrl + option* keys on Mac or *Ctrl + Alt* keys on PC and clicking and dragging left and right will adjust the brush size, and if the brush has a hardness attribute, dragging up and down will adjust the brush's hardness.

Next up is the **Stabilizer** option. This option will stabilize and smooth out your paint strokes as you paint them. It attempts to average out your hand movement to produce smoother paint strokes as you paint. The stabilizer option has two different modes: icon **b** – **Rope Mode** and icon **c** – **Window Mode**. Rope Mode produces sharper corners than Window Mode.

Length and **Window** are the amounts of stabilization each option's effect has. Rope length and Window size - The higher the number, the stronger the effect. This can be input numerically or by using the slider dropdown. The stabilizer option in Pixel Paint mode is noticed and works best with thinner, harder edged brushes. The **Symmetry** option allows you to paint strokes in a symmetrical circular or mirrored pattern along with a number of central axes you define in the numerical input or drop-down slider. **Mirror** requires the **Symmetry** option to be checked with an axis number of one and places a repositionable single axis where a drawing on one side is mirrored on the other side. *Figure 7.20* illustrates both the **Symmetry** and **Mirror** options in two examples:

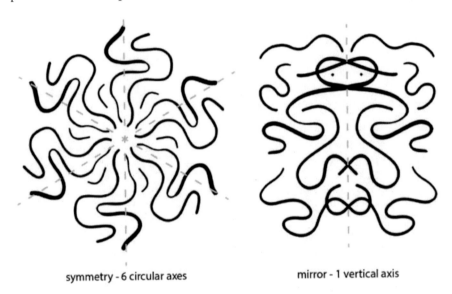

symmetry - 6 circular axes   mirror - 1 vertical axis

Figure 7.20 – The Symmetry and Mirror options

Lock will prevent accidental repositioning of the axes as you paint. Unchecking this enables you to reposition the axes.

- **Section 3** – Options include the **Blend Mode** control for how the brush's color interacts with other colors in the document. Experimenting with this may lead you to achieve some unexpected creative results. **Protect Alpha** locks or masks off the transparent (alpha) pixels on the current layer so any painting will only occur where there is already some color. This is handy if you want to paint or shade inside of a shape you have already laid down, as in *Figure 7.21*. It allows you to apply painterly styles or rough textured brushes to an object while maintaining its original shape:

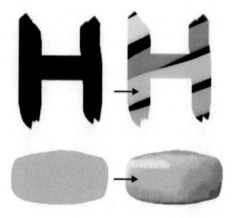

Figure 7.21 – Use Protect Alpha to paint inside the lines of created shapes

Alternate is unique to the Pixel tool. It allows you to assign one of three handy options to use while painting. The options are **Erase, Background color**, and **Undo from snapshot. Erase** is my preference. It allows you to press the *Command* key modifier to toggle the current brush into an eraser. The great thing about this option is that it uses the same brush that you were painting with, rather than switching to some default eraser brush; it just erases instead of paints. **Background color** enables you to press that same modifier key to access the background color. This is convenient if you are using two colors often and don't want to keep going to the **Swatches Panel** to change color. **Undo from snapshot** allows you to return (undo) to a specific earlier version of what you are working on. This is good for experimenting, with the ability to quickly revert back to an earlier state (snapshot) in case you change your mind.

Similar to the Pixel Tool, the Paintbrush tool is used to paint antialiased paint strokes.

The Paint Brush tool

The **Paint Brush** tool (shortcut *b*) is used to paint anti-aliased or smooth paint strokes:

Figure 7.22 – The Paint Brush tool

The **Paint Brush** tool behavior is very similar to the Pixel Brush tool but it lays down brushstrokes that appear smoother because it applies anti-aliasing or smoothing to the pixels as it paints. This allows for a somewhat smoother transition when applying a stroke over or beside other areas of color. The Paint Brush tool shortcut (*b*) is the same as the Pixel Brush tool. Pressing it repeatedly will toggle between the two tools. See *Figure 7.18* for a comparison example of the Pixel tool and Paint Brush tool.

With the exception of the Pixel tool's **Alternate** option, the options available for the Paint Brush tool in the context toolbar are identical to the Pixel tool, so I will list them here but won't cover them all again (please refer to *Figure 7.19*). The Paint Brush tool options are **Width**, **Opacity**, **Flow**, **Hardness**, **More** (advanced option popup), **Force Pressure**, **Stabilizer** (rope and window), **Symmetry**, **Mirror**, **Lock**, **Blend modes**, and **Protect Alpha**.

The Paint Brush tool does have one additional option, an option that allows for **Wet Edges** (See *Figure 7.23* for an example). When this is checked, it will simulate a wet paint or watercolor brush effect by building up or pushing paint along the edges of a painted area. It can be especially convincing when using a watercolor style brush as I have done here. Some brushes are designed to work with wet edges on and some aren't. You may find certain brushes will automatically turn this feature on by default when selected. If that is undesired, just uncheck the option in the **context toolbar:**

Figure 7.23 – The Paint Brush tool with and without Wet Edges examples

The illustration of a White Tailed Deer in *Figure 7.24* is a visual example of the level of realism that is attainable using a combination of the Pixel and Paint Brush Toolsets. This in combination with various types of brushes available for Affinity Designer allow you to achieve results previously only reserved for dedicated painting applications:

Figure 7.24 – Deer illustration showcasing the painting tool capabilities

As good as the Pixel and Paint Brush Tools are, sometimes you will want to remove some of the marks you've made and the Erase Brush Tool is perfect for that.

The Erase Brush tool

The **Erase Brush** tool (shortcut *e*) is used to erase vector or pixel paint strokes:

Figure 7.25 – The Erase Brush tool

I will only list the options available for the Erase Brush tool in the context toolbar here as they are identical to the first 11 Pixel tool and Paint Brush tool options and are described under the Pixel tool options and shown in *Figure 7.19*.

The Erase Brush tool options include **Width**, **Opacity**, **Flow**, **Hardness**, **More** (advanced options), **Force Pressure**, **Stabilizer** (rope and window), **Symmetry**, **Mirror**, and **Lock**.

They *do not* include **Alternate**, **Blend Mode**, **Wet Edges**, or **Protect Alpha**.

The **Erase Brush** tool in the Pixel Persona is used to erase pixels or vector objects. The main difference between erasing pixels versus vectors is that with the Erase Brush tool, pixels are completely removed to transparent as you would expect, and vectors just appear to be removed and are actually masked by adding a nested mask layer, so they aren't truly removed. This can be good if you prefer to work non-destructively when erasing your vector work and like having the option of bringing back your work by adjusting the mask. This method is not so good if your intention is to remove the vector areas you are erasing. At the time of writing this book, there are no options for truly erasing vector artwork, although I think we may see that feature added sometime in the future. See *Figure 7.26* for an example of the differences between the two methods. The gray rectangle below the shapes does show that both methods erase to transparency, but if you wanted to continue to modify those new vector edges, you couldn't because they aren't there:

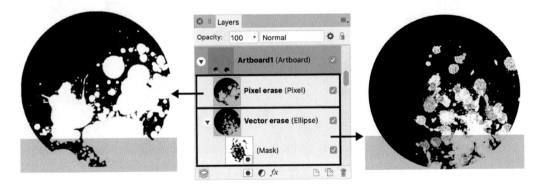

Figure 7.26 – The Erase Brush tool Pixel versus Vector comparison

To quickly add color or a fill to an area, reach for the Flood Fill Tool.

The Flood Fill tool

The **Flood Fill** tool (shortcut *g*) is used to fill in areas of your layer, object, or selections with the selected color from the color panel:

Figure 7.27 – The Flood Fill tool

With the **Flood Fill** tool selected, the following options are available in the context toolbar:

Figure 7.28 – The Flood Fill tool options

Tolerance uses a percentage to control the number of pixels that are selected based on the color of the pixel that is clicked on. A lower number will select pixels closer to the color and a higher number will broaden the selection range to include colors that vary more from the source pixel. If **Contiguous** is checked, the flood will only affect pixels in the same area as the pixel clicked on no matter where in the document or current layer they are. When this option is unchecked, it will select all pixels of a similar tonal range or color on the same layer:

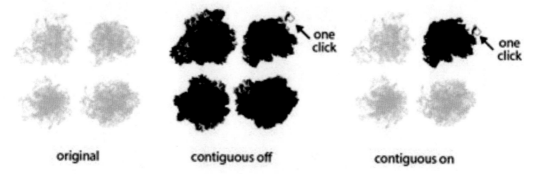

Figure 7.29 – The Flood Fill tool Contiguous comparison

The **Blend Mode** option was discussed in *Section 3* of *The Pixel tool* and is shown in *Figure 7.19*. The **Source** option enables you to target the Flood Fill tool in specific layers, choosing from **Current Layer**, **Current Layer and Below**, and **Layers Beneath**.

Let's now move on to the Pixel Persona's five retouch tools. These tools are designed to alter or modify existing pixel work. The retouch tools enable you to Lighten, Darken, Smudge, Blur, or Sharpen pixels. These tools are exclusive to pixel layers only.

Need to lighten or darken an area? The Dodge and Burn Brush Tools allow you to make subtle tonal adjustments to your pixels areas or selections.

The Dodge Brush tool and Burn Brush tool

The **Dodge Brush** tool and the **Burn Brush** tool (shortcut *o*) are used to lighten (**Dodge**) and darken (**Burn**) areas of your layer, object, or selections:

Figure 7.30 – The Dodge Brush tool and the Burn Brush tool

The **Dodge Brush** tool and the **Burn Brush** tool options are identical in terms of what they provide. They also both share the same shortcut of *o* and pressing it repeatedly will toggle each of the tools. The only difference between the two is that the Dodge Brush tool lightens pixels and the Burn Brush tool darkens pixels:

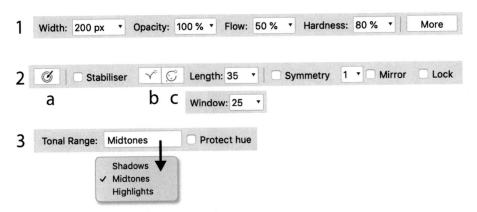

Figure 7.31 – The Dodge Brush tool and the Burn Brush tool options

- **Sections 1** and **2** are exactly the same options as with the Pixel tool so I won't repeat them here. For a full description please refer to the full descriptions following *Figure 7.19*.

- **Section 3** is unique to the Dodge Brush tool and the Burn Brush tool. **Tonal Range**, with the drop-down options of **Shadows, Midtones,** and **Highlights,** controls or limits the tonal ranges that the tools will affect to one of those three areas. **Protect Hue** keeps any color tonal adjustments true to the original color hue.

Figure 7.32 illustrates a couple of simple examples of how the Dodge Brush tool and the Burn Brush tool can be used to lighten or darken an area or add some textural or tonal shading interest to shapes and objects. This is how I use these tools. They are traditionally used for photographic retouching but can also come in pretty handy for adding effects and shading for illustration work:

Figure 7.32 – The Dodge Brush tool and the Burn Brush tool illustrative examples

As well as affecting the lightness or darkness of an area there are times when you will want to smooth areas adjacent to one another. The Smudge Brush Tool is perfect for blending areas of pixels together.

The Smudge Brush tool

The **Smudge Brush** tool (no default shortcut) is used to smudge color around to soften area edges or to blend areas together:

Figure 7.33 – The Smudge Brush tool

With the **Smudge Brush** tool selected, the following options are available in the context toolbar:

Figure 7.34 – The Smudge Brush Tool options

All of these options except for **Strength** been discussed in full under *The Pixel tool* options *Sections 1 and 2*. **Strength** is the new option here and it controls the amount of smudging the tool will apply. Higher numbers apply more of an effect than lower numbers.

The Smudge Brush Tool behavior works more like a blender than a smudger. Smudge tools in other applications usually smear or stretch pixels, this Smudge Brush Tool blends by scattering the brush randomly as you use it as shown in *Figure 7.35*. In fact, there are specific brushes that you use when you use the Smudge Tool and they are usually called Blenders. You'll know if a brush is a blender brush by seeing the Smudge Tool icon beside the brush in the Brushes panel:

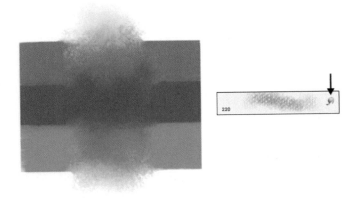

Figure 7.35 - The Smudge Brush Tool using a 'Blender' brush

Similar to the Smudge Brush Tool, the Blur and Sharpen Brush Tools move pixels around to either soften (blur) or harden (sharpen) pixel areas or selections

The Blur Brush tool and Sharpen Brush tool

The **Blur Brush** tool and the **Sharpen Brush** tool (no default shortcuts) are used to blur and sharpen areas of your layer, object, or selections:

Figure 7.36– The Blur Brush tool and the Sharpen Brush tool

The **Blur Brush** tool and the **Sharpen Brush** tool options are identical in terms of what they provide. The only difference is that the Sharpen Brush tool has an additional **Mode** selection with 3 options:

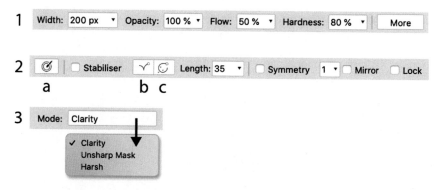

Figure 7.37 – The Blur Brush tool and the Sharpen Brush tool options

- **Sections 1** and **2** have exactly the same options as the Pixel tool so I won't repeat them here. For a full description, please refer to the full descriptions following *Figure 7.19*.

- **Section 3** is unique to the Sharpen Brush tool. The modes are **Clarity**, which will increase the local contrast; **Unsharp Mask**, which will increase the edge pixel contrast; and **Harsh**, which will increase the contrast on all pixels.

> **Quick Sharpen or Blur toggle**
>
> With the Blur Brush tool active, pressing the *Option* key on a Mac or the *Alt* key on a PC will temporarily activate the Sharpen Brush tool. Conversely, with the Sharpen Brush tool active, pressing the *option* key on a Mac or the *Alt* key on a PC will temporarily activate the Blur Brush tool.

Sometimes you will want to quickly select a color from an area of pixels, the Color Picker Tool handles this task with ease.

The Color Picker tool

The **Color Picker** tool (shortcut *i*) samples color from your document or anywhere on your screen:

Figure 7.38– The Color Picker tool

It then stores it in the swatch next to the **Color Picker** icon either on the various **Color** or **Swatch** panels.

With the **Color Picker** tool selected, the following options are available in the context toolbar:

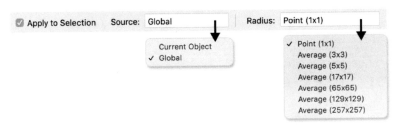

Figure 7.39 – Color Picker tool example and options

The **Apply to Selection** option will immediately apply your sampled color to the selected object. This is the default behavior. **Source** controls where the sample is picked from. **Current Object** restricts the sample to the current object only, and **Global** will sample from all objects or layers. **Radius** determines how wide an area your sample is collected from based on the cursor location when clicked. It starts with a single **Point** sample of one pixel in size and goes up from there. **Average** averages the color sampled as the size increases. **Point** is the most accurate and is the default.

The View tool

The **View** tool (shortcut *h*) is used to pan or move the view of your document:

Figure 7.40 – The View tool

The spacebar can be used as a view tool toggle to quickly move the view around without leaving the current tool. Pressing the spacebar to move then releasing it:

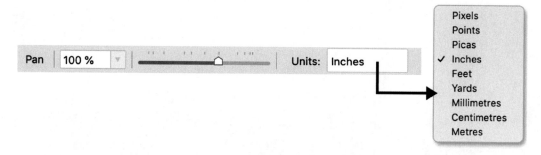

Figure 7.41 – The View tool options

With the **View** tool selected, the following options are available in the context toolbar.

The **Pan** percentage is your current document zoom level. You can either input it numerically or adjust the slider. **Units** is the current measurement system of units of your document.

The Zoom tool

The **Zoom** tool (shortcut *z*) is used to zoom in or out on your document:

Figure 7.42 – The Zoom tool

When the tool is selected, the zoom default is set to zoom in. In order to switch that to zoom out, press and hold the *Option* key (Mac) or the *Alt* key (PC). Letting go resumes the default zoom-out function. I rarely ever use the actual Zoom tool to zoom in or out as there are many other quicker ways to achieve this, as covered in *Chapter 1, Getting Familiar with Affinity Designer's Interface*:

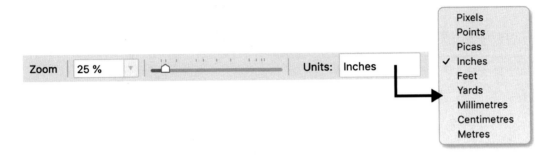

Figure 7.43 – The Zoom tool options

With the **Zoom** tool selected, the following options are available in the context toolbar.

These options, incidentally, are identical to the View tool. The **Zoom** percentage is your current document zoom level. You can either input it numerically or adjust the slider. **Units** is the current measurement system of units of your document.

Summary

In this chapter, we have taken a look at the Pixel Persona toolset. We covered the selection tools, the painting tools, the retouch tools, and the navigation tools.

As with the *Chapter 6, Tools – Designer Persona*, I encourage you to go back and put into practice or experiment with some of the Pixel Persona features and options we discussed in this chapter. I hope covering these two Tools chapters has given you a sense of the power and flexibility of Affinity Designer's Vector and Pixel toolsets. Its true strength is its ability to create a seamless vector and pixel workflow environment. Let's now take a closer look at Affinity Designer's Export Persona toolset in the next chapter!

8
Tools, Panels, and Process – Export Persona

Welcome to the eighth chapter of *Up and Running with Affinity Designer*.

In the previous Designer Persona and Pixel Persona tool chapters, the tools we discussed covered a wide range of functions and uses. The Export Persona is different, however; it is designed specifically for a single task – exporting. While you don't have to be in the Export Persona to export your artwork, the options available in the Export Persona greatly enhance and streamline the process. It is especially useful for UI/UX asset exporting for screen, web, or game design applications where you are exporting many assets to different sizes, formats, and resolutions. Currently, the export formats include PNG, JPEG, GIF, TIFF, PSD, Open EXR, HDR, TGA, and SVG, EPS, PDF.

> **Breakdown of export types and general usage**
>
> **PNG**: print and online usage, transparent backgrounds, broad ranging color.
> **JPEG**: widely used online, high compression (small file size) ability. **GIF**:
> transparent backgrounds, widely used online for short animations. **TIFF**: high
> quality often used in print, not for online. **PSD**: Photoshop format, multiple
> layers including vector layers, used to create online and print formats. **Open
> EXR** and **HDR**: high dynamic range color, used in film and 3D art production.
> **TGA**: older format often used in video game production. **SVG**: versatile XML
> vector format used online and for user interface design and for print. **EPS**: high
> quality vector graphics, logos. **PDF**: highly versatile format used to display
> graphics and images across many formats and applications including print
> production and online documents.

In the Export Persona, you'll essentially find one main tool, the Slice tool, with three supporting tools. The Slice and the Slice Selection tools work in combination with the Layers, Export Options, and the Slices Panels for exporting your artwork. In fact, most of the work takes place in those three panels.

In this chapter, we will look at the **Slice**, **Slice Selection**, **View**, and **Zoom** tools first, and then we will discuss the process of exporting with **Layers**, **Export Options**, and **Slices Panels**.

The specific areas we will be discussing in this chapter are as follows:

- **Export Persona Tools** – Slice Tool, Slice Selection Tool, View Tool, and Zoom Tool
- **Export Persona Panels** – Layers Panel, Slices Panel and Export Options Panel

> **Note**
> I will attempt to cover as much information as is relevant to the scope of this
> book. However, there are quite a few options when it comes to exporting in
> the Export Persona. If you find that you require more information than is
> available in this book, please go to **HELP | AFFINITY DESIGNER HELP |
> EXPORTING** for a thorough and up-to-date look at exporting.

Export Persona tools

As with the previous two Persona tool chapters, we will be discussing the Export Persona tools in the order that they appear in the tool panel from top to bottom. For this chapter, with only four tools, we'll start with the Slice tool and conclude with the Zoom Tool.

Figure 8.1 – The Export Persona tool panel

The Slice tool

The **Slice** tool (shortcut *s*) is a slice creation and editing tool:

Figure 8.2 – The Slice tool

The Slice tool allows you to create custom slices by clicking and dragging out an area in your document. Use this tool when you want to create a slice in a specific area or edit an already created slice by dragging the slice's corner points. The Slice tool is also the tool to select and move or reposition slices in your document. Clicking and dragging the slice's upper blue title area will move the slices around. When moving, the default behavior is to snap, pressing the *option* or *Alt* key down as you drag to disable the snapping.

> **Note**
> You must first select the slice to move it. Moving slices in this way will only move the slice, not the object. To move the object, you will need to return to the Designer Persona.

When the Slice tool is selected, the following options are available in the Context toolbar:

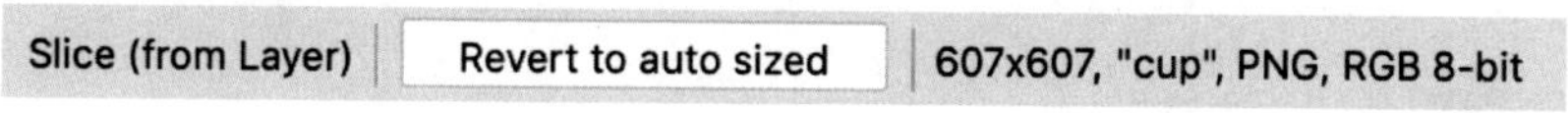

Slice (from Layer)	Revert to auto sized	607x607, "cup", PNG, RGB 8-bit

Figure 8.3 – Options for the Slice tool

There aren't many options for the Slice tool in the Context toolbar. The first option, **Revert to auto sized**, will only appear if you have resized an automatically created slice, as discussed in the previous paragraph with the Slice tool. Clicking on it will revert it to the automatically created size. The rest of the Context toolbar displays the currently selected slices – **size, name, format,** and **color space.**

The Slice Selection tool

The **Slice Selection** tool (shortcut *l*) allows you to select your slices by clicking on them:

Figure 8.4 – The Slice Selection tool

The Slice Selection tool may look the same as the Move tool in the previous two Personas, but although it shares the same black arrow cursor, it is, in fact, an entirely different tool. The Slice Selection tool cannot move your selection or slice around in the document; it can only select it. To move any elements around, you will need to go back to Designer Persona, move your object, and return to the Export Persona. When you do return to the Export Persona, the slice will move and stay with the object.

> **Note**
> One thing I've noticed, however, is that any slices I've made with the Slices tool that are inside automatic slices, as in *Figures 8.9* and *8.10*, did not move with the object upon returning to the Export Persona. I had to reposition them manually, so watch out for that.

There are no options available in the Context toolbar when the Slice Selection tool is selected.

Once again, the familiar View and Zoom Tools can also be used within the Export Persona.

The View and Zoom tools

The View and Zoom tools are the same as the two personas covered previously:

Figure 8.5 – The View and Zoom tools

The **View** tool (shortcut *h*) is used to pan or move the view of your document. The *spacebar* can be used as a view tool toggle to quickly move the view around without leaving the current tool, pressing the *spacebar* to move and then releasing it.

The **Zoom** tool (shortcut *z*) is used to zoom in or out of your document. When the tool is selected, the zoom default is set to zoom in. To switch that to zoom out, press and hold the *Option* or *Alt* key. Letting go resumes to the default zoom-out function. I rarely ever use the actual Zoom tool to zoom in or out as there are many other quicker ways to achieve this, as covered in *Chapter 1, Getting Familiar with the Affinity Designer's Interface*:

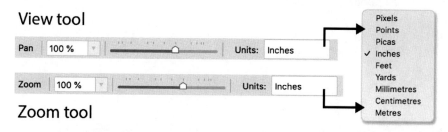

Figure 8.6 – The View and Zoom tool options

With the **View** tool selected, the following options are available in the Context toolbar.

The **Pan** percentage is your current document zoom level. You can either input it numerically or adjust the slider. **Units** are the current measurement system units of your document.

These options, incidentally, are identical to the View tool. The **Zoom** percentage is your current document zoom level. You can either input it numerically or adjust the slider. **Units** are the current measurement system units of your document.

Export Persona panels

Here we will discuss how the panels specific to the Export Persona allow you to completely control every aspect of exporting your files or "slices" out of Affinity Designer.

The Layers panel

To illustrate the process of exporting using the Export Persona, I have created a simple document with a few objects that we will use. *Figure 8.7* shows four selected individual layers containing four groupings of elements ready for export. To the right of them is the Layers panel. In this current state, before creating any slices to export, the Layers panel looks the same as it did in the previous tools chapters. Once we start selecting and making slices to export, its appearance will change somewhat. A **Create Slice** button will appear in the bottom right-hand corner of the panel and a **Layer is Exported** icon will appear in the left-hand column per layer, as shown in *Figures 8.8* and *8.10*:

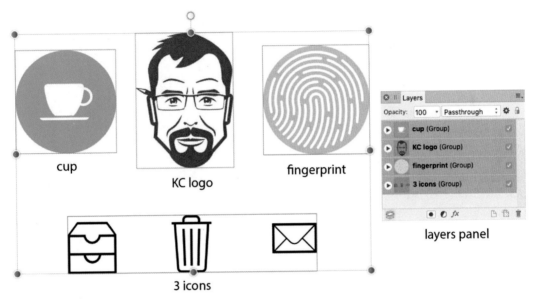

Figure 8.7 – A document to illustrate the Export Persona tool panel and the exporting process

Affinity Designer makes creating and exporting slices fairly simple and flexible, once you grasp the process. After a slice is created, you are free to resize it using the Slice tool, as well as change its export format or resolution at any time. The true strength of the Export Persona is setting up and exporting single or multiple slices in different sizes, formats, and resolutions at the same time in one click.

Most of the time, when creating slices, you will use the **Layers** panel. The Layers panel in the Export Persona has a **Create Slice** button in the lower-right corner enabled when an object or layer is selected to create slices in a single click. This in turn, automatically creates slices based on the dimensions of the selected layer and the default options set up in the **Export Options** panel, as shown in *Figures 8.10* and *8.14*:

layer selected →

enabled

Figure 8.8 – Export Persona Layers panel with the Create Slice button

This automatic Create Slice method is usually the desired workflow and works for most occasions. Sometimes, however, you may want to crop or add certain areas not selected by the automatic selection. This is where the **Slice** tool can assist you in either resizing your slice or creating an entirely new slice inside the bounds of an already automatically created slice, as shown in *Figure 8.9*. As mentioned in the Slice tool description earlier, the Slice tool can also be used to edit the size of a slice:

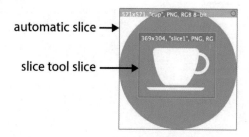

automatic slice →

slice tool slice →

Figure 8.9 – Using the Slice tool to create a new slice not automatically created

Once a slice has been created, it will show up in the Slices panel and its options will be listed in the Export Options panel. The blue boxes around these objects indicate slices. Notice that I've added another Slice tool selection around the trash can icon as an additional slice and see how each slice is displayed as its own slice in the Slices panel. The same four layers in the **Layers** panel now have a new **Export Slice** icon in the left column of the panel:

Reminder

Of course, as always, it's important to label your objects and slices with names that make sense, otherwise a complex document generating lots of slices may get confusing.

We will continue using this simple document setup to illustrate the slicing and export panels workflow.

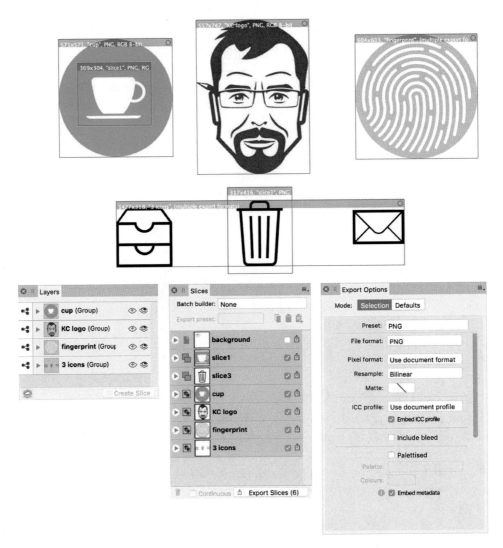

Figure 8.10 – The Layers, Slices, and Export Options panels

Figure 8.10 shows a view of our object slices, with the Layers panel, the Slices panel, and the Export Options panel beneath. Each panel plays a role in the Export Persona, but none are as important as the Slices panel. We'll take a look at the Slices panel next and the various available options. I will attempt to explain, or at least point out, all of these options in a series of screenshots on the next few pages. I admit that these screenshots may look a little on the complex side visually because of all of the arrows and letters, but once you grasp the concept and the setup, these options will make sense. Trust me, if you plan on doing a lot of exporting from your Affinity Designer documents, you're going to love all of these options. Of course, the best way to explore the Export Persona is to create your own simple file with a few objects and start clicking on the various buttons and options to see what they offer.

The Slices panel

Okay, let's dig a little deeper into the Slices panel using the **Fingerprint** slice as an example.

With the Fingerprint slice selected, I have expanded the Fingerprint Slice layer, exposing some of the initial options available. More options are shown in *Figure 8.13*.

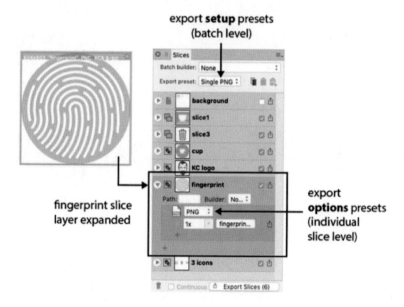

Figure 8.11 – The Slices panel with the Fingerprint slice layer expanded

I have opened the Fingerprint slice layers expand arrow to show a few options for this selected slice. **export setup presets** (batch level) and **export options presets** (individual slice level) are all of the possible options available for **Batch** slice exporting and **Individual** slice exporting and are shown in *Figure 8.12*:

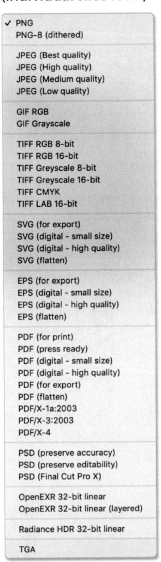

export **options** presets (individual slice level)

✓ PNG
PNG-8 (dithered)
JPEG (Best quality)
JPEG (High quality)
JPEG (Medium quality)
JPEG (Low quality)
GIF RGB
GIF Grayscale
TIFF RGB 8-bit
TIFF RGB 16-bit
TIFF Greyscale 8-bit
TIFF Greyscale 16-bit
TIFF CMYK
TIFF LAB 16-bit
SVG (for export)
SVG (digital - small size)
SVG (digital - high quality)
SVG (flatten)
EPS (for export)
EPS (digital - small size)
EPS (digital - high quality)
EPS (flatten)
PDF (for print)
PDF (press ready)
PDF (digital - small size)
PDF (digital - high quality)
PDF (for export)
PDF (flatten)
PDF/X-1a:2003
PDF/X-3:2003
PDF/X-4
PSD (preserve accuracy)
PSD (preserve editability)
PSD (Final Cut Pro X)
OpenEXR 32-bit linear
OpenEXR 32-bit linear (layered)
Radiance HDR 32-bit linear
TGA

export **setup** presets (batch level)

Single JPEG (High quality)
Retina JPEG (High quality)
Single PNG
Retina PNG
Apple Universal Icon
OSX Application Icon
iOS Application Icon [iOS 7-9]
iOS Application Icon [iOS 5-9]
Apple Universal Icon part - @1x image
Apple Universal Icon part - @2x image
Apple Universal Icon part - @3x image
OSX Application Icon part - 16px (16x16 @1x)
OSX Application Icon part - 32px (16x16 @2x, 32x32 @1x)
OSX Application Icon part - 64px (32x32 @2x)
OSX Application Icon part - 128px (128x128 @1x)
OSX Application Icon part - 256px (128x128 @2x, 256x256 @1x)
OSX Application Icon part - 512px (256x256 @2x, 512x512 @1x)
OSX Application Icon part - 1024px (512x512 @2x)

Figure 8.12 – The many export setup presets and export option presets available

Specifically, **export setup presets (batch level)** are for the Apple app icon design. **export options presets (individual slice level)** are the export formats available to individual slices for all applicable platforms.

Figure 8.13 displays the same Slices panel in two states, before and after adding a few options on the Fingerprint slice layer:

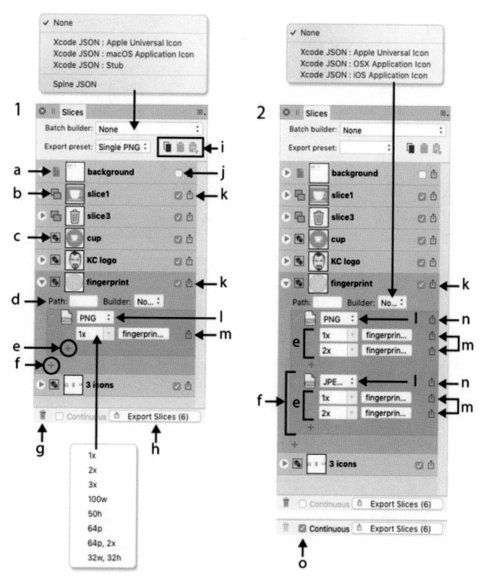

Figure 8.13 – The many Export options available in the Slices panel

Starting on the left **Slices** panel (1), the icons a, b, and c denote the type of slice it is. **Icon a** is a page slice, in this case, named **background**. If a slice is created from this layer, everything on the page or artboard would be exported as one file. **Icon b** is simply called a slice. These are made by clicking and dragging with the **Slice** tool. **Icon c** is known as a **Slice From Layer**. These are created when you press the **Create slice** button in the **Layers** panel to create a slice from a selected layer.

Moving down to **icon d**, **Path** this creates the folder name and location where the JSON image set will be written to. This is for Xcode UI development only.

Icon e, when pressed, will create an additional slice for that image format. In this case, it will add another **PNG** file where you can assign it a different size. See **icon e** on **Slices** panel (2) for an example where I have added a **2x** version of the slice. **Icon f** does something similar. Pressing it allows you to add an additional file format. Refer to **icon f** on **Slices** panel (2) for an example. In this case, I've added a **JPEG** file format and added both **1x** and **2x** sizes (**icon e**). **Icon g** will delete the currently selected slice. It will not delete the object, just the slice. **Icon h** will export all of the slices that have been checked or enabled. See **icon j**.

Icon i has three different icons. The first icon is **Copy Export Setup to Clipboard**. This will copy the selected slice's complete export setup so that it can be pasted to any other slice that you want the same setup to be applied to. The second icon when clicked will **Replace an Export Setup** with a copied export setup of a slice from the clipboard. The third icon will **Add an Export Format from Clipboard** to another slice. This last option is achieved through the Panels preferences drop-down menu in the upper right-hand corner. Experiment with these to see the differences between them.

Icon j is a tick box that enables or disables the slice from being exported when **icon h** is pressed.

Clicking **icon k** will export that individual slice. If you have different formats and sizes, they will all be exported. Notice as well on **Slices** panel (2) that **icon k** will export everything inside the gray area of the Fingerprint slice layers.

Icon l is a dropdown where you can assign different **export options presets** (see *Figure 8.12*) or image formats to export. On **Slices** panel (2), I added a couple of different sized **JPEG** formats that will also be exported if **icon k** is clicked.

Icon m allows you to individually export one format size at a time if you need to. Refer to **icon m** of **Slices** panel (2) for an example of a few more sizes added, each with an individual export icon. The amount of control is pretty comprehensive.

Icon o, when checked, will continuously re-export any previously exported slices that have been modified.

There are three drop-down menus in *Figure 8.13* that also need to be covered here. The first menu above **Slices** panel (1) is the **Batch builder** menu. I'm not familiar with this menu, so I'm quoting directly from the Help menu here. This menu *"Creates Xcode JSON batches from multiple Apple Universal or Application icon slices."* - Affinity Designer Help Menu.

I'm also not familiar with the second **Builder** dropdown above **Slices** panel (2). The Help file says *"Builder generates supplementary Xcode JSON files along with the exported slices for Apple icons."* - Affinity Designer Help Menu. Both of these menus pertain to Xcode UI development only.

The third drop-down menu indicated below **Slices** panel (1) is known as the **Size Scaling** menu. It allows you to select scaling or size options by either scaling up the size 1x–3x or by choosing a set size from the menu.

Moving on from the Slices Panel, let's now take a look at extensive options offered by the Export Options Panel.

The Export Options panel

Now we'll take a look at the final panel in the Export Persona chapter, the **Export Options** panel.

The **Export Options** panel is the panel where you can set up options for any currently selected slice or set up your default export options.

For example, if you consistently export a lot of SVG files, then this panel is where you would set up the defaults for the SVG format, ensuring that each time you create a slice, it will use those default settings and export accordingly.

Currently, there are 38 different formats available to choose from for your file format, with an impressive array of options for each for further configuration. There are so many options that I will not attempt to list them here. Again, go to **HELP | AFFINITY DESIGNER HELP | EXPORTING | EXPORT OPTIONS PANEL** for an explanation of the export options and a list and explanation of all possible formats available for your chosen format.

Figure 8.14 shows just 3 of the 38 format presets available with a list of those format presets on the right-hand side. As you can see, each format comes with its own list of specific options related to each format, giving you a great degree of control over what gets exported:

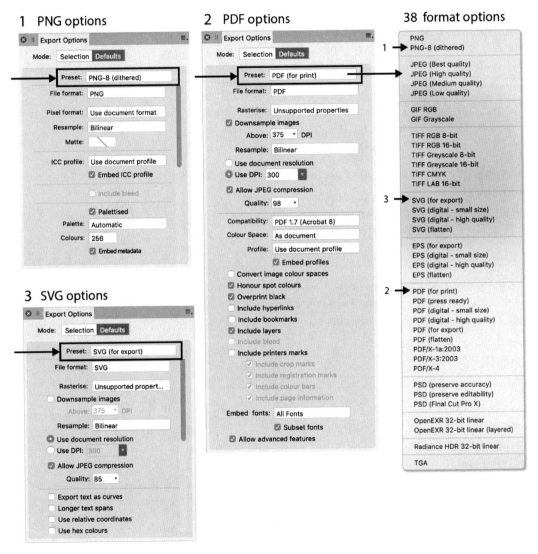

Figure 8.14 – The Export Options panel showing 3 of the 38 possible format presets

As you can see, the Export Persona takes exporting to a whole new level. Using a combination of the Slices panel, the Export Options panel, and the Slices tool, and with all of the options available, exporting your Affinity Designer documents using the Export Persona is powerful and efficient.

Summary

In this chapter, we have taken a look at the Export Persona toolset and, in particular, the Slices tool, along with the Layers, Slices, and Export Options panels.

We didn't cover all of the possible settings, but hopefully, we've covered enough to give you a good sense of how the Export Persona is perfectly designed for exporting your work out of Affinity Designer with flexibility and proficiency.

Chapters 9 and 10 are dedicated to workflow. In the next chapter, we'll cover the mighty Layers panel.

9

Workflow: Layers and Objects

Welcome to the ninth chapter of *Up and Running with Affinity Designer*.

In this chapter, we are going to cover Affinity Designer's Layers workflow. This will also involve a discussion on object management. Primarily, we will discuss the Layers panel and how we can use it to not only organize and manage the objects in our projects but also to apply effects, control visibility, work with vector and pixel assets, apply non-destructive layer adjustments, and blend modes.

> **Workflow**
>
> The term "workflow" here refers to the process or working method of how best to achieve desired, predictable results when it comes to using Affinity Designer. Usually, there is more than one way to get a similar result and depending on your own particular needs, my workflow suggestions may not necessarily work for you. However, over the years, through trial and error, I have developed a few habits that may help you avoid some of the pitfalls I've encountered. At the very least, it may give you ideas that you can base your workflows on.

In this chapter, we will be covering the following topics:

- The Layers panel and the types of layers
- Objects in Affinity Designer

The Layers panel and the types of layers

In this chapter, we will look at the **Layers** panel (*Figure 9.1*), the four basic types of layers, and the behavior and creative features of what layers can offer. The use of layers in creative applications has been around for quite some time now, so you are probably pretty familiar with the general concept of layers and how they work at their basic level.

What are layers and how do they contribute to a good workflow?

Essentially, the layers in Affinity Designer contain all of the elements of your project. There are four types of layers available – the Vector, Pixel, Mask, and Adjustment layers. Layers are arranged in the **Layers** panel as a stack, from top to bottom, and in your document view in the form of the viewing stacking order. In its most basic form, the set of layers in the **Layers** panel dictates which elements are seen in front or behind one another. In Affinity Designer, the topmost layer will appear in front or in the foreground. As you progress down the layer, stack elements will appear progressively behind the previous layer until you get to the bottom, or the base layer. This is called the **order** and in *Chapter 1, Getting Familiar with Affinity Designer's Interface*, we discussed the order of elements when covering the toolbar. See *Figure 9.15*.

Take a look at the following diagram. At first glance, you might think that these four basic shape examples are all on the same level or layer. Upon closer inspection of the **Layers** panel, you'll notice that each shape is on its own layer. Notice that when I move them so that they overlap, their stacking order becomes more obvious. Every element in Affinity Designer, in most cases, gets its own layer. That's the default behavior. There is an exception to this called Sublayers, which I will cover later in this chapter, but for now, having one element per layer is normal:

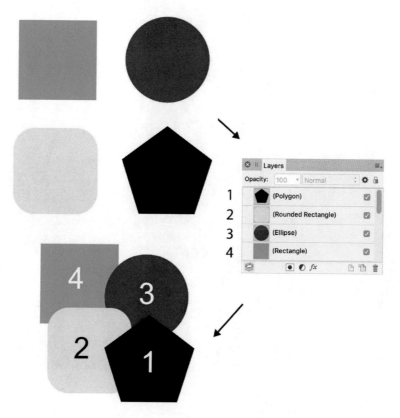

Figure 9.1 – The Layers panel showing the hierarchy of the stacking order

Let's take another look at this stacking order setup but with a slightly more complicated, practical example. The following figure, which has been created for a brewery, shows how this layer stack compares to the simpler example shown in *Figure 9.1*, as well as how important it is to keep your work organized with meaningfully named layers as you build it. We will discuss how I set up this layer stack after we discuss a few of the **Layers** panel's settings:

Figure 9.2 – The Layers panel showing the stacking order in a slightly more complicated piece

Before we spend too much time discussing the stacking order and the organizational aspects of the **Layers** panel, let's step back and have a look at the features of the **Layers** panel itself. Like other panels in Affinity Designer, this panel has a lot of functionality packed into it. This is where you will be spending a lot of your time when you are working with this application.

If we take another look at our simple four-shape file layer stack, we can see that it highlights some of the **Layers** panel's features:

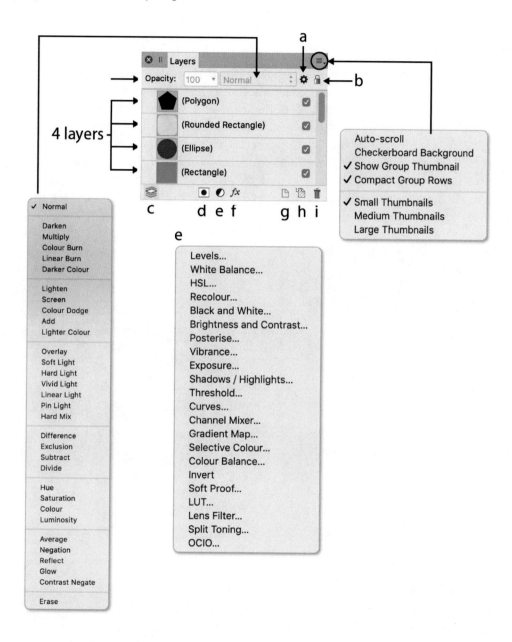

Figure 9.3 – The Layers panel with icons and menus

Starting from the top left-hand corner of the preceding figure, we can see the **Opacity** input area, along with its dropdown slider arrow. We can use this to adjust the selected layer's opacity. You can either input a specific percentage or click and drag along the opacity slider. The lower the opacity, the more transparent the element on the selected layer will become.

Just to the right of the **Opacity** input area is the **Blend Mode** dropdown menu. This is shown as a long list on the left-hand side of the figure. Blend modes alter the appearance of the elements on the selected layer, blending them with the pixels on the layers beneath it. As you can see, there are quite a few blend modes to choose from. There is even one called **Erase** at the bottom of the list that will erase anything placed below it. I use this blend mode to mask one shape from another, as shown in *Figure 9.4*. It's a quick and effective way to create clean silhouettes or edges, without having to create the necessary paths or cut anything away. In this figure, I used oval shapes along the top and bottom and two rectangles on each side to create clean, defining edges. Notice how the effect goes through to the transparent background in the image on the right. Experiment with the other blend modes on different layers to see the effects in real time as you drag over each one in the list:

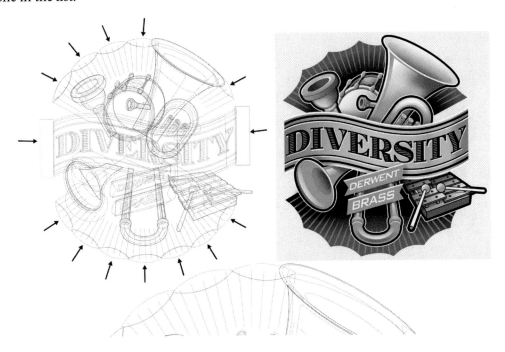

Figure 9.4 – Oval shapes set to Erase Blend Mode

Still looking at *Figure 9.3*, next to the blend modes, we have a settings icon (**a**) , where we can choose **Blend Range Panel** (*Figure 9.5*). This feature allows us to control various aspects of the currently selected layer's blend mode. The amount of control that's provided is fairly extensive. I'm not going to get into this here, though I will say that you should experiment with it to see how it affects your work. Truth be told, I don't think I have ever used it, but it's good to know it is there if you do need to make those types of adjustments:

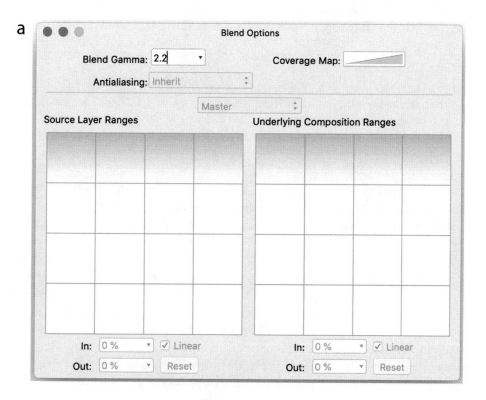

Figure 9.5 – The Blend Range panel's options

Next up, we have icon **b** (as labeled in *Figure 9.3*), which is the **Lock/Unlock** button. When a layer is selected, clicking this button will either lock or unlock it. This is a very handy workflow option if you're working with multiple layered, complex files. To lock or unlock more than one layer at a time, *Shift + click* or *Command + click* multiple layers and then click on the lock icon to either lock or unlock them all in one go. This works on layers, groups (multiple layers made into a group of layers), artboards, and objects. We will cover groups and artboards in more detail later. To lock or unlock multiple layers at a time, *Shift + click* to select the layers you want and click once on the lock to affect them all.

Next, we have icon **c** (as labeled in *Figure 9.3*), which we touched on briefly in *Chapter 7, Tools – Pixel Persona*, when we discussed the **Edit All Layers** button. At the risk of repeating myself, it is simply a toggle button that, when clicked, allows you to access all the layers in your document when you click and select any element (providing you haven't locked it, as described previously). When not pressed, it locks all the layers except for the currently selected layer in the **Layers** panel. This can be handy in situations where you may be having a difficult time selecting an item or a group of items in one layer. Locking the other layers makes this easier. I don't use this very often.

Edit All Layers Note

It can be tricky to see when this feature is on or off as the icon's background, when selected, is barely different than when it isn't selected. I'd like to see this icon get an update with a more obvious color change to indicate whether it's on or off as I've been stumped more than once, not being able to select anything and not realizing that I had toggled it off.

Icon **d** (as labeled in *Figure 9.3*) is the **Mask Layer** button. This button allows you to apply a mask to the selected layer. This will essentially mask away portions of the layer's opacity when you paint with the mask selected using a grayscale color, usually black or white, with the mask icon selected. Black will erase or lower the opacity with the layers below visible, while white will do the opposite. This workflow can be a very powerful way to add interest, organic detail, soft edges, or shading to an otherwise flat graphic element. For example, in the following figure, I have hidden all the other shapes to focus on the magenta circle. I selected the magenta circle layer and pressed the mask layer icon to add a mask layer to it. The new mask layer will be indented beneath the target layer in the layer stack. I then chose a watercolor brush and applied some pixel painting, via the pixel persona, to the mask layer with the brush while using pure black as my color. Black, when painted on the mask layer, will erase or mask the target layer. The mask layer is shown both hidden and unhidden here to show you the clear difference a mask layer can make with a few short paint strokes. The great thing about this method is its non-destructible workflow, meaning that you can hide the effect if need be or repaint the selected layer using white to remove the mask to reveal the original element, unaltered. Given the variety of brushes available, this workflow is virtually limitless in terms of the kinds of effects you can achieve:

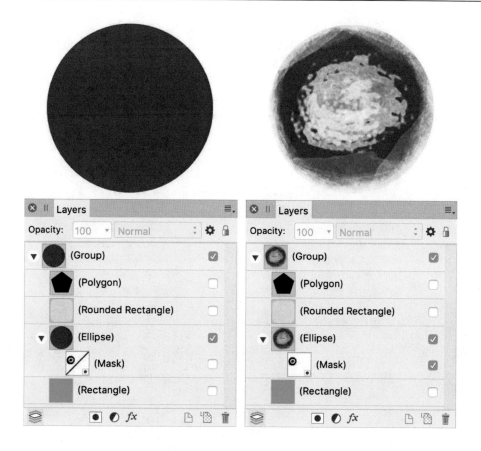

Figure 9.6 – The Mask Layer using a pixel painted workflow

Masks are not limited to pixels only. They can also be used with your vector elements. The vector workflow just behaves a little differently than a pixel mask layer does.

The following figure shows how this method works. I created a few rectangles and then grouped them, which you can do using *Cmd G* or *Ctrl G* (*1*). Next, I selected the blue rectangle layer (*2*) and clicked on the **Mask Layer** button, as I did earlier, to create a mask for the blue rectangle (*3*). Finally, I selected the **Group** layer in the **Layers** panel and dragged it just to the right of the **Mask** layer's icon (*4*), creating the final masked shape you can see here (*5*). The trick here is dragging the vector group to the correct spot, just to the right of the icon:

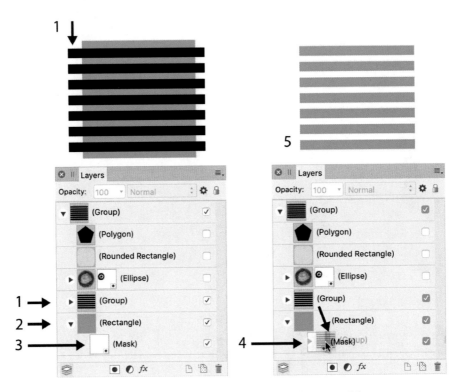

Figure 9.7 – The Mask layer using a vector shapes workflow

Continuing with *Figure 9.3*, icon **e** is the **Adjustment Layer** icon. Adjustment layers are layers that apply various kinds of non-destructive adjustments to either a whole layer or to parts of a layer. Most of these adjustments deal with color or tonal adjustment options, as shown in the drop-down list. Some adjustments that I use on a fairly regular basis are **Levels, Recolor, Black and White, Brightness and Contrast, Vibrance, Curves**, and **Color Balance**.

Huge Workflow Improvement

Before I started using Affinity Designer for my illustration work, I would have had to take my illustrations into another program to make these kinds of adjustments, thereby incurring extra time and not having a seamless workflow that doing it all in one application allows. Having these powerful adjustment layers right inside Affinity Designer is a game-changer.

The following screenshot shows the **Recolor Adjustment** layer being applied to one of the eyes of my Scottish gentleman:

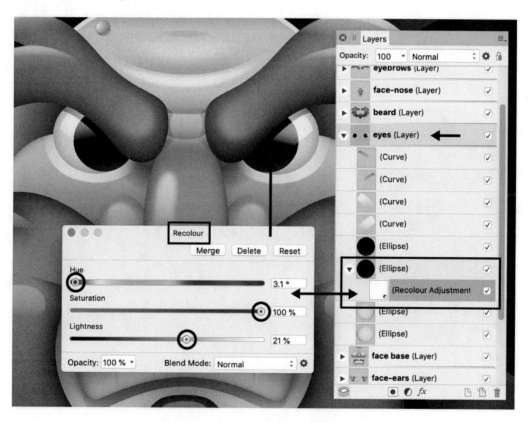

Figure 9.8 – The Recolor Adjustment layer example with the Recolor panel

What's Up with Those Extra Layers?

If every object is its own layer, as I stated earlier, you may be wondering how I seem to have multiple "sublayers" in my layer stack. This is part of the workflow I employ when I first start a project, and I will explain this once we've covered all the icons and features of the **Layers** panel shown in *Figure 9.3*.

Icon **f** (as labeled in *Figure 9.3*) is the **Layer Effects Panel** (**fx**) popup button. This panel displays the same effects as **Effects Panel**, which we covered in *Chapter 5, Main Studio Panels and Managers,* and provides access to all Affinity Designer effects. These effects can be applied to an entire layer or just to selected objects. It is accessible here as a convenient shortcut. Rather than forcing you to go back to *Chapter 5, Main Studio Panels and Managers,* to look at this panel, I am presenting it again here:

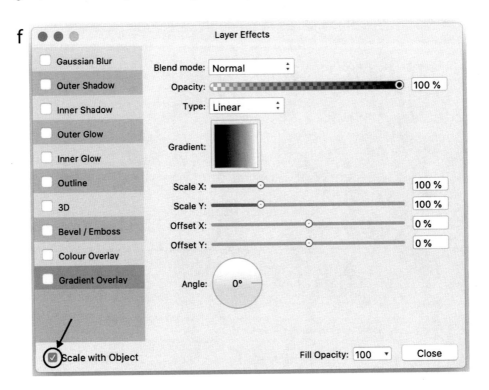

Figure 9.9 – The Layer Effects panel

Scale with Object!

One thing that is crucial to point out on this panel is the **Scale with Object** feature in the bottom left-hand corner. When this is checked, it will scale all the effects associated with the object if you decide to change the size of that object. Otherwise, if unchecked, the effect will remain its original size, and that is usually not the desired result. This is the same idea behind the **Scale with Object** feature we discussed in *Chapter 5, Main Studio Panels and Managers,* for the **Stroke** panel. One more thing: it's important to know that this feature is not a global feature. In other words, switching it on only affects the element it is attached to, unlike other, similar applications, it can be switched on for certain items and switched off for others.

> **Layer Visibility Tick Boxes**
>
> The small tick boxes on the right-hand side of all the layers are the layers' **Visibility** tick boxes – checked for visible, unchecked for hidden. To control the visibility of more than one layer at a time, *Shift + click* or *Ctrl* or *Cmd + click* to select your layers and then check or uncheck just one of the tick boxes to affect all of them.

Let's have a look at the last three icons highlighted in *Figure 9.3*. Icon **g** , **Add Layer**, will add a new vector layer immediately above the selected layer. Alternatively, if a layer hasn't been selected, the new layer will be placed at the top of the layer stack. Icon **h**, **Add Pixel Layer**, adds a new Pixel layer immediately above the selected layer. Alternatively, if a layer isn't selected, the new layer will be placed at the top of the layer stack. Finally, we have icon **i**, **Remove Layer**, which will delete the currently selected layer, or layers if multiple layers are selected, removing everything that was on that layer or layers.

Creating a layer stack plan and taking advantage of Sublayers

It's unrealistic to think you will get very far with keeping every single element on its own layer. Technically, it is possible, and it does seem to work that way as you start creating your elements, but it doesn't make for a very efficient workflow. We need to come up with a more organized way that makes more sense and allows us to hide or lock layers if we need to, move groups of elements around, or even be able to easily make selections when we need to. Unless we come up with a system to do this, we will run into a confusing mess pretty fast.

My solution to this is as follows: I have a look at and review the sketch of the piece I am about to start working on before I do anything, and then break it down into its main layers. If you don't have a sketch, try to visualize how your project's layer order should be set up.

Then, I think in terms of the top to bottom nature of the layer stack and which areas I will want up-front and those I will want behind. Often, this changes as the illustration develops, and I usually make adjustments and move layers around as I go if I need to.

Let's take a closer look at how to set up an efficient layer stack by revisiting the Full Kilt beer label piece from earlier. Here is the rough sketch I used as a guide for this piece. These sketches don't have to be a final finished idea – they just need to provide enough visual information to get me started as the concept generally evolves throughout a project, once I start building elements and playing with color:

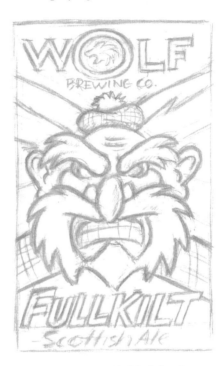

Figure 9.10 – Ale label sketch

If we look again at the Full Kilt ale label pieces' layer stack (*Figure 9.11*), we can see that the main layers are arranged from top to bottom in the order that they will be seen.

I usually place my scanned sketch as the topmost layer, with a **Multiply Blend Mode** set to around 50% so that I can still see the sketch as I create the piece, with none of the elements covering it up. Hiding the sketch layer is easy when I need to have it out of the way, as shown in the following figure, by deselecting the scan layer's visibility tick box. You'll notice how the piece has evolved from the initial sketch. The type elements and the logo are completely different. The character's face, however, has stayed pretty true to the original idea:

Figure 9.11 – Ale label final with layer stack

Looking at the finished label (*Figure 9.11*) and comparing it to the **Layers** panel, you can see how the stacking order, starting with the dark blue background on the bottom layer, going all the way up to the type layer, reveals all the content in one seamless image. Separating your work using layers in this way makes it extremely easy to not only create but also edit or make any changes to it as you work.

Setting up and managing Main and Sublayers

To set up my main layers, I create the number of new layers I think I'll need by clicking the new (vector) layer icon. That's the icon on the left of those three in the bottom right corner. In this case, according to my sketch, I clicked the **New Layer** button 11 times and made 11 new blank layers. Then, I name those layers according to the elements that will be on them – eyebrows, nose, eyes, and so on – in the order that I need them to be in. This naming step is very important for maintaining an efficient workflow. These new layers will be the "containers" for all the individual paths and pieces that come together to create the final illustration.

Next, I begin adding components and start to build the piece. To do this and to ensure that the new objects get placed on the appropriate main layer as sublayers, I "target" or select the correct main layer first. Then, once I start adding a shape object or start clicking with the pen tool, the element will be placed automatically under that selected main layer. This is why, in the **Layers** panel, you will notice the little arrow flyouts just to the left of each of the layer icons, indicating that there are additional sublayers below. You can think of these main layers as folders with content inside. As you build up your work, you keep targeting the layers you need to. If you find you need to add a new main layer from time to time, you only need to hit the **New Layer** button, name it, and off you go.

If we look at the twirled-down **wolf logo** main layer in the following screenshot, we can see the sublayers nested inside it. Notice that there are two group layers containing groups of the required type for the logo, with their own sublayers and two additional unnamed layers. I don't usually name my sublayers unless I think I need to stay organized at that level. Generally, naming the main layers is all you will need to do:

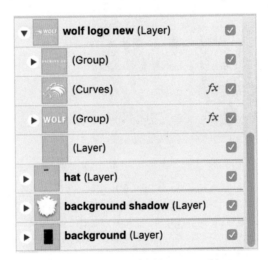

Figure 9.12 – Layer stack showing sublayers

If you have created a new layer with an object that you would like to be part of another main layer's sublayer, simply drag it to that main layer, just below and to the right, until you see an indented horizontal gray bar. Dropping it there will insert it into the main layer as a sublayer. In my example, in Figure 9.13, I dragged the green cog shape up into the main group layer. Actually, as long as you drag it to any of those sublayers in the same fashion, it will add it to that main layer. For instance, if you wanted to position it in-between the black pentagon shape and the yellow rounded rectangle, you would drag it to just below the black pentagon shape. The following figure illustrates this method of creating a new sublayer. Notice as well that the main layer's thumbnail icon updates to show the green cog:

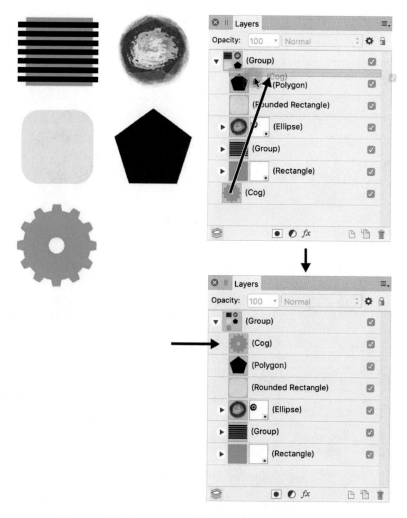

Figure 9.13 – Dragging and dropping to create a sublayer

You can remove sublayers from the main layer by dragging them out of the group, thereby turning them into normal layers. Drag the sublayer just above the main layer until you see a horizontal gray bar that is the whole width of the layer and not indented. This tells you that it has been dragged outside of the main layer it was nested inside. Experiment with moving your layers around or nesting them under other layers to see how it changes the behavior or location in the viewing stacking order. In Affinity Designer, layer placement, as we've seen, can make a real difference to the appearance of your elements and whether they are visible or not.

Layer Context menu

The Layer Context menu can be accessed by *right-clicking*, if you are using a standard three-button mouse, or *Ctrl + clicking* on the selected layer you want to affect. A drop-down menu will appear with quite a few options for you to choose from. Figure 9.14, right-clicking on a layer (*1*) – in this case, a sublayer in the group – and (*2*) a mask layer below the blue rectangle, showing the options that are available.

For both of these layer context menu dropdowns, at the bottom of the list, there are options to apply one of seven colors so that you can color tag your layers for yet another way to organize your layer stacks. This gives you another powerful option for selecting layers by color tags:

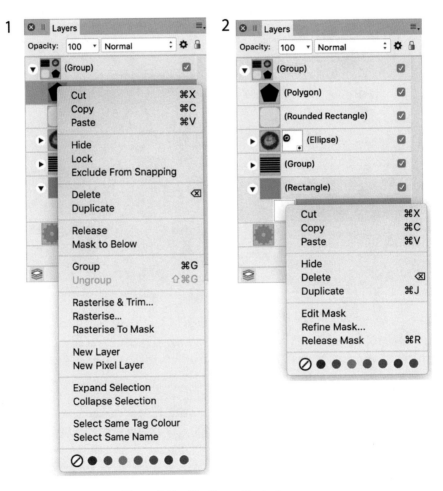

Figure 9.14 – The Layer Context menus

Moving or repositioning layers

Moving or repositioning any layer or layers is just a matter of clicking and dragging them around to the desired position in the stack. You can also move a selected layer up or down the stack by selecting it and pressing the **Move Forward** or **Move Back** icons in the upper toolbar:

Figure 9.15 – The toolbar order icons

Sometimes, the layer stack is so long that it may be impractical to drag and drop a layer to move it. In that case, I usually cut *(Cmd or Ctrl + X)* the selected layer, select the layer just below where I want to paste the layer, and paste *(Cmd or Ctrl + V)* the copied layer into place.

Clipping

One of the most commonly used techniques that's available from the **Layers** panel is clipping. This works with both vector and pixel objects. Clipping is similar to masking, where shapes or elements are used to hide a portion of another shape or element (clipping). Whereas masking uses a mask layer to "cover up" elements with the use of black or white pixel paint or vector shapes, clipping uses a clipping object and a clipped object, where one clips the other. Any portion of the clipped object that falls outside the clipping object will be hidden.

Use mask layers to control the inside and outside of a shape, and clipping when you just need to clip the outside boundaries of an object or painted area. Masking is more complicated but offers more control.

The following figure shows me clipping a pixel layer with a vector sphere or circle shape:

Figure 9.16 – Clipping Pixel brush marks example

The following figure shows me clipping six vector layers with a vector sphere or circle shape:

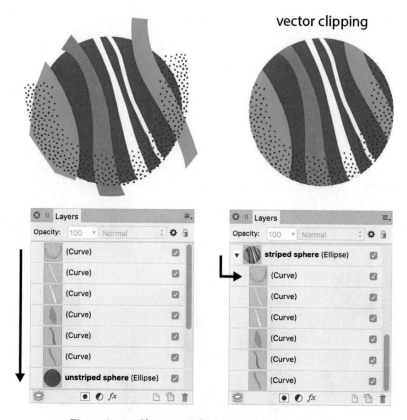

Figure 9.17 – Clipping multiple vector shapes example

To achieve this, simply press *Shift* and select the layers that you want to clip. Then, drag these layers underneath and slightly to the right of the clipping layer until you see an indented horizontal gray bar. Letting go at that position will nest the selected layers inside the clipping shape. This can take some practice as sometimes, it can be a little tricky to trigger the hotspot that tells Affinity Designer to insert the chosen layers inside the clipping layer.

To unclip a layer, drag it outside the clipping layer or go to **LAYER | ARRANGE | MOVE OUTSIDE**.

Artboards and the Layers panel

If you work with single or multiple artboards, the workflow is pretty much the same as it is for non-artboard documents, as far as the **Layers** panel and objects are concerned. Each artboard is like a main layer, with the content of each artboard nested below the main artboard layer's name. With artboards, the **Edit All Layers** function toggles the ability to work with or move objects between other artboards on and off. When **Edit All Layers** is off, to work on or "activate" a different artboard, you must either click on the other artboard's name in the **Layers** panel or click on the other artboard's name in the top-left corner, above the artboard, in the document view. For a more comprehensive look at artboards, see the *Artboards* section of *Chapter 4, Document Setup and Modification*:

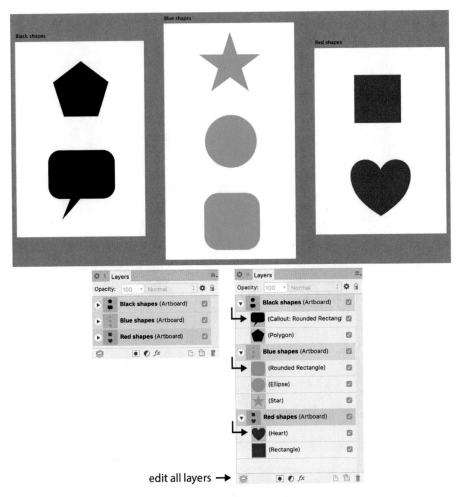

Figure 9.18 – Artboards layer behavior

Closely related to any good layer workflow practice is having first-hand knowledge of how to manage objects in your documents. As you add more and more elements to your projects, the ability to stay organized and maintain control can mean the difference between a successful, enjoyable experience or one of frustration. In addition to managing objects, there are also specific types of objects and special unique ways of placing objects that allow you to do certain things. In the next section, we'll take a closer look at Affinity Designer's objects.

Objects in Affinity Designer

We have discussed objects and object-related topics throughout this book, in terms of how they relate to other subjects and features. However, there are some particular aspects of working with objects that I thought belonged alongside a discussion regarding layers and layer management.

So far, we've talked about selecting objects, aligning and distributing objects, and the object hierarchy. Here, we will touch on some of these topics while we cover a few more important specific characteristics of working with objects, some related to a layer's workflow and some not.

Finding objects

With all the layers that you will be creating in your work and with all the various layer-related workflows we've been discussing in this chapter, you are going to want to be able to find your selections quickly and efficiently in the **Layers** panel. Affinity Designer's default solution for this is something called Auto Scroll. When you select an object, the **Layers** panel scrolls automatically to its position in the layer stack. This initially sounds ideal, but I found it to be a bit distracting as it scrolls every time you select something, and the constant movement in the **Layers** panel was a visual distraction for me. Luckily, there is an easy solution for this. To quickly locate a selected element in your **Layers** panel, you can right-click on the element and choose **Find in Layers Panel**. Or, if you like to use keyboard shortcuts, you can assign one for this. I have assigned the *f* key, as in "Find," for this.

Grouping and ungrouping objects

Grouping objects is a great way to organize separate elements into a cohesive unit, making it easier to select, move, or transform them either as a single unit or separately. Creating groups is a great way to keep your long layer stack in order.

Grouping is pretty straightforward in that you select two or more objects and group them by pressing either *Cmd* or *Ctrl G*, select **Group** in the **Context** toolbar or select **Group** in the **Layers** menu, or right-click and select **Group** from the menu options. In the **Layers** panel, you'll notice a new main layer called Group with the objects of the group nested as sublayers. You can double-click Group to rename it.

Once you've grouped your objects, if you select any of the objects in the group, you will see a group selection box around the whole group. To select one object from the group, double-click on it; it will be selected with its own selection box. At this point, making subsequent selections will allow you to select additional individual objects. Try this for yourself to get comfortable with this workflow:

Figure 9.19 – Group object selected on the left and the double-clicked individual selection on the right

To ungroup objects, select the group and press *Cmd* or *Ctrl + Shift + G*, click **Ungroup** in the **Context** toolbar, select **Ungroup** in the **Layers** menu, or right-click and select **Ungroup** from the menu options. Be careful not to select **Ungroup All**; otherwise, every group in your document will be ungrouped.

To keep the group but just remove one or more objects from a group, select the object or objects in the **Layers** panel, right-click, and choose **Release**. If you selected more than one object layer, they will all be released from the group at the same time.

Finally, to create a layer from a group – or, as Affinity Designer calls it, "*Promote a Group to Layer*" – simply click on the group and go to **LAYER | PROMOTE GROUP TO LAYER**. This turns the group into a normal layer, with the former objects of the group nested under the new layer.

Duplicate and Power Duplicate

We have touched on duplicating objects throughout this book, when we discussed other topics, but I will cover this again here, as well as mention the Power Duplicate feature.

To **Duplicate** an object, you can either drag a selected object with the *Cmd* or *Ctrl* key pressed to copy the selected object, group, or layer; or copy and paste an object, group, or layer and right-click or *Ctrl + click* on the object, group, or layer in the **Layers** panel and choose **Duplicate**. The keyboard shortcut for duplicating is *Cmd* or *Ctrl + J*.

To **Power Duplicate** an object, select the object and duplicate it using one of the methods just mentioned. Now, move it or transform it. Pressing **Duplicate** again will repeat the last duplication. Keep duplicating to create more copies of the duplication. Depending on what you do with that object, you can create some interesting shapes or patterns. The following figure shows a simple example of this:

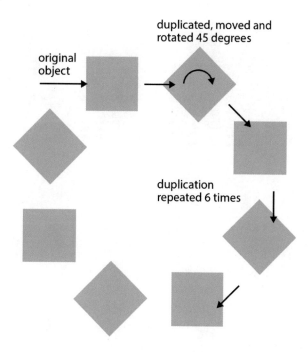

Figure 9.20 – Using the Power Duplicate function to repeat a duplication

It can be a little tricky to get the desired result, and you may find that you need to attempt this a few times. Using the *Cmd* or *Ctrl + J* shortcut will speed up the process of duplicating your shapes.

Compound objects

Compound objects are objects that are created from two or more objects using a non-destructive approach. They are similar and operate in the same fashion as the boolean operations we discussed in *Chapter 1, Getting Familiar with Affinity Designer's Interface*, but they remain live and can still be edited and transformed once they have been created. They can be added to, modified, or removed from the compound object at any time and will retain their original shape. This flexibility comes in handy when you don't want to commit to a shape right away, giving you a bit more creative freedom to experiment.

To create a compound object, select two or more shapes and go to **LAYER | CREATE COMPOUND**. The topmost object in the layer stack will show a compound boolean icon. Clicking and holding this icon will make a small pop-up appear that provides four different boolean options. In the following figure, I used the **Add** and **Xor** options:

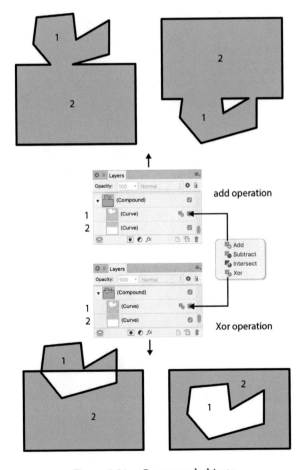

Figure 9.21 – Compound objects

What makes this flexible is that you can freely move the shapes around and the boolean will update since it's a non-destructible effect. To remove the compound effect, go to **LAYER | RELEASE COMPOUND**.

Isolating object layers

You can isolate or show a chosen single layer and temporarily hide all other layers by choosing **Option** or using the *Alt* key and clicking once on a chosen layer in the **Layers** panel. This will hide all the other layers except the layer you clicked on. The idea is that you can view and/or work on this visible layer. Clicking on any other layer or anywhere else in the document or pressing the *Esc* key will unhide all the hidden layers. In theory, this isolation mode works, but it is very difficult to work on the isolated layer as it is too easy to click out of isolation mode. In the future, I would like to see a more robust version of this where you have more control over exiting isolation mode. As it is now, its use is more of an isolation **view** mode than an isolation **work** mode. Hopefully, this will be improved in subsequent updates of the application.

Rasterize

Sometimes, you will need to rasterize a vector object. You may want to preserve certain complex aesthetic qualities or vector effects of an element to ensure accurate reproduction. Alternatively, there may be pixel painting effects that you want to add to an object that require it to be pixel-based. To do this in the **Layers** panel, right-click on the selected object's layer and chose **Rasterize**. Alternatively, you can go to **LAYER | RASTERIZE**. This is an undoable operation, so either make a copy of the layer or immediately undo (*Cmd* or *Ctrl + Z*) this if you want to keep a vector version of the layer.

Converting shape tools or text objects into curves

When working with Affinity Designer's shape tools or text, often, you will need to make edits to shapes that require you to change them from parametric objects to bezier curve objects. For example, you may need to adjust the points of a star, use a boolean operation on a circle shape, or make custom edits to a font. To make these types of modifications, you will need to convert these shapes or text into curves:

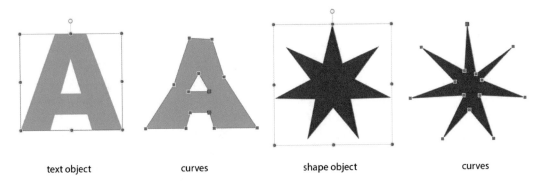

Figure 9.22 – Text and shape objects converted into curves

Converting can be done by selecting the shape or text and clicking on **Convert to Curves** in the **Context** toolbar or going to **LAYER | CONVERT TO CURVES**.

Copying, pasting, and inserting objects

Affinity Designer has some unique copying and pasting methods for working with objects and layers.

Copying is pretty much the same as any other similar application. In **PREFERENCES | GENERAL**, you can specify whether to **Copy items as SVG** or not as a global preference. Pasting has a few options, however, and they are as follows:

- **Paste** *(Cmd or Ctrl + V)*: This is a standard paste procedure that makes a duplicate of the copied object.

- **Paste Inside** *(Option, Cmd or Alt + Ctrl + V)*: This will paste the copied object inside another object. This is great for quickly creating those clipping objects we discussed earlier in this chapter.

- **Paste Style** *(Shift, Cmd or Shift + Ctrl + V)*: This is a super handy operation that's used to copy an object's stroke, fill, and any effects to another object. Basically, you are pasting the style of one object to another object.

- **Paste Effects** *(Ctrl, Cmd or Alt + Shift + V)*: This will only paste the effects from another object, which is also super handy.

- **Paste Without format** *(Option, Shift, Cmd or Alt, Shift + Ctrl + V)*: This will paste unformatted text, ignoring the copied text's formatting and keep the formatting of the targeted text.

Targeting or inserting objects is yet another way of moving or repositioning your objects. By default, when you copy and paste an object, it is pasted directly above the current selection. Alternatively, if there is no selection, it is pasted at the top of the stack on that layer. With targeting, you can select a different object for the copied object to either be pasted inside, pasted above, or pasted behind. To do this, select your object and copy it. Select your target object and from the toolbar, select one of the options, as shown in the following figure. Choosing **Insert Inside** is a quick way to make a clipping shape and this is the option that I use most often. In the **Layers** panel, you will see that choosing **Insert Inside** has created a nested object that's indented below your target object:

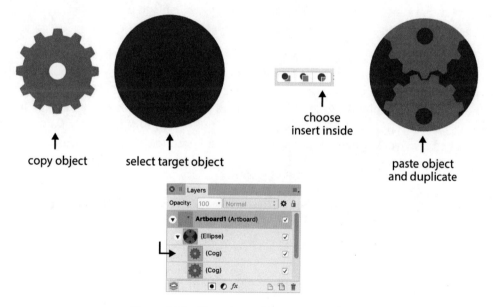

Figure 9.23 – Targeting and inserting an object

This concludes our look at the layers and objects workflow. As you get more accustomed to Affinity Designer, you may find that you will come up with your own versions of setting up or keeping your files manageable when working with layers and objects, as there are usually more than a few ways of doing things in Affinity Designer. The workflow and methods discussed in this chapter have worked well for my illustration work over the last few years when using Affinity Designer, and it's basically the process (as far as layers and objects go) that we will be using for the three practical chapters later in the book: *Chapter 11, Creating a Professional Logo, Chapter 12, Creating Astronaut Ricky and Sidekick K9,* and *Chapter 13, Rocketing into the Pixel Cosmos.*

Summary

In this chapter, we looked at how to harness the **Layers** panel to create a smooth and predictable workflow. We discovered the differences between working with vector and pixel layers and how to take advantage of mask and adjustment layers. We saw how sublayers and groups can extend the options we have available to us, and we also covered how to use the clipping function to control the appearance of our objects.

We also took a more specific look at Affinity Designer's objects features and functions and how to manage them within the **Layers** panel. We learned about finding objects with Auto Scroll, how to create and take advantage of compound objects, how to isolate layers, and how to move objects around within the **Layers** panel through copying and pasting, targeting, and inserting. In short, we've taken a deep dive into how to use the **Layers** panel by using regular layers, sublayers, and artboards to help us manage our document objects and streamline our workflow.

In the next chapter, we'll continue with the second of two chapters on workflows by discussing the power of symbols, the convenience of assets, and the History panel.

10
Workflow: Symbols, Assets, and History

Welcome to the tenth chapter of *Up and Running with Affinity Designer*.

In this chapter, we are going to take a look at Affinity Designer's powerful symbols workflow, as well as the incredibly handy **Assets** panel and **History** panel, three workflow features that enable you to work more efficiently and more effectively.

Symbols

Put simply, symbols are objects that affect other objects. Symbols are especially useful when you have a lot of repeating objects or elements in your project, and you want to have the flexibility to be able to make edits or updates to those objects all at once. The Symbols panel allows you to change one symbol, such as scaling or changing its color, and all of its symbol instances will get updated to reflect that change.

Creating symbols

To create a symbol, you will need to have the **Symbols** panel onscreen. Go to **VIEW | STUDIO | SYMBOLS** to make the **Symbols** panel appear. As far as I can tell, using the **Symbols** panel is currently the only way to create a symbol. On the **Symbols** panel there are three buttons, **Create**, **Detach**, and **Sync**, which we will discuss in detail in the following visual examples:

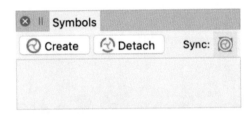

Figure 10.1 – The Symbols panel

Once you have the **Symbols** panel onscreen, select the object you want to become a symbol and click the **Create** button in the upper-left corner of the panel. Immediately you will see a new symbol icon of your selected object in the **Symbols** panel with the title **Symbol** under the icon. To rename it, right-click or *Ctrl* + click on the icon and you will be presented with the option to either delete the symbol or rename it. I suggest you rename each symbol to something that makes sense, especially if you are going to have a lot of symbols in your document. Here, in *Figure 10.2*, I wanted the light- and dark-colored trees to be separate, so I selected each one individually before creating each symbol:

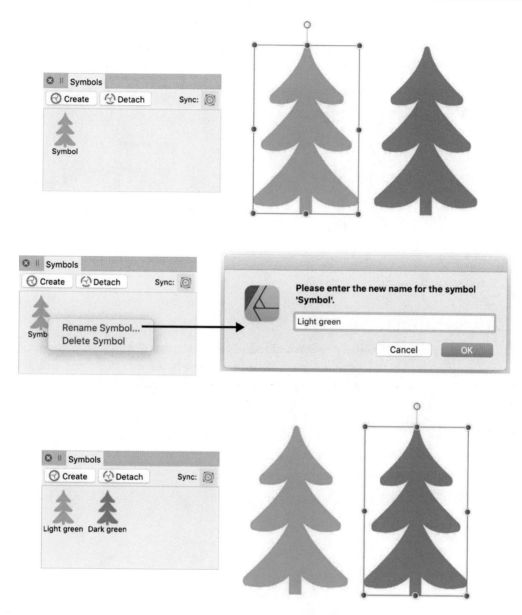

Figure 10.2 – Creating and renaming a symbol

Symbols are indicated in the **Layers** panel, with a thin vertical band on the left-hand side of the layer, colored either orange in the UI's dark mode, or dark gray in the UI's light mode:

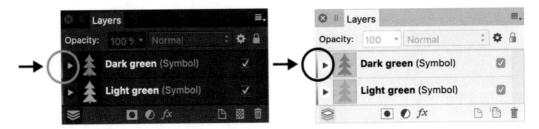

Figure 10.3 – Symbol layer indication

Trees are a good example to use as symbols. Typically, you may use quite a few in an illustration, and if you need to make adjustments or changes to lots of them, symbols are a quick and efficient way to achieve this.

Using symbols

When you drag a symbol out of the **Symbols** panel and into your document workspace you are creating a copy or an *instance* of the symbol. This instance can then be duplicated or copied from the instance you initially dragged out into your document and it will retain the symbol's behavior. In other words, you don't necessarily need to keep dragging your symbols from the **Symbols** panel. Editing any one of the instances will apply the same changes to all of them, creating a powerful way to edit many copies of the object at once. In *Figure 10.4*, I have created a simple infographic type of forest, by first creating the background hill shape, and then dragging and duplicating a few of the light and dark green tree symbols I created earlier:

Figure 10.4 – Simple forest created using symbols

The hill shape is not a symbol. Editing and working with symbols may be confusing at first, but it's more than worth it once you grasp the concept and adopt it into your workflow.

To double-click or not to double-click?

There are generally two ways to edit symbols in Affinity Designer. The first method involves exercising your clicking finger with a fair amount of double-clicking. I will cover it so that you know this method if you need to use it, and of course it's always good practice to know alternate ways of doing things. The second method is easier, less confusing, uses fewer steps, and involves the **Layers** panel.

Editing the object versus editing the symbol

In *Figure 10.4*, you may have noticed that some of the trees in the forest are different sizes. How is this possible if they are instances? Shouldn't any edited instances be reflected across all instances? Not exactly, and here's why. Just selecting a symbol instance and editing it doesn't affect all of the other symbol instances. In order to affect the other symbol instances, you need to double-click on the symbol instance you are editing to go into a sort of symbol **edit** level, then any edits you make to it will be distributed across all instances of that symbol. Double-clicking a second time will give you access to the base curve, allowing even more editing options (*if you don't see any base curve nodes, check to see if your shape has been converted to curves*). Any changes made to a symbol instance at the base curve level will change all of the symbol instances' base curves:

1 - single click (object editing)   **2 - double click** (symbol editing)   **3 - double click again** (symbol editing curve)

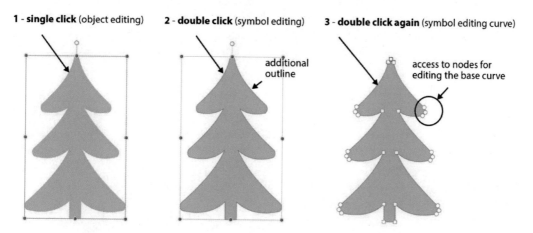

additional outline

access to nodes for editing the base curve

Figure 10.5 – Double-click on the symbol instance to enter symbol edit mode

In the forest scene (*Figure 10.4*), I *single-clicked* with the **Move** tool to select each object to scale them up or down; this allows for individual or local changes when using symbols without affecting all of the symbols. Then I *double-clicked* on one of the light green tree symbols and adjusted its width. Notice in *Figure 10.6* how all of the light green trees are now narrower? I then changed the color of those same trees to a dark orangey-brown by just changing a single tree. This would be an easy method to indicate in our forest infographic that some of the trees are not growing and are slowly dying:

Figure 10.6 – Scale and color adjustments made to the symbol

You can see that the trick with working with symbols efficiently with this first method is remembering when to single-click and when to double-click. This is especially the case when your symbol is made up of more than one element. Our initial pine tree is basically just a single curve element. For objects that contain more than one element, you will need to group them first before creating your symbol, otherwise you'll create separate symbols for all of the objects you have selected. *Figure 10.7* shows this with a second type of tree, one made up of two separate objects. Notice in the left **Symbols** panel, ungrouped elements created as separate symbols. This isn't usually the desired result:

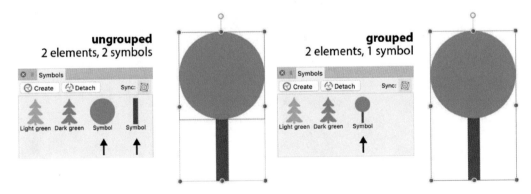

Figure 10.7 – Grouping elements to create one symbol

To add to the confusion with this method, editing grouped symbols requires one extra step compared to editing a single object based symbol. If you recall *Chapter 9, Workflow: Layers and Objects*, we discussed grouping and ungrouping objects, and how to access individual elements or objects within a group in order to edit them. To recap, to edit an object inside a group, you need to double-click on that group to get access to the individual nodes and curves of the object inside it.

So when the symbol is a group as in our tree example in *Figure 10.7*, you will need to first double-click the grouped symbol to access the individual element level, then double-click it again to access the symbol element level to edit from, then, with the symbol element level still selected, you will need to *Shift* + select all of the other symbol element-level objects that are inside the group, in this case just the tree trunk. This, as you can imagine, has the potential to get a little cumbersome and confusing, especially if you are working with some complex symbols. So, let's discuss the second method using the **Layers** panel.

Using the Layers panel for selecting

Using the grouped tree symbol, let's see how using the **Layers** panel can simplify our workflow. We know from our discussion in the previous chapter about Affinity Designer's layer stack that every single element can be accessed by selecting it in the **Layers** panel. This includes any symbol that we have in our document and the elements that make up the symbol.

If we take a look at the grouped tree symbol in the **Layers** panel (**Summer tree**) in *Figure 10.8*, we can see the structure of this symbol's layers setup. The selected top layer, denoted as a symbol, contains the group of the two shapes that make up the tree group indented and below it:

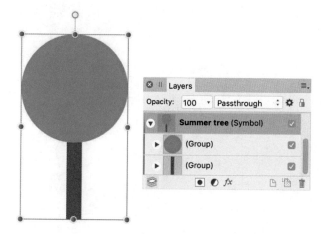

Figure 10.8 – Grouped symbol in the Layers panel

Using the **Layers** panel allows easy access to the group's individual elements. Selecting these elements enables us to edit our symbols in a much less confusing manner than all of the double-clicking and *Shift* + selecting of the first method. By selecting the elements of the group, you can scale, rotate, change color, or even quickly access the individual curve nodes to affect all of the symbol instances simultaneously. This can be seen in *Figure 10.9*:

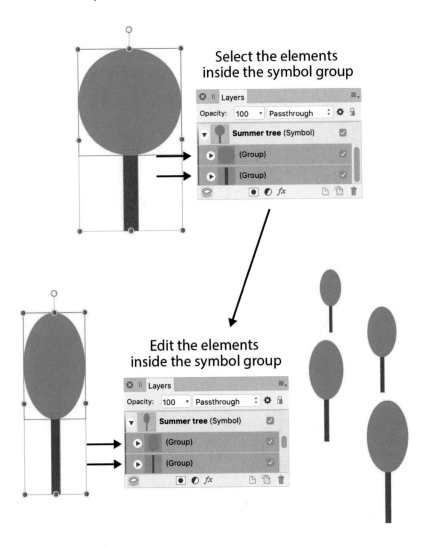

Figure 10.9 – Editing a grouped symbol using the Layers panel

These tree examples are a simple illustration of how you can approach working with symbols. Working with more complex symbols may involve more careful attention to how you go about making your selections, but the core fundamentals will remain the same.

I suspect most readers will prefer to use the second method (the **Layers** panel workflow) when it comes to working with symbols in Affinity Designer. But now you are acquainted with both, you might find yourself using each of them depending on your needs. If you are working with fairly simple symbols, using the first method (double-click) can save you a lot of back-and-forth trips to the **Layers** panel over the course of a project.

Detaching, deleting, and un-syncing your symbols

Let's look at how we can use all three in the following section.

Detaching

In order to detach or cut the relationship of a symbol to one of its instances, you must *select the instance* in the document and click on the **Detach** button on the **Symbols** panel. Detaching a selected instance of a symbol will revert that specific instance to a normal object. Only the instance that you selected will revert to a normal object; the symbol itself that it was connected to will still remain a symbol. You can select more than one instance to detach if you need to, and they will all be detached at the same time:

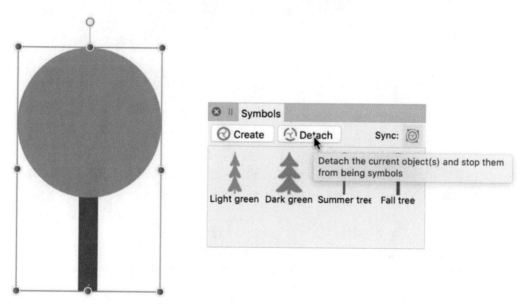

Figure 10.10 – Detaching a selected instance of a symbol

Deleting

If you want to remove or delete a symbol completely from the document, right-click or *Ctrl* + click on the chosen symbol in the **Symbols** panel and choose **Delete Symbol**. All instances of that deleted symbol will remain in the document and will revert to being normal objects:

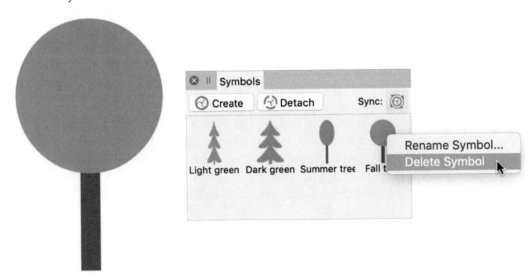

Figure 10.11 – Deleting a symbol

Un-syncing

Syncing occurs automatically when you create an instance of a symbol by dragging a symbol out into the document window. However, sometimes while working with symbols you will want to edit a symbol instance separately from the symbol it belongs to, and yet still keep a link to it. This is what un-syncing will allow you to do.

> **On or off?**
> The **Sync** button on the **Symbols** panel is a toggle. It allows you to sync or un-sync an instance of a symbol. However, currently it may be difficult to tell if it is on or off because the on or clicked state is very close in tone to the off state. I am hoping this gets addressed in updated versions of the application.

This workflow comes in handy in design application projects that use a lot of UI elements such as icons or navigational buttons that need to be similar or consistent with one another yet still require unique individual elements, such as color, size, or titles.

We can take a simple logo symbol I created as an example. *Figure 10.12* shows how I used one symbol to create a different instance that is still linked, yet is also different, by toggling on and off the **Sync** button and making edits or adjustments. This is a very powerful way to work with design elements that are both linked and still uniquely editable:

1- Create the logo symbol

2- Un-sync and edit instance type and rectangle shape

3- Re-sync and edit symbol rectangle color

Figure 10.12 – Sync and un-sync workflow

But wait, there's more – patterns and symmetry using symbols

There are a couple of more interesting and unique workflow options when it comes to symbols in regards to pattern creation and working with symmetry, which we will discuss next.

I'm not going to go into a full-blown pattern tutorial here, as there are many tutorials online that go into more depth. But I will show you the basic concept behind creating a repeating pattern using symbols in Affinity Designer. Understanding the basic premise of how symbols work, we can exploit that knowledge to create symbols that when repeated in certain ways can form repeatable patterns that otherwise might be difficult to replicate or edit. In *Figure 10.13*, I created five circles and arranged them in the corners and center of a perfect square:

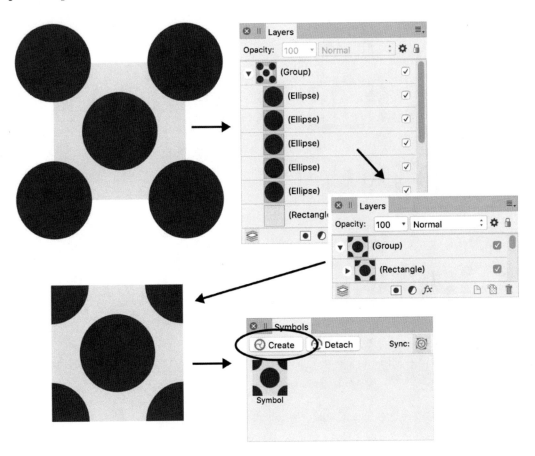

Figure 10.13 – Setting up a symbol for a simple repeating polka dot pattern

When creating patterns, you'll want to be as precise as you can, so I enabled snapping to make sure the object placements are accurate and snap to the underlying vector path nodes. Using the **Layers** panel, I nested the circles inside the square shape by dragging the circle shapes underneath the square shape to clip them. Then, using the **Symbols** panel, I created a symbol by clicking on the **Create** button:

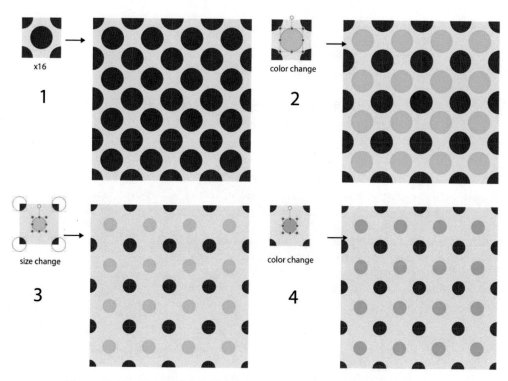

Figure 10.14 – Creating and editing a simple polkadot pattern using symbols

Copying the symbol 16 times and with snapping still enabled, I lined them up into a pattern as shown in *Figure 10.14, Number 1*. The power of symbols for pattern making comes in handy for making quick and easy edits, as shown in *Number 2*, where I changed the color of the central circle shape to blue, and again in *Number 3*, where I reduced the size of all five of the circle shapes for a more visually pleasing design, and finally in *Number 4*, where I changed the blue circle into a green color.

Using a symbol-based workflow allowed me to make these edits quickly and easily.

Once you get your pattern looking the way you like, the easiest way to use it is to export it out of Affinity Designer to your hard drive, either as a PNG or a JPG, and import it back into a selected shape using the **Fill** tool. Choose **Bitmap** from the list of options in the **Fill** tool options in the context toolbar, with **Maintain fill aspect ratio** turned on, and **Wrap** selected in the **Extend** options dropdown:

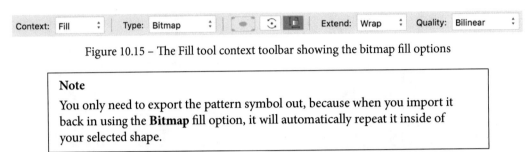

Figure 10.15 – The Fill tool context toolbar showing the bitmap fill options

> **Note**
>
> You only need to export the pattern symbol out, because when you import it back in using the **Bitmap** fill option, it will automatically repeat it inside of your selected shape.

To ensure your pattern looks the best it can, try to create the pattern symbol large enough so that it retains a sharp resolution when you export it out to import it back in as a PNG or a JPG. These are currently the two formats that can be imported using the **Fill** tool.

Creating and saving multiple patterns this way allows you to quickly import your own custom patterns to fill any shape you create:

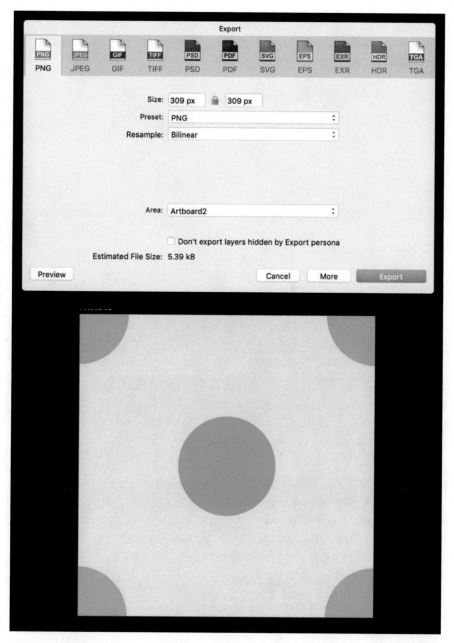

Figure 10.16 – Exporting the pattern symbol artboard as a PNG

Selecting the **Fill** tool and going to the context toolbar, I import and resize the pattern symbol back into the document as a bitmap fill as seen in *Figure 10.17*. It can also be rotated using the **Fill** tool. The imported pattern automatically repeats itself:

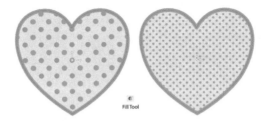

Figure 10.17 – Filling the heart shapes with the imported repeating pattern symbol

Symbols and symmetry

The last aspect of a symbols workflow that I will cover is perhaps its most unique: the ability to work in a sort of **Symmetry** mode. I say "sort of" because it isn't really a dedicated symmetry mode, but more of a work-around or a "hack" that takes advantage of how symbols work. This is not the symmetry painting feature that we discussed in *Chapter 7, Tools – Pixel Persona*, but rather a way to use symbols in Designer Persona to achieve a similar effect, except with vector elements.

It's easier to show you what I mean than to try to explain it, but basically it's drawing or editing a symbol that is mirrored or flipped on the opposite side by duplicating an instance of the symbol and flipping it vertically, so that when you edit either the symbol or the instance, the flipped position creates a mirror effect.

In *Figure 10.18*, I attempt to use this method to create a face using just the **Pencil** tool and simple line brush. I first create an eyebrow line, then I create a symbol from it, copy it, and flip it vertically. Now, if I select the symbol and continue drawing with the pencil tool, I can add to the face symmetrically. Of course, you are not limited to the **Pencil** tool and simple line work. You can choose any tool or shape you want, just as long as you are adding to the symbol. It's a fun and interactive way to create symmetrical objects:

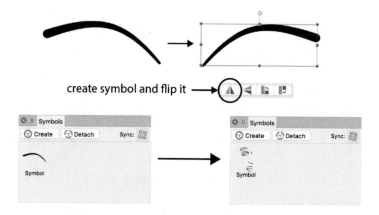

create symbol and flip it →

select symbol and add to it

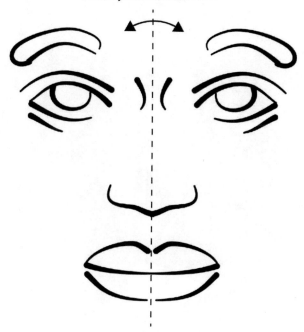

Figure 10.18 – Creating symmetrical objects using a flipped symbol workflow

I have just scratched the surface of what you can do with symbols in these few examples. Depending on the sort of work you do, you may find working with symbols becomes a large part of your workflow. If you tend to work with lots of repeating objects where you need to make global changes to specific items, such as UI/UX work, web design, map making, or infographic work, the power of symbols could be a game changer.

I encourage you to experiment and further explore working with symbols to discover how you can take advantage of a symbols workflow. There are many tutorials online that will expand on what we've covered here, and as always check out Affinity Designer's **Help** system for a full rundown of the options and features.

Assets

Assets in Affinity Designer are basically reusable objects or components that can be stored and accessed from within any Affinity Designer file in the **Assets** panel, and can be dragged into the document at any time when the **Assets** panel is onscreen:

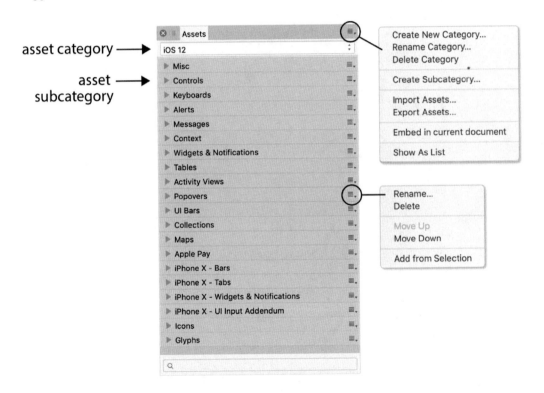

Figure 10.19 – The Assets panel

Affinity Designer ships with a pretty comprehensive assortment of iOS 12 icon assets to get you started. To use them, simply click and drag them out of the **Assets** panel into your document window:

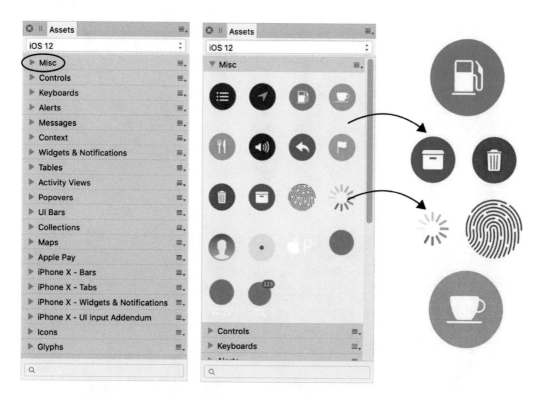

Figure 10.20 – Dragging assets out of the iOS 12 subcategory lists

Of course, any object or element you create can be saved as an asset. Assets are great for objects that you use often and need to have access to, without having to search for a file or having to recreate each time. To create your own custom asset, simply select any object or element that you want to become an asset, and then go to the top-right corner drop-down menu of the **Assets** panel, and select **Add from Selection**. Alternatively, you can drag your object into the **Assets** panel to create an asset.

It's a good idea to create a new category to store your assets in which makes sense to you, especially if you are going to create a lot of assets. Here, I have created a category called **My assets**, and a subcategory called **starbursts** to put my asset into. See *Figure 10.19* to see where to access the **Create New Category** and **Create Subcategory** menus:

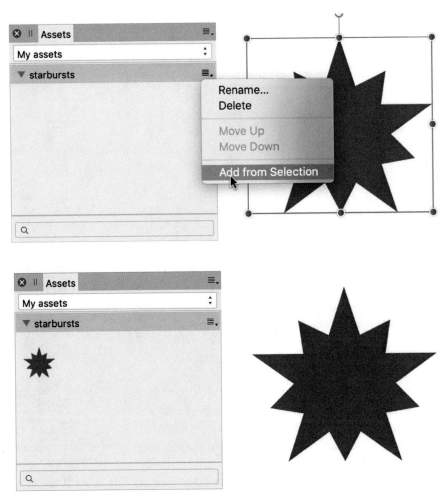

Figure 10.21 – Creating a custom asset

Assets in the **Assets** panel can be displayed as a grid of thumbnails or in a list, and can also be shared by exporting or importing them using the same top-right corner drop-down menu. If you export any assets, you will notice that they are exported as their own `.afassets` file type. I encourage you to check out places online where you can either purchase assets or download free assets. A good place to start searching is the Affinity Users forum at `https://forum.affinity.serif.com/`.

Depending on the type of work you do, using assets can allow you to work more efficiently. If you find yourself using a lot of the same objects or elements in your work, or if your work calls for regular collaboration with others in a team, an asset workflow will streamline and simplify, leaving you more time for being creative.

History

The last brief section of this workflow chapter is about the **History** panel. The **History** panel tracks all of the individual changes you make over the course of either a session or the entire length of a project. Each change is recorded as an entry in a list with the earliest or oldest entry at the top of the list.

Usually, I typically just track the history of a session, and this is the default behavior. I have never had the need to track every single change in a complete project. If you do want to track your changes throughout the entire length of your project, go to **File | Save history with document**. This will save everything you do over the course of your project, including access to history before closing and reopening the document.

The **History** panel basically allows you to scroll through time back to the beginning of a session, or to the very beginning of the creation of the project if you are saving your history with the document. To go back to a certain point, you can either use the slider at the top of the panel (*left is for undoing, right is for redoing*), or you can scroll down through the list to a particular point or state in your session or project's history.

Using the **History** panel can be a lifesaver if you need to revert to a particular state. It's good to know that beyond the normal undo and redo there is something a little more powerful tracking all of your changes in case you need it:

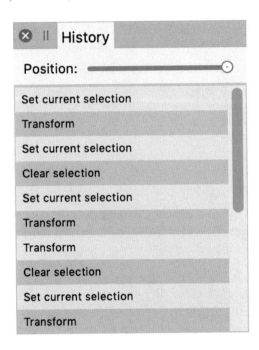

Figure 10.22 – The History panel

Summary

In this second workflow chapter, we introduced and got familiar with the **Symbols** panel, and discovered how the use of symbols can be exploited to do some heavy lifting when it comes to editing repeated elements globally across a project efficiently and quickly. We explored briefly how to put symbols to work creating repeating patterns, and also helping to generate unique and fun designs using symmetry in the Designer Persona.

Then we took a look at Affinity Designer's **Assets** panel, learned what assets are, and when and how to use them. We talked about a workflow using assets, enabling us to store and retrieve commonly used objects, and allowing us to work smarter when it comes to reusing or sharing elements, either personally or collaborating within a team environment.

Finally, we touched on the nature of the **History** panel, and saw how tracking the changes you make as you create your projects can allow you to go back in time to repair or revisit any aspect of your document.

In the next chapter, we are going to start putting what we've learned into practice. We'll start the first of three practical exercise chapters: creating a professional logo.

Section 3: Bringing It All together

In this section, we will tackle three practical exercises using the skills and knowledge covered in the previous chapters, but in a more "real-world" application. The first will be a beginner-level professional logo, the second a more advanced professional illustration, and for the third, we will create the rocket for our character Ricky. We'll put into motion the workflow and best practices discussed previously.

This section comprises the following chapters:

11
Creating a Professional Logo

Welcome to the eleventh chapter of *Up and Running with Affinity Designer*.

The idea behind this first of three exercise chapters is to build a fun, simple project using some of the skills, knowledge, and workflow practices we've been discussing over the last 10 chapters. The concept is a logo (which could also be described as a sign or poster) promoting Astronaut Ricky and her dog K9 Rover and their adventures as Rocket Racers.

The finished logo project should look something like the example in *Figure 11.1*.

Prerequisites and expectations

The goal of this chapter is designed to allow absolute beginners to start to gain confidence creating and using Affinity Designer's shapes and tools to create something that's a little bit more like a real-world project. We will be getting familiar with the tools again while creating our logo using basic and custom shapes. We'll create additional linework using the **Pen** tool and spend some time working with, and manipulating, text.

> **Note**
>
> Although you are welcome to create any logo you want from your own sketch or another reference, for the sake of the exercise here, we will be creating a particular line style for this logo that may or may not work with the example you have.

We will be placing the hand-drawn logo sketch I created (shown in *Figure 11.2*) into Affinity Designer as a guide or blueprint and will reference it as we create the logo in a step-by-step format:

> **Save. Save. Save.**
>
> As a general rule, save your files often. Go to **FILE** | **SAVE** or press *Cmd* or *Ctrl* + *S*. Don't run the risk of losing work.

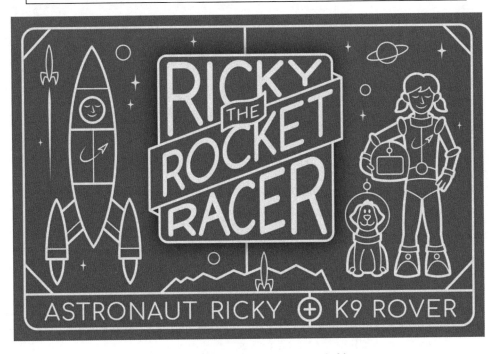

Figure 11.1 – The finished blueprint styled logo

As you can see, the final logo is comprised of many simple basic and custom shapes built up over the piece. In keeping with the graphic quality of a good logo, I decided to just have a simple one-color background and make use of a bold white line. This style is meant to mimic a traditional blueprint or plan drawing. I thought it worked well with the subject matter and the combination of simple shapes and lines makes for a nice introduction to drawing and creating shapes in Affinity Designer. Feel free, however, to use any combination of line and/or background color you wish. Experiment with different combinations to see what you can come up with.

In the next chapter, *Chapter 12, Creating Astronaut Ricky and Sidekick K9*, we will take the idea of this concept a little further than strictly linework with a deeper exploration into color and shading. We will create Astronaut Ricky and her faithful travel companion, K9 Rover, with a bit more detail and expression than what you see here. You can always skip to the next chapter if you feel confident and ready to tackle something a little more involved. However, if you feel like you want to start here on the basics and work your way up to the more challenging second part, stick around and let's get started on this logo for Ricky the Rocket Racer.

Let's get started – downloading the sketch

Okay, let's make a start on this project. To follow along using the logo sketch provided, you will need to download it from the download link and save it to somewhere on your hard drive where you will be saving your Affinity Designer file for this project. The sketch can be downloaded from the following link: `https://github.com/PacktPublishing/Up-and-Running-with-Affinity-Designer/tree/main/Chapter11`.

Workflow tip

For a best practice workflow, placed images such as this sketched image should either reside in the same folder as the Affinity Designer file or at least be close to each other. If the sketch gets moved around on your hard drive after you have placed it in your file, Affinity Designer will say that it's missing the next time you open the file and you will need to relink it. A good way to avoid this is to keep it close to your file and try not to move it or rename it. You can always embed image files into your Affinity Designer file, but that can sometimes create a larger file than you may want. The image can be deleted from the file upon completion:

Figure 11.2 – Ricky the Rocket Racer sketch

Document setup

Once you have the image downloaded and saved, let's create the Affinity Designer document that we will be using to build the logo. With Affinity Designer open, go to **FILE | NEW**. For my setup involving this sketch, and because I am in North America, I am going with the very standard **Letter**-sized document. This is a horizontal **11 x 8 ½ inch** format. I am going horizontal because the sketch is set up as horizontal and it will allow me to maximize the document size.

It really doesn't matter what size you decide to go with, just as long as the sketch fits nicely in the document without too much wasted space. You can always resize the document later if you find you need to. Your settings don't have to be the same as mine here. The key element in this chapter is the creation of this logo; the document setup, while important, isn't necessarily critical to the success of what we're going to create.

Refer to *Figure 11.3* for the document settings that I chose for this logo project. I'm using a **horizontal** version of the **Letter** size at **300 DPI** using **Inches** for **Document units**. I'm not using the **Create artboard** option and I've set **Image placement policy** to **Prefer Linked**. I'm going with an **RGB/8** color format and an **sRGB** color profile. I'm deselecting **Transparent background** without any margins or bleed settings:

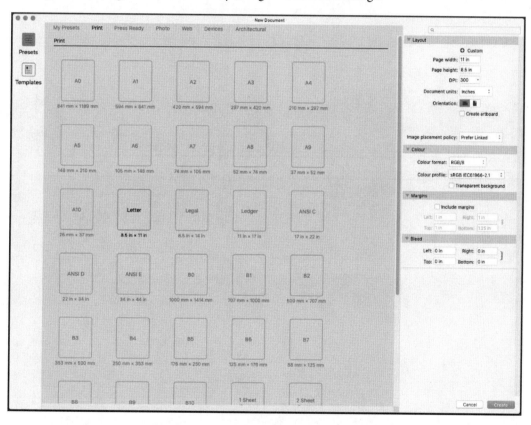

Figure 11.3 – My document settings

Placing the reference sketch

Once you have your document created, let's add the sketch image by going to **FILE** | **PLACE** or by clicking on **Place Tool** in the Tool panel and selecting the sketch to place it in our document.

Once the sketch has been placed, I scale it up a little bit to fill the document window. Use the **Move** tool to select it and drag on the corner handles *without* the *Shift* key pressed to scale it without stretching it. Then, in the **Layers** panel, I reduced the **Opacity** setting of the layer to **50%**, changed the blend mode of the layer to **Multiply**, and then locked the layer.

Basically, what this setup allows us to do is to use the sketch as a guide for us to draw all of the shapes and lines on layers below while still seeing the sketch because it's on the top layer. The multiply blend mode allows us to see through the sketch as we build the logo. If we need to hide the sketch for any reason, we just have to hide the sketch layer in the **Layers** panel. Locking the sketch layer prevents us from accidentally selecting or moving it:

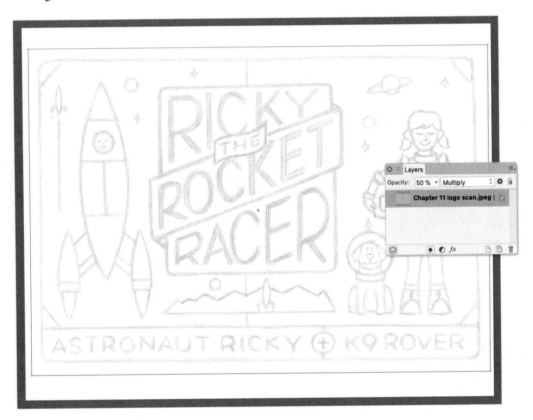

Figure 11.4 – The sketch in the document set to 50% opacity in multiply blend mode and locked

Creating the layer stack hierarchy and adding a background color

Now is the time to have a look at the sketch and decide how to divide up the layers. For every project, before I create anything, I always determine which elements are to be given their own layers. This not only forces you to organize how to build the piece, but it also gives you the ability to hide or lock any layer you need to as you build. For this logo project, it might not be as necessary as some projects because it isn't as complicated, but it is still going to come in handy I suspect and it's a great habit to get into. *Figure 11.5* shows how I decided to break up the layer stack to begin with.

I have left the sketch layer at the top of the stack, as explained earlier. The rest of the layers are placed top to bottom at this point, with the background layer at the bottom to be behind everything that will be built in the layers above. On the background layer, I will add a blue-colored rectangle shape. This might be changed later, but it's close to the blueprint color I'm wanting and it will enable the white linework of the logo to be easily visible:

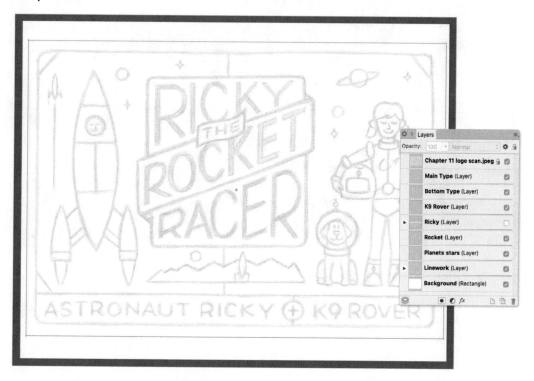

Figure 11.5 – The layer stack

Because we will be using white linework for the logo, let's start by adding a deep blue background to provide some good contrast. Select the **Rectangle** tool from the **Tools** panel, select the background layer in the **Layers** panel, and click and drag out a background shape that fills the entire screen. Now, using the **Color** panel, select an appropriate blue color. The blue I am using is **RGB Hex 00798D**. Feel free to use any color you want as long as it's dark enough for the white linework to be easily visible. You can access the Hex color input fields from the upper-right corner of the **Color** panel. See *Figure 11.6*:

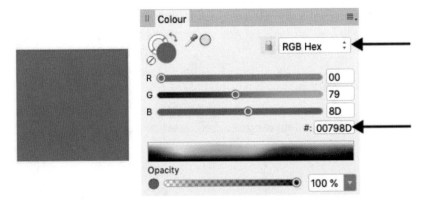

Figure 11.6 – The Hex input field in the Color panel

Building the simplest shapes and forms

Let's start by creating all of the simplest shapes first – the ellipses, rectangles, straight lines, and so on, before getting into any custom or hand-drawn shapes. This is a nice way to ease into things. I am thinking at this stage of using two different line widths. Based on the size of your piece, your line widths may be different. For my piece, I think two different line widths of 4 points and 2 points might be a good place to start. I'll use the narrower line to do areas that are smaller and closer together. The wider lines are good for most of the other areas and will make great outlines around shapes that you might want to highlight or direct the eye toward.

Remember to select the appropriate layer before you start to create your shapes and lines so that they end up on the proper layer.

> **Moving elements to another layer**
>
> If you accidentally place something on the wrong layer, one quick way to move it to the correct layer is to select it either in the document or in the **Layers** panel and press *Cmd* or *Ctrl* + *X*. This will cut or remove it, but it will also place it on your computer's clipboard. Then, just select the layer it should be on in the **Layers** panel and press *Cmd* or *Ctrl* + *V* to paste it. It will be pasted to the correct layer and it will show up in the exact same spot in your document.

Rectangles, lines, and circles… using the sketch as your guide and selecting the correct layer before starting to create each of your shapes, let's use the **Rounded Rectangle** tool to drag out a large rounded rectangle shape for the main border of the logo. I am using the Linework layer for all linework that has to do with the logo's containment shapes. With the **Rounded Rectangle** tool, you have the ability to adjust the corner radius amount at any time. Either use **Corner Widget** while the tool is still active, or adjust the corner percentage in the **Context** toolbar with the shape active. Mine is set at 4%.

Now, let's continue to create a few of the logo's straight lines. The easiest way to achieve a straight line is by using the **Pen** tool. Select the **Pen** tool and click to add the first node location to start the line, and then shift-click to add the end location of the line. Shift-clicking will create either a horizontal or vertical straight line, or lines at 45-degree angles. It all depends on the location where you click that second node point. With the **Pen** tool selected, you can also choose the **Line** or **Polygon** modes in the **Context** toolbar to ensure straight lines, but these won't guarantee that the line will be perfectly horizontal or vertical unless, again, you hold down the *Shift* key as you click to add those nodes.

Figure 11.7 shows how it's looking so far. These white lines are showing up nicely on the blue background. Let's continue creating all of the basic shapes we can find. Remember that if it's supposed to be on a specific layer, such as the dog or the rocket, don't forget to select that layer first. You can also select an element that is on the layer to make that layer active:

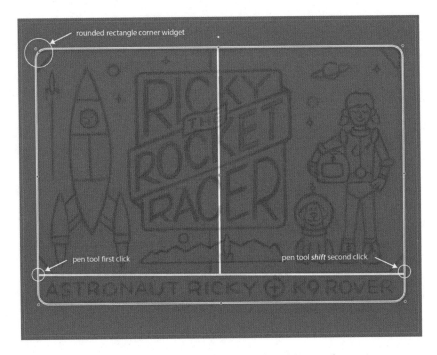

Figure 11.7 – Starting the basic shapes linework

You may notice that the sketch centerline is not entirely accurate. This is a good case of the type of correction that often takes place when working from a hand-drawn reference like this. I left it in rather than correcting the sketch to illustrate how we can make adjustments as we build as you will no doubt encounter similar types of situations yourself and it's good to see how to deal with them. This one isn't too bad though and we'll correct it as we continue to build the logo. The solution will most likely be to extend or widen the area the rocket is in over to the left a bit. I will do this later on after I have used the reference to build everything first. Once everything has been built, we can reposition any elements exactly where we need them.

A reference is only a reference

Using a reference is only a guide. In most cases, as you build your projects, you will need to make adjustments that are not necessarily included in your reference to make the piece work well. This is fairly normal and occurs in just about all creative work. It's a natural part of the process and it allows you to improve or radically change your original idea if need be. Don't be afraid to experiment and try out different approaches.

Here is a screenshot showing most, if not all, of the basic shapes created using ellipse and rectangle shapes and straight lines with the **Pen** tool:

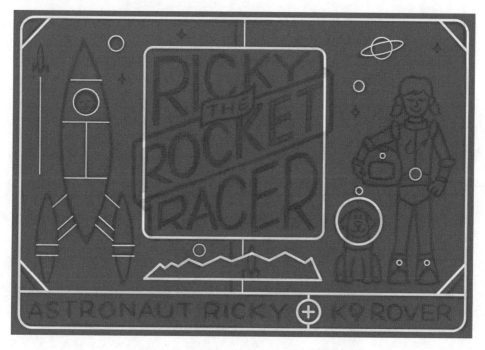

Figure 11.8 – Basic shapes and linework in place

All of these basic shapes so far should be straightforward enough to create. Try to place them as close to the reference as you can as we slowly build up the elements. Here, you can start to see the appearance the two line widths are making.

Remember that copying and pasting or pressing *Cmd* or *Ctrl* while dragging elements will copy them. They can then be flipped horizontally or vertically using the **Flip Horizontal** or **Flip Vertical** buttons in the toolbar. They can also be centered or lined up with each other using the **Alignment** options in the **Context** toolbar:

Figure 11.9 – Flipping and alignment buttons

Next, we will use some of Affinity Designer's unique **Shape** tools to create the rocket shapes and the stars in the space background. For the rocket shape, we will start with the crescent-shaped tool in the **Shape Tools** pullout of the **Tools** panel:

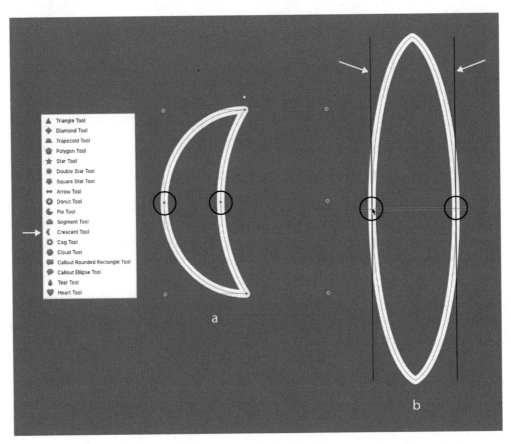

Figure 11.10 – Using the crescent-shaped tool to create a rocket shape

Adjust the two sides of the crescent shape until you see the two red symmetry lines and you'll know that the shape is symmetrical. You will also likely need to increase the height of the overall shape to get something closer to the rocket shape.

To create the side thrusters and the flames on the rocket, follow the sequence in *Figure 11.11*. Copy the main rocket shape and reduce it to the size based on the sketch. Then, with this selected, convert the shape to curves from the **Convert to Curves** button in the **Context** toolbar. Once it has been converted to a curve object, select the bottom-most node on the shape and delete it (**a**). This deletes the node but leaves the line intact as a smooth curve (**b**). To straighten the bottom curve out, select the bottom two left and right nodes and click on the **Convert Sharp** button in the **Context** toolbar (**c**). Finally, for the flame element, copy the shape you just made, flip it vertically, reduce it in size a little, and place it as shown (**d**). Hopefully, yours looks similar to mine pictured here:

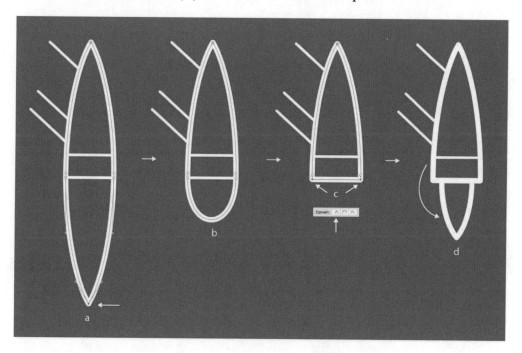

Figure 11.11 – Creating the thruster shape and flame

When you reduced the flame in size, if the width of the line became narrower, this is because the **Scale with object** setting is on in your **Stroke** panel. You will most likely want that off for all of the linework you will be creating for this piece. If we need to turn it back on for whatever reason, we can, but for now, let's turn it off. Part of the success and charm of this style is to have consistent line widths, and the two line widths of 4 and 2 points we assigned at the beginning are working well.

The **Scale with object** setting in the **Stroke** panel is not a global setting, meaning it can be on for one element and off for another. So, in our case, to make sure all of the linework in our document has this option turned off, as there is no global switch to turn it on or off, select all of the linework and switch it on then switch it off. This is a sort of override that turns it on for all of the elements and then turns it off, effectively working like a global switch. It's not a perfect workaround but it seems to do the trick. It's good to keep an eye on it though if you notice the linework sizing changing as you scale elements up or down:

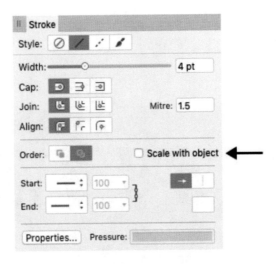

Figure 11.12 – Scale with object option turned off

Continuing with the stars for the space background, the easiest and most flexible way to create these is again with the use of one of Affinity Designer's unique Shape tools. I'm constantly amazed at how many objects I create have started out from one of these super useful shapes.

This time around, it's the **Star** tool. The star tool's default is a typical five-point star. We will reduce it to four points by using the input field or slider in the **Context** toolbar. Then, we'll make some adjustments using the adjustment points on the shape itself to add smoother curves in between the points, as shown in *Figure 11.13*:

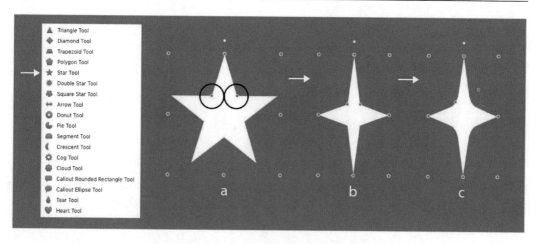

Figure 11.13 – Using the star shape tool

Now, at this point, you should have all of the simple basic shapes as well as the rocket and star shapes in place. As you can see in *Figure 11.14*, I have all of these shapes in place and I have sprinkled a few more stars around in areas that I thought could use them. Varying the size is a good idea, too, to add a sense of far-off distance to some of them. When you size them with the **Move** tool, make sure you press *Shift* to keep them in proportion:

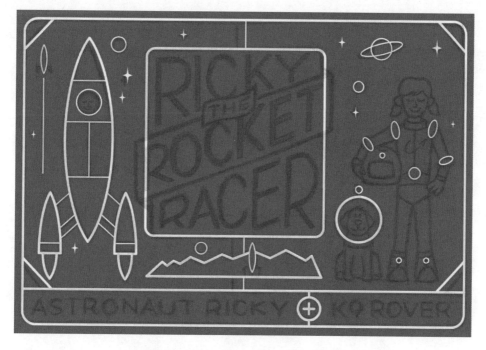

Figure 11.14 – The logo is taking shape

Before going further with more shape creation, this is a good time to double-check whether all of our current elements are on their proper layers.

Layers housekeeping

When you create or copy objects here and there, it's easy to accidentally place things on the wrong layers. An easy way to tell whether your objects are on the correct layer is to turn off the visibility of a layer in the **Layers** panel. Only elements on that layer will be hidden. If an element is still visible that should be hidden, then it's on the wrong layer.

For example, I had all of my stars on the rocket layer, and when I turned off visibility for the Planet and stars layer, they didn't get hidden, but they did get hidden when I turned off the rocket layer. To fix this, I selected all of the stars and pressed *Cmd* or *Ctrl + X* to remove and copy them to the clipboard. Then, I selected the Planet and stars layer and pressed *Cmd* or *Ctrl + V* to paste them onto the correct layer.

Go through each layer in turn and use this trick to see whether you need to make any layer fixes.

Once our layers have been straightened out and we get back to building our logo, let's tackle the next stage of form building.

Building more complex shapes and forms

Let's turn our attention now to some of the slightly more complicated forms, mainly the shapes that make up our fearless leader and her trusty companion.

> **Old dogs. New tricks.**
>
> The methods I use may not work for everyone, and you are welcome to develop your own way of creating shapes and forms as you see fit for your working style. In fact, I encourage you to explore and experiment with alternative ways of getting results that work for you as you get more comfortable with the tools and gain more confidence. That said, although I have been using these methods for years now and they have held up pretty well, I do recognize when someone points out a better way of doing things and I try to improve my skills as well. You're never too old to learn something new.

In tackling more complicated shapes, I usually start out by seeing whether there are any symmetrical areas I can quickly create by building one side and then duplicating and flipping for the opposite side. Fortunately for us, most of Ricky and the Dog can be built up this way.

If we look at Ricky in the sketch, her face, body, and legs right down to her boots are basically symmetrical, and likewise with K9 Rover. His entire head and body are basically symmetrical. Being able to recognize this will help us in the creation of these shapes. We can create one side, copy it, and then flip them horizontally for the opposite side. Often, you'll want to avoid being overly symmetrical in a design for aesthetic purposes, especially as regards characters, but our graphic logo style will work well with a symmetrical stylized treatment.

Getting back to the logo, I've added a centerline guide on both characters to aid in creating one side of each of the characters. This gives me a good indication of where to create the linework. I hid the blue background temporarily to allow you to see the faint guideline.

To create a guideline, click and drag from inside the left-hand side ruler on the left side of your document window. You should see a faint line indicating a guide is being created as you drag it out. I placed my vertical guides as close to the center of each character as I could and then let go of the line. These will serve as design aids helping us to create and then flip our linework to build our characters.

If your rulers aren't visible, go to **VIEW | SHOW RULERS** or press *Cmd* or *Ctrl + R*. You can lock your guides so that you don't accidentally move them by going to **VIEW | LOCK GUIDES**.

We will then use the **Pen** tool to draw all of the various shapes we need, paying careful attention to following the sketch reference as we create our shapes and lines:

Figure 11.15 – Adding center guides

Before we use the **Pen** tool to create these character shapes, let's take a look at how the **Pen** tool works and how to make the kinds of shapes we will need.

For the graphic style of our logo, we want to be able to control how and where we put our lines, and the **Pen** tool is ideally suited for making precisely controlled straight and curved lines. The **Pen** tool sometimes gets a bad rap as being difficult to use. While it is a more controlled way of making linework, it is also the best way to put down the fewest number of points to create a line. It's worth practicing to get the hang of the **Pen** tool. You may be tempted to draw lines freehand with the pencil tool, but the pencil tool can be hard to control, and generally, it creates more points than are required. The more points you have, the more difficult it can be to edit or manipulate your line. Plus, that's not the look we are going for here. We want nice smooth curves and perfectly straight lines:

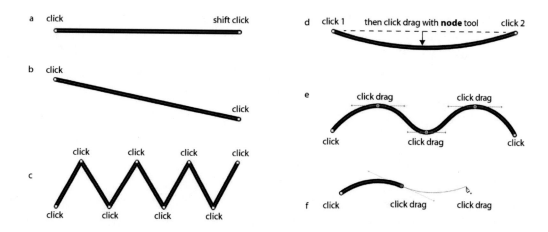

Figure 11.16 – Creating straight and curved line segments using the Pen tool

The left column Pen tool behavior will produce straight lines, while the right column Pen tool behavior will produce curved lines. Let's break down what is happening in *Figure 11.16*:

- **a** – This is a simple click followed by a second click while holding down the *Shift* key to constrain the line to a horizontal axis.

- **b** – This is the same as example **a** but without the *Shift* key pressed. You will still get a straight line but it won't be constrained to any axis.

- **c** – Repeating clicks can produce a zig-zag type of line with straight line segments.

- **d** – This starts out like example **a**, with two clicks as a straight line, but after selecting the line with the **Node** tool, you can click and drag on the line to apply a curve to it.

- **e** – This starts by clicking your first point with the **Pen** tool, and then adds to your line by repeatedly clicking and dragging to add nodes with bezier handles, allowing for smooth flowing curves. These handles can be further selected and manipulated to make adjustments, while the points themselves can be moved, changing the nature of each curve. End the line by single-clicking again without dragging.

- **f** – This is the same basic technique as **e**, but this time the **Rubber Band** mode is activated in the **Context** toolbar of the **Pen** tool. This feature will give you a preview of the line as you create it. Some people find this helpful when getting used to the **Pen** tool as it shows you just where the line will be placed before you click each point.

All of the examples in *Figure 11.16* are executed using the **Pen** mode behavior for drawing paths with the **Pen** tool. This is the default behavior allowing for the most control and variety of lines. For a recap or more information on each of the modes used by the **Pen** tool, refer to the extensive *The Pen tool* section in *Chapter 6, Tools – Designer Persona*:

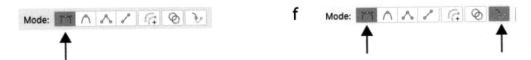

Figure 11.17 – Pen mode for all examples and the Rubber Band mode setting for example f

With that lesson on the **Pen** tool and with our symmetry center guidelines in place, let's begin building the linework for our two characters. We'll start with Ricky.

Starting to build our two characters

Through a series of step-by-step incremental screenshots, we'll create the boot and continue up the leg. Then we'll do the torso and head area until finishing with the arms, helmet, face, and any smaller details.

I'm going to unhide the blue background and start building using the **Pen** tool and a 2 point white line for now starting on her left side. Later, I'll pick and choose which lines to thicken up to a 4 point width when we do the overall fine-tuning of the entire logo:

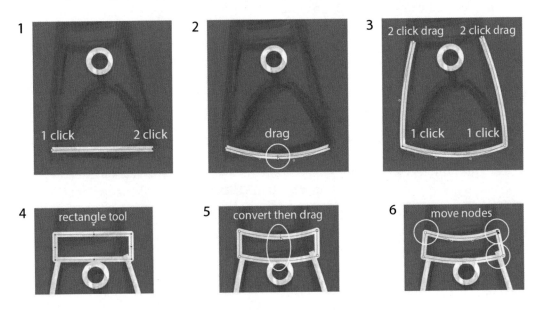

Figure 11.18 – Ricky character, steps 1 – 6

- **1** – With the **Pen** tool, click twice as shown to create a straight 2 point width line.

- **2** – Select the **Node** tool and click in the center area of the line and drag it down to create a nice curve for the bottom of the boot.

- **3** – With the **Pen** tool active, press on the *Cmd* or *Ctrl* key to temporarily activate the **Move** tool and then click on the left node to select it. Release the *Cmd* or *Ctrl* key and the **Pen** tool should still be activated. Making sure that the node is still selected, click on it now with the **Pen** tool. This will connect the next line you create to that node. Click a second time toward the top of the boot and, while clicking, drag it a little to create a subtle curve as shown in screenshot 3. Repeat these actions for the right-hand side, being careful to follow along the curve of the sketch.

- **4** – Select the **Rectangle** tool and draw out a rectangle as shown in screenshot 4.

- **5** – Convert the rectangle to curves using the **Convert to Curves** option in the **Context** toolbar. Then, using the **Node** tool again, click and drag down on each center area to create curves as shown in screenshot 5. This is to mimic the top of the boot as it goes around the leg.

- **6** – Select the **Move** tool and reposition the top two nodes on the rectangle to angle inward slightly. Move any line ends that need to be tucked away:

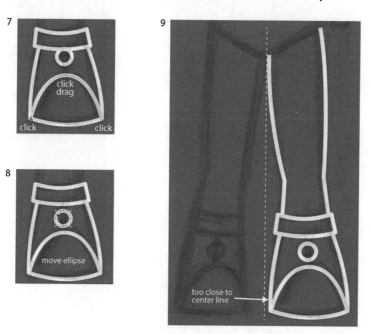

Figure 11.19 – Ricky character, steps 7 – 9

- **7** – With the **Pen** tool, click once to start the boot foot arch. Click and drag out to curve the line. Finish the curve by clicking once in the bottom right position. You can always go back and adjust any bezier curve by clicking on any one of the nodes and adjusting the bezier curve handles.

- **8** – With the **Move** tool, select the ellipse and move it down slightly to reposition it. Yours may be fine; mine just happened to be a little high and in the way.

- **9** – Because the leg is a little too close to the centerline, let's shear it a bit to the right. We want to just move the bottom of the leg's position, the top is good as is:

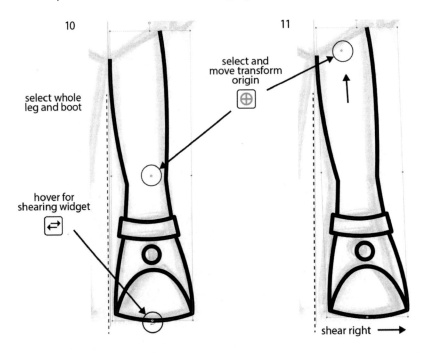

Figure 11.20 – Ricky character, steps 10 – 11

- **10** – I've reversed the coloring of the lines and hidden the blue background to make it easier for you to see some of the very small details of the UI here. To just shear or skew the bottom of the leg and boot, we need to activate **Transform Origin** from the **Context** toolbar. Refer to the following *Figure 11.21*:

Figure 11.21 – Transform origin button in the Context toolbar

The transform origin is a circle with a cross inside it. This allows us to sort the target where the transform is based. By moving it up to the top, we will affect more of the bottom portion of the leg and boot. After moving the transform origin and with the entire leg and boot selected, hover your mouse just below the bottom center of the selection box (see the circled area at the bottom of the boot in step *10*). This has a very touchy 'hot spot' so be patient. When you see the double arrows appear, click and drag them to shear the selection slightly to the right.

- **11** – This step shows the sheared leg and boot repositioned:

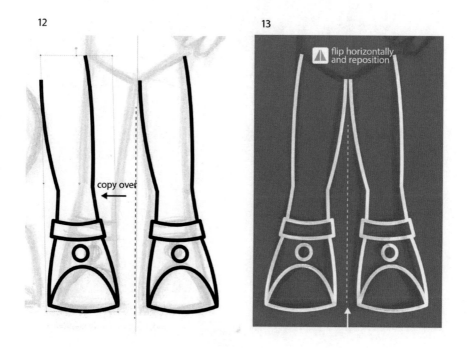

Figure 11.22 – Ricky character, steps 12 – 13

- **12** – After you have sheared the leg and boot over, while it is still selected, with the Move tool and the *Cmd* or *Ctrl* and *Shift* buttons pressed, move and copy the selection to left.

- **13** – Finally, let's flip it vertically using the **Flip Horizontal button** in the main upper toolbar. Once flipped, and with it still selected, gently move it into place, similar to what I have done in *step 13*:

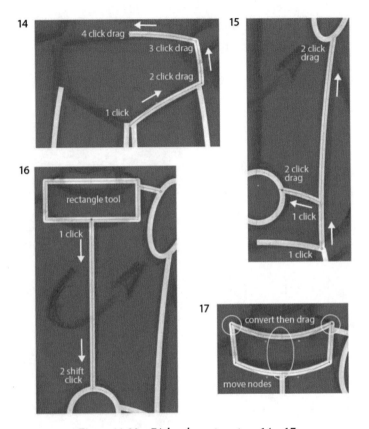

Figure 11.23 – Ricky character, steps 14 – 17

- **14** – For this area, starting with the first click in the center area, click and drag out a small curve for the top of the leg (2), followed by a click and drag for an almost vertical curved line (3), and finally a click and drag for the waistline (4). Re-adjust the curves if you need to.

- **15** – In this screenshot, there are two lines. One is a long tall vertical line going from the hip to the armpit, and the other is a short horizontal line from the right side into the circular shape. Both are two clicks, with a subtle click and drag curve on the second click.

- **16** – Here, we have a straight vertical line using a shift-click from the circle shape up to the bottom of the collar. Then we use the Rectangle tool to create the collar area, and finally, a short gentle curve connecting the shoulder ellipse to the collar.

- **17** – With the collar rectangle selected, click on the **Convert to Curves** button in the **Context** toolbar, and then, with the **Node** tool selected, click and drag two curves down in the collar's center area to form a nice rounded curve.

Let's continue building up our Ricky character by copying and flipping what we just built. The method is the same as before. Copy and drag the linework off to the left-hand side and, while it's still selected, press the **Flip Horizontal** button in the main top toolbar. Then, gently move it into place. In *Figure 11.24*, you can see how everything is looking after I copied, flipped, and moved my linework over:

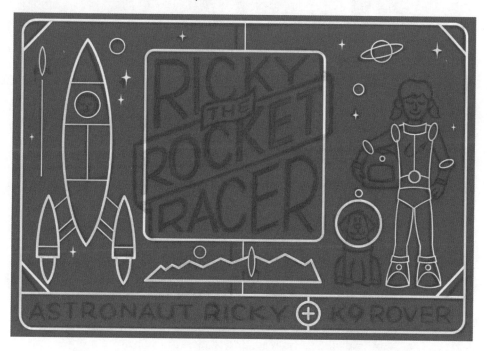

Figure 11.24 – Ricky character progress with the rest of the logo so far

Things are starting to take shape, literally. After flipping the one side over to the opposite side, there is a little cleanup to do.

Next, we'll move on to her hair and face before we create her arms, hands, and finally her helmet:

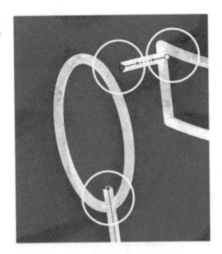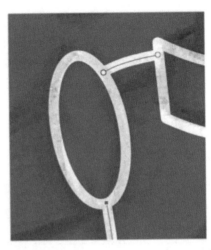

Figure 11.25 – Making small cleanup adjustments

- **18** – After flipping, it's natural to make some small adjustments to connect the lines.

Are we there yet?

When creating this type of stylized logo, there can be a lot of repetition… clicking, click-dragging, adjusting, and so on… This is a good thing. It allows you to get familiar with the tools and the process and forms great muscle memory. Learning new skills takes time. Take breaks now and then if you need to and come back to it when you feel refreshed. Soon you will get to the point where you are not even thinking about how to do it anymore and find yourself just enjoying the creation aspect.

Let's continue with Ricky and give her a bit of personality.

The next series of steps is all about Ricky's hair and face. I have broken it down into a series of screenshots showing the paths, clicks, and edits. Owing to size constraints, I am not going to label every click as before. I think you are probably getting the hang of the **Pen** tool and this next series of steps is continuing the same processes as with all the previous techniques.

I will discuss everything in each of the description steps, however, so if you get stumped or confused, just have a look at the text covering each of the screenshots:

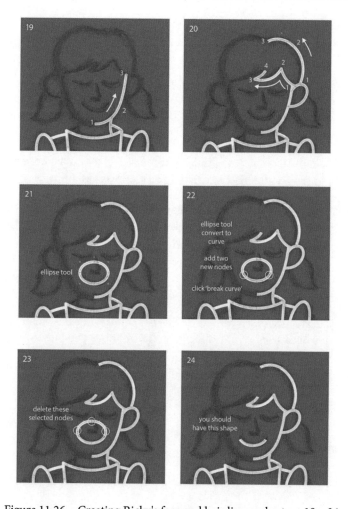

Figure 11.26 – Creating Ricky's face and hair linework, steps 19 – 24

- **19** – Next, create the linework for the back of the collar, the curve of her neck, and the side of her face. Each path is a gentle curve using the click and click and drag methods.

- **20** – Create her hair and ears in the same manner.

- **21** – The smile is a sort of perfect curve shape, so let's use the **Ellipse** tool to create this. Drag out an ellipse so the bottom sits nicely on the smile in the sketch.

- **22** – Convert the ellipse into a curve by pressing the **Convert to Curves** button in the **Context** toolbar. Select the **Node** tool and add two new nodes to form the corners of her smile (see the two little circles). Select both of these new nodes and, on the **Context** toolbar, click on the **Break Curve** action. This cuts the line at the location of the two nodes.

- **23** – Now, select the three nodes as shown and delete them.

- **24** – You should be left with this perfect curved smile shape. We could have used the **Pen** tool again to create this, but I wanted a perfect curve here and it was an opportunity to try an alternative way to create a particular curve.

Before going any further, we should check again to make sure all of this Ricky character linework we're creating is actually on the Ricky layer. Go ahead and use the 'hiding the layer' method from earlier to see whether you need to move any recent linework onto the Ricky layer. Once you've checked this, let's resume and finish up her hair and face:

> **Sharpen it up!**
>
> To quickly create nice sharp corners or sharper bends while drawing with the **Pen** tool, clicking a second time directly on the last node you put down with the **Pen** tool will create a sharp corner.

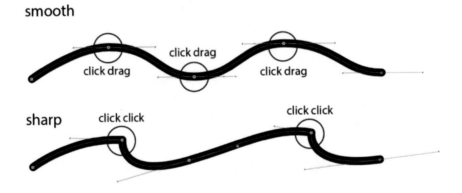

Figure 11.27 – Creating sharper corners

Let's finish up Ricky's face and hair now:

Figure 11.28 – Creating Ricky's face and hair linework, steps 25 – 30

- **25** – Using the **Pen** tool, create her nose and eyes. You can copy and drag the first of her eyes for the second one so they are the same. The nose will involve the creation of a sharp corner. See *Figure 11.27* for a way to create sharp corners while you draw with the **Pen** tool.

- **26** – Using the **Stroke** panel, with the eyes, nose, and mouth selected, change **end caps** to the **round** option. This just makes them look a little softer.

- **27** – Now, create her pigtail. Use the sharp corner method on that third click.

- **28** – Select the ear, pigtail, and side of the face, copy and drag with the *Shift* button pressed to make a copy, and then flip the selection horizontally.

- **29** – Position in place and clean up the gap at the chin if you have one.

- **30** – Add the remaining hair to complete her face.

Let's just make one more adjustment to Ricky's eyes, nose, and mouth. This is not mandatory, but I think it might look better if we vary the line thickness in these areas:

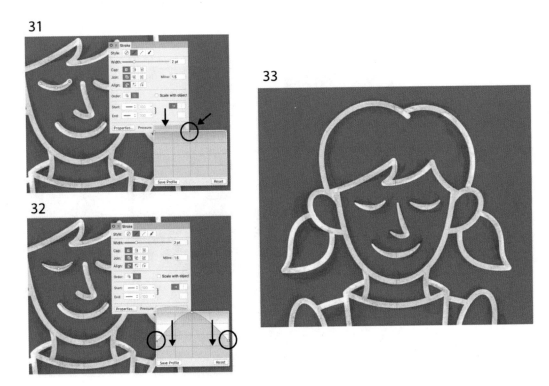

Figure 11.29 – Adjusting line widths, steps 31 – 33

- **31** – Select the eye line. Using the **Stroke** panel, click on the **Pressure** field in the lower-right corner. Click to add a point in the top middle area of the graph area. There should now be three points on the top of the graph.

- **32** – Click and drag either the left or the right point in the graph down. You'll notice that both the right and left points will move down together. Essentially, what this is doing is that it's changing the profile or thickness of the selected curve (the eye), giving you a nice varied thickness to your line. The left and right points define the beginning and end of your selected line.

You can add as many points to the graph as you want just by clicking on the curve in the graph. For now, we just need the three we have. To move the points independently of one another, press the *Option* or *Alt* key while dragging.

- **33** – To quickly apply this same line profile to the second eye, nose, and mouth, select the first line (eye) with the new profile attached to it and then press *Cmd* or *Ctrl* + *C* to copy it. Now, select the second eye, nose, and mouth and press *Cmd* or *Ctrl* + *Shift* + *V* to paste the attributes of the first line, in this case, the adjusted line width profile, to the other eye, nose, and mouth simultaneously. Affinity Designer allows you to transfer many attributes of one or more objects this way.

You could have also selected all four of these objects at once and then applied the pressure option from the **Stroke** panel. Either way will give you the same result.

Experiment with both the **Stroke Panels Pressure** feature as well as the copying and pasting of different attributes from one object to another. It works on color, effects, gradients, basically, all kinds of different attributes, and you can copy attributes to multiple selected objects as mentioned.

Both of these features can speed up your workflow while allowing you to customize your linework's expressive qualities.

Let's now finish up Ricky's arms and helmet:

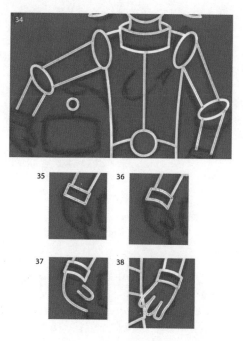

Figure 11.30 – Adjusting line widths, steps 34 – 38

- **34** – Continue using the **Pen** tool to add straight lines to make up the arms. Make any adjustments or repositioning as required after you place the straight lines.

- **35** – Add rectangles to form the cuffs just above the hands.

- **36** – Convert these rectangles to curves from the **Context** toolbar and, once again with the **Node** tool as we've done before, create subtle curves to add a bit of a curved form to the cuffs.

- **37** and **38** – Use the **Pen** tool to create the hands as shown:

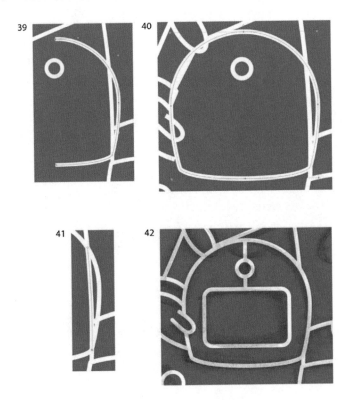

Figure 11.31 – Creating the helmet, steps 39 – 42

- **39** – Use the **Pen** tool to create one side of the helmet. Starting at the top or the bottom, as in previous sections, create just half of the helmet and flip it horizontally to create the other side.

- **40** – Copy and drag half of the helmet off to the side and flip it horizontally using the flip horizontal button from the upper toolbar. Position the flipped portion so that it appears to be joined. Adjust if needed. Add a rounded rectangle for the visor and a straight line centered above the visor going to the top of the helmet, as shown.

- **41** and **42** – Where the helmet lines intersect with some of the arm and body, use the **Node** tool to add nodes that we can use to cut those lines to make the helmet look like it's in front. Remember to use the **Break Curve** button in the **Context** toolbar with the **Node** tool selected to break the portions you need to delete. Make sure to leave the thumb intact and cut that portion out of the helmet instead. Make adjustments and close any gaps you might have after you make your cuts.

Figure 11.32 shows a completed Ricky character. Our logo is certainly coming together. We still need to adjust some line thicknesses, but we can do that later once everything in the logo is built and we're in the fine-tuning stage:

Figure 11.32 – A completed Ricky character

K9 Rover

I went ahead and created K9 Rover as I think it would be a good exercise for you to tackle this one with the knowledge you've acquired thus far. In terms of complexity, he's pretty simple I think. I would approach it the same way we did for Ricky. Remember to select the correct layer before starting to build K9 Rover. When you're ready, start by using the **Pen** tool to create curves by clicking and by clicking and dragging. He's basically completely symmetrical. Complete one side, and then copy and drag that half off to the side, flip it horizontally, and place it up against the first side.

For this logo exercise, we don't need to attach or join the flipped lines to each other once they are flipped because we are just dealing with simple linework for this style and that amount of work isn't necessary here.

Figure 11.33 shows a look at our finished K9 Rover:

Figure 11.33 – The completed K9 Rover character

Adding type to our logo

The final section of the logo to be built is the wording or type. For the font, I am recommending we use a nice rounded font called **Comfortaa**. You can download this free font from Google Fonts at `https://fonts.google.com/specimen/Comfortaa?preview.text_type=custom&preview.size=50&query=comfortaa&preview.text=RICKY%20the%20ROCKET%20RACER`.

This font will complement our design and the linework styling very nicely.

Download the font and make it available from within Affinity Designer. Let's begin with an easy application of the type, the bottom row of the logo, with the words `ASTRONAUT RICKY` and `K9 ROVER`.

Select the **Artistic Text** tool in the **Tool** panel and make sure you have the correct layer selected in the **Layers** panel. Mine is named **'Bottom Type'**:

With the correct layer selected and the **Artistic Text** tool selected, click to place your cursor somewhere near the A in ASTRONAUT in the bottom-left part of the logo. Type the word ASTRONAUT in all CAPS, select the word, and then, with the text tool still active, you should see a section for **Font** selection in the **Context** toolbar. Scroll to **Comfortaa** or type in Comfortaa in the text field. For our purposes here, we will use the **Regular** weight.

Rather than typing both ASTRONAUT and RICKY, we'll just do one word at a time as this will give us more control over placing each word. I ended up with a font size of **38 points** for my wording to fit comfortably within the allotted space; yours, of course, may be different depending on what size you created your document at initially:

Figure 11.34 – Type setup for the bottom row

I added a little bit more letterspacing between each letter by selecting each word and then pressing Option or *Alt* plus the right arrow on my keyboard. Then I adjusted each word to fit nicely within each space. Use the align tools if you need to align your type.

For the plus sign, rather than use a font, I just created two straight lines with **Round End Caps** using the **Pen** tool and rotated one of them 90 degrees to form a plus sign. Then, using the alignment tools, I centered everything up with the ellipse shape they are inside of as well as the two lines above and below the ellipse.

Before we get rolling with the main type component, we first need to finish building the type containment shapes, in particular, the angled rectangle in the middle section surrounding the word **ROCKET**:

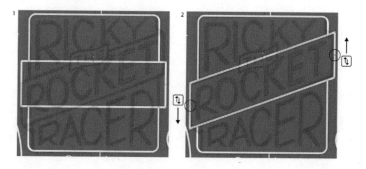

Figure 11.35 – Rectangle in place and skewed using the shear feature

Place a rectangle using the **Rectangle** tool with a white stroke and blue fill. The blue fill covers up the rounded rectangle below. Then, hover your cursor over the center areas of the left and right sides until you see the shearing double arrows. Click and drag to shear or skew the rectangle as shown in *Figure 11.35*. Try to line up the top and bottom roughly with the word **ROCKET**. My line width is set to 4 points for my heavier line; yours may vary.

Let's add the word **ROCKET** now. Select the **Artistic Text** tool, and click and type the word ROCKET in all caps. Change the font to Comfortaa if it isn't already and size it by selecting the corner handles to fit comfortably within the width of the rectangles.

Next, we will shear it into place using the same method as we sheared the rectangle by first selecting it with the **Move** tool in order to get those handles and then hovering over the left- and right-side center areas to activate the shearing widget. See *Figure 11.36* for an example. You may or may not need to use the *Shift* key while sizing your type to fill it properly so that it fills most of the rectangle shape it is inside of. Normally, I am against distorting the type and would recommend sizing your type without the *Shift* key to keep it from getting stretched or squashed. This case is an exception, however, because we want it to fill the rectangular containment shape evenly and we will be distorting the words RICKY and RACER quite a bit to fit into their containment areas as well:

Figure 11.36 – Placing ROCKET into the logo and shearing it to fit

In *Figure 11.37*, I show my **Character** panel ROCKET type settings to give you an idea of what I used for this situation. Yours may vary depending on the size of your document and the dimensions of your rectangle. Just as long as you get it looking similar to mine, you should be fine. Experiment with the sizing to get something pleasing to the eye:

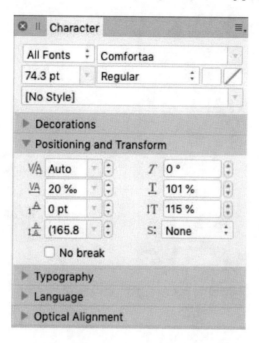

Figure 11.37 – My ROCKET type settings

The next part we'll tackle is the word **THE** in its small containment shape. To create the containment shape, using *Figure 11.38* as a guide, start by creating a simple wavy curve with the **Pen** tool for the top curve. Copy and drag it down for the bottom curve. Then, using the **Node** tool, select the right points of each of the curves and, from the **Context** toolbar, click on **Join Curves Action** in the **Context** toolbar to join the curves on the right side. Then, with the **Node** tool still active, select the two remaining open points on the left side and click on **Close Curve Action** to create a closed shape. You could also have used the **Pen** tool and clicked on one point and then the other to close the curve.

I make my line width 4 points for this shape and fill the shape with the same blue color to cover up anything below it (4):

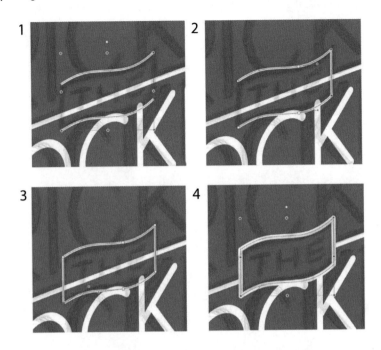

Figure 11.38 – Creating the 'THE' containment shape

For the word **THE**, we are going to place each letter individually instead of as one word. This will give us easier control over the positioning of each of the letters. Select the **Artistic Text** tool and click to add the letter **T** inside the containment shape. Use the same Comfortaa font or whichever font you are using for all of the types. Repeat this again for **H** and **E**. Again, make sure that all three letters are individual letters. With the help of the **Move** tool, size and position each the letters in a similar fashion to what I have done in *Figure 11.39*. They should all be the same size, so when sizing them, select and size them all at the same time:

> **Housekeeping!**
>
> This might be a good time to save your file and also to check to see whether all of the type and containment shape work you've done so far is on the correct layer. My work is all on the Main Type layer.

Figure 11.39 – The 'THE' type as individual letters in place

Okay, let's start on the word **RICKY** next. This will basically be the same as the word **THE**, where we will place individual letters to be easier to manipulate and position but, in addition, this time we will create curves or outlines out of the type so we can further manipulate each letter to fit the sketch and the design a bit better than just the normal type would. This workflow of customizing or distorting type and form is very common in the world of logo design. The word **RACER** will also be done this way, but slightly differently.

If we look at the sketch, the word **RICKY** is horizontal on the top of the letters and angled at the bottom of the letters. We'll need to customize the letters to achieve this.

We'll get started by selecting the **Artistic Text** tool and creating individual letters for the word **RICKY**. Once you have done this, go about sizing the letters to fit in a similar fashion to what I have in *Figure 11.40*. Use the *Shift* key or the handles with the move tool to fit the letters all together in a visually pleasing way. Follow the sketch and try to give each letter an equal or appropriate amount of room. We don't want any of the letters looking out of place.

One thing we will need to do is to make sure that even though the letters will be different sizes, they should all still look like they have the same thickness. Basically, the idea is that it is one word, so we don't want the letters to have different thicknesses. This can be achieved by adding a white stroke to the letter from the **Stroke** panel. For example, in my final version, the **R** and **I** don't have a stroke, but the **C**, **K**, and **Y** do. This makes sense as they are being reduced in size the most and needed some thickness added to them to make them look like they are part of the whole word, all with the same thickness. The second thing I did to make my letters conform to the containment shape is that I converted each letter into a curved shape by selecting each letter and going to **LAYER | CONVERT TO CURVES**. This essentially will convert the font into a vector path, complete with nodes and curves. This allows you to manipulate the letters into anything you need. In this case, it allows us to stretch or elongate the **R** and **I** and shorten the **K** and **Y**:

Fonts to curves!

Once you convert a font into a curve, you will lose the ability to change any of the letters as it is no longer a font.

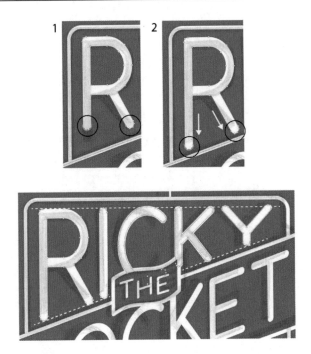

Figure 11.40 – Fitting the word 'RICKY' in place

In *Figure 11.40*, I added a couple of dashed lines here just to indicate roughly where the top and bottoms of each letter should fall. This isn't always an exact science. In the end, it should be based on what looks the best visually, especially where letterforms or words are concerned. Sometimes, having everything line up exactly might be 'correct' but will look 'off'. Always go by your eye on these things to ensure that it looks right.

Also, you can see how, when we converted the font into vector paths, we got access to the nodes of the path that allow us to make adjustments that would otherwise be impossible with a straight font. If you look closely at **C**, **K**, and **Y**, you will see the strokes I have added to thicken each letter up so that the whole word has a consistent thickness.

Let's continue now and complete the last of the type components for this logo by adding the word **RACER** to the logo by using the same method as we did for **RICKY**.

We'll start by typing each individual letter as before and then sizing them to fit as best as possible to the allotted space we have. Remember when sizing each letter to keep the whole word in consideration, visually speaking. We don't want anything to look out of place:

Figure 11.41 – Setting up the word 'RACER'

Once you are happy with the placement or position of each letter, you'll need to shear each letter to line up with the angled top, as shown here in *Figure 11.41*. Even the **A** and **C** get sheared even though they don't have a flat top to their letters simply because they need to fit in visually with the rest of the letterforms and **A** does have a middle crossbar.

Do this shearing to each letter individually using the hover method over the right-hand center sides of each letter. For these letters, we want the middle horizontal parts of **R**, **A**, **E**, and **R** to be angled as well. In this case, I also think the bottom of the **E** will look better angled rather than flat to go with its two upper horizontal lines.

Once you have your letters sheared to your liking, select them all and convert them to curves by going to **LAYER | CONVERT TO CURVES**. Now we can get access to the path nodes and manipulate these letters to fit the sketch.

In *Figure 11.43*, you will see that I am using the **Transform** widget to reposition and correct some of the distortion we created when we sheared the letters to line up to that top angle. When you have access to the nodes of an object using the **Node** tool, you will also allow access to the **Transform** widget *(Figure 11.42)* to shear, rotate, or scale selected nodes:

Figure 11.42 – The Transform widget

Here, you can see that the **Transform** widget is used to not only move nodes after they have been selected but also to shear them to try to remove some of the stretching and distortion caused when we sheared the letters to align with the top angle. Don't forget to use the **Node** tool to move or even remove specific nodes if you need to refine the shapes further:

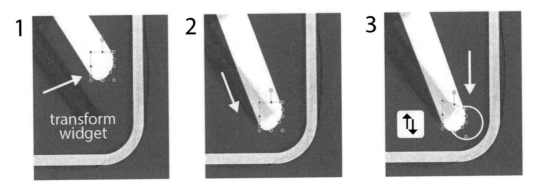

Figure 11.43 – Using the Transform widget to move and shear some nodes

After correcting the distortion with the **Node** tool and the **Transform** widget, I ended up with a fairly satisfying result in *Figure 11.44*:

Figure 11.44 – The final version of 'RACER'

The final thing I added to the main type layer is a couple of small wrap-around details to the central angled rectangle shape to add a sense of dimension to this section of the logo. It's often these small details that can add a lot in terms of interest to this type of linework:

 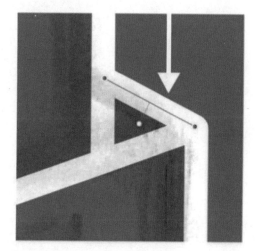

Figure 11.45 – Wrap-around details

Well, that's it for the type components and we are just about at the finish line for this logo and this chapter. The last bits I'd like to do are mainly fine-tuning touches and, of course, that centering correction I mentioned way back when we first started this chapter. *Figure 11.46* shows where we are at currently:

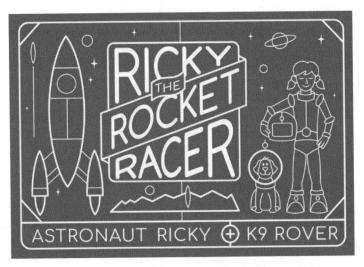

Figure 11.46 – Type components complete

Let's fix that centering issue now.

Select everything in the document except the blue background layer. Next, select the top-left corner handle and, with the *Shift* key pressed, drag down to the right and reduce everything by approximately 90%. This should open up more room on the left-hand side. Next, select the outer rounded rectangle and drag the left side center handle to the left to add some room to the rocket area. Next, start moving elements to the left. Re-align the two angled lines above and below the left-hand side of the rocket. Select the rocket layer in the **Layers** panel; this should select the whole rocket and recenter it inside the new wider space. Select the bottom row of the type and re-center that as well. You may also need to move the plus sign and circle. Finally, center the central vertical lines that intersect the main type area in the middle of the logo. Make any other visual adjustments you need to. I didn't move Ricky or the dog at all.

Figure 11.47 shows the adjusted and properly centered setup. Compare this to *Figure 11.46* to see what changes I made:

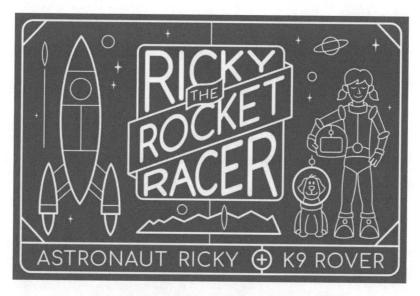

Figure 11.47 – Recentered logo setup

Fine-tuning

The last part of this logo will be to make some fine-tuning adjustments to improve on what we currently have. See *Figure 11.48* for the final logo with all of these adjustments made. I also added a rocket logo to Ricky's uniform and removed part of the orbit line going around the back of the planet Saturn.

To achieve the heavier outline around Ricky, I copied and dragged her off to the right to make a copy of her, and then, while the copy was still selected, I converted all of the linework into fills by going to **LAYER | EXPAND STROKE**. After this, I applied the **Add** Boolean command from the **Main** toolbar to join or unite all of the expanded strokes together.

Then, with the **Node** tool, I selected and deleted all of the inside shapes, leaving a silhouette or a shadow of just her outline. This was a slow process as there is no way to just select and delete the inner nodes in one go, so I had to select and delete them all by hand with the **Node** tool. In the end, though, it was worth it. Be careful not to delete the shapes that define the areas between the arms and the body. Then, I added a heavy white stroke, in my case, a 4 point stroke width, to the silhouette shape, and removed the white fill.

Then I dragged the new outlined silhouette into place behind the existing Ricky character, creating a nice heavy outline around just the outside of her. Do the same procedure for K9 Rover:

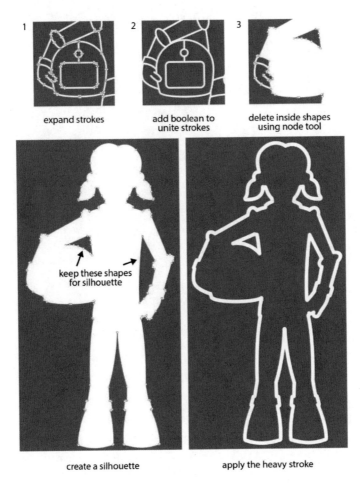

Figure 11.48 – Ricky heavy outline steps

Figure 11.49 shows the completed logo. See whether you can make out all of the fine-tuning adjustments I added:

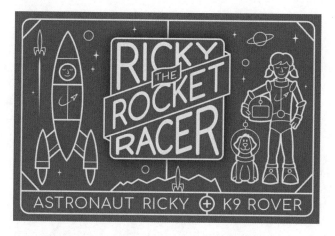

Figure 11.49 – The completed blueprint styled logo

The list of final improvements and adjustments

In addition to the thickening of the linework on Ricky and K9 Rover as discussed above, here are the changes I made:

- I added some landing gear to the two small rockets. I edited the blast trail on the small flying rocket in the upper-left corner with the **Stroke Panels Pressure** feature to add varying thicknesses to the line.

- I moved the mountain shape and small rocket down to sit on the baseline above the type.

- I added a blue fill to the main type's rectangular shape and then I added a large dark blue 200 pixel **Outer Shadow** to the shape using the **Effects** panel.

> **Note**
> The **Radius** slider on the outer shadow only goes to 100 pixels, but you can override this by typing in a higher amount.

- I added a nice flying swoosh mini logo to Ricky's uniform and to the large rocket.

- I copied Ricky's eyes, nose, and mouth to the Rocket layer and placed them in the window.

- I thickened the two center lines and also some of the lines on the large rocket to 4 points.

- I removed the part of Saturn's ring that goes behind the planet.

- I changed K9 Rover's helmet to a thinner 2 point line.

- Finally, I added a **Noise** texture to the whole piece by adding a new layer at the very top of the layer stack. On that layer, I dragged out a rectangle to cover the entire layer. I gave the rectangle a white fill with no stroke. I set the layer to **Multiply Mode**. The white rectangle will disappear because white won't show up using **Multiply Mode**. With the rectangle selected, I went to the **Color** panel and, in the lower-left corner, clicked on the little round swatch below the word **Opacity**, which toggles it to a **Noise** slider. I set the layer all the way to 100% noise. This is a nice easy way to add some subtle texturing to the whole piece.

The noise layer addition is a step you don't have to add if you don't want to. I just really like how it adds a nice subtle visual texture to everything and brings the composition together. I find it adds a sort of retro feel to the piece as well.

Summary

In this first practical exercise chapter of creating a professional logo, we started by planning our document setup. We followed this by learning how to place an external image to use as a template or guide. Then we put our knowledge of how to use the Layers panel into practical use to keep our work organized and discussed how to use the Layers panel to also hide or lock objects and layers.

Throughout this chapter, when we started building our logo, we got pretty familiar with the Pen tool and the various ways to create shapes and different types of lines. We explored how to plan and build our logo, first with basic shapes, before getting into more complex multi-part objects.

We then explored the Artistic Text tool and how to add type components to our logo, eventually learning how to customize and manipulate some of the text's letterforms to conform to our logo's distinct containment shapes.

We've tackled a lot in this long chapter and the lessons learned here will come in handy when we move up a level for the next chapter, where we are going to create more complete and detailed versions of Ricky and her trusty companion K9 Rover. We'll also learn about color, shading, and lighting. When you're ready, let's get started.

12
Creating Astronaut Ricky and Sidekick K9

Welcome to the twelfth chapter of *Up and Running with Affinity Designer*. In this second exercise chapter, we will build on what we learned in the previous chapter and cover some more advanced illustration techniques. The finished illustration project should look something like the example in *Figure 12.1* and carries on with the Ricky and K9 Rover theme from the previous chapter's logo project.

Figure 12.1 – The finished illustration

As you can see, this final illustration is very different from the previous exercise. In this illustration, we'll be taking the finished look much further than the simpler linework of the logo. With this illustration, we are trying to create a sort of stylized or idealized realism with dimensional form, color, highlights, and shadows. Fortunately, Affinity Designer has the tools and features to make this not only possible but a whole lot of fun.

Prerequisites and expectations

The goal of this second exercise chapter is to use the skills discussed and acquired throughout the book as well as skills specifically just covered in the last chapter. We are going to continue building on using the Shape Tools and the Pen tool to create shapes. We'll cover how to prepare and organize these shapes for use in a complex multilayered illustration. We'll also work with different methods of shading using **Gradients** and **Effects** to enhance and bring our shapes to life. We have a lot to cover so buckle up and get ready to blast off!

We will start as we did in the previous chapter by placing the illustration sketch I created shown in *Figure 12.2* into Affinity Designer as a guide, referencing it as we create the illustration shape by shape.

Let's get started – downloading the sketch

Okay, let's make a start on this project. To follow along using the provided logo sketch, you will need to download it from the download link and save it to somewhere on your hard drive where you will be saving your Affinity Designer file for this project. The sketch can be downloaded from the following link: `https://github.com/PacktPublishing/Up-and-Running-with-Affinity-Designer/tree/main/Chapter12`.

Figure 12.2 – Ricky and K9 Rover sketch

> **Workflow tip worth repeating**
>
> For a best practice workflow, placed images like this sketch image should either reside in the same folder as the Affinity Designer file or they should at least be close to each other. If the sketch gets moved around on your hard drive after you have placed it into your file, Affinity Designer will say it's missing the next time you open the file and you will need to relink it. A good way to avoid this is to keep it close to your file and try to not move it or rename it. You can always embed image files into your Affinity Designer file but that can sometimes create a larger file than you may want. The image can be deleted from the file upon completion.

Document setup

Once you have the sketch downloaded, let's create the Affinity Designer document that we will be using to build the illustration. With Affinity Designer open, go to **FILE | NEW**. For my setup using this sketch, I am once again going to start out with an **8.5 in x 11 in** format. This time I am going vertically because the sketch is set up as vertical. Remember you can always resize the document if you need to later on by going to **FILE | DOCUMENT SETUP**.

Refer to *Figure 12.3* for the document settings that I chose for this logo project:

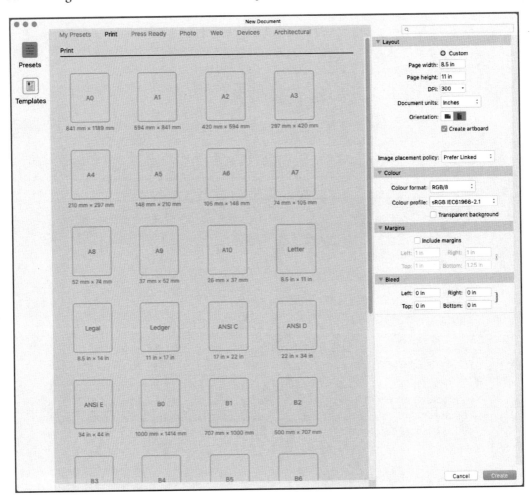

Figure 12.3 – My document settings

I'm using a vertical version of the **Letter** size at **300** DPI using **inches** for **Document units**. Similar to the previous chapter, I'm not using the **Create artboard** option and I've set my **Image placement policy** to **Prefer Linked**. I'm also again going with an **RGB/8 Color format** and an **sRGB** profile and I'm deselecting **Transparent background** without any **Margins** or **Bleed** settings.

Placing the reference sketch

Once you have your document created, let's add the sketch image by going to **FILE | PLACE** or clicking on **Place Tool** in the Tool Panel and selecting the sketch to place it in our document.

Once again, scale the placed sketch up or down to fill the document window if you need to. Use the Move Tool to select it and drag on the corner handles *without* the *Shift* key pressed to scale it without stretching it. Then, in the **Layers** panel, I reduced the **Opacity** of the layer to **50%** and changed the **Blend mode** of the layer to **Multiply**, and then locked the layer.

We are going to once again use the sketch as a guide for us to draw all of the shapes and lines on layers below while still seeing the sketch because it's on the top layer. The multiply blend mode of the sketch layer allows us to see through the sketch as we build the logo. If we need to hide the sketch for any reason, we just have to hide the sketch layer in the **Layers** panel. Locking the sketch layer prevents us from accidentally selecting or moving it.

Figure 12.4 – The sketch in the document with the rest of the layers set up and named

Creating the layer stack hierarchy and adding a background color

Some of the file's structure will be basically repeated from the previous chapter because it is how I set up every one of my files. Have a look at the sketch and decide how to divide the layers. *Figure 12.4* also shows how I've decided to break up the layer stack.

I have left the sketch layer at the top of the stack as explained earlier. The rest of the layers are placed from top to bottom in the order that they will appear in the illustration with the background layer at the bottom of the stack. When planning your layers, study the sketch and pay close attention to which shapes you think will be in front and which shapes will be behind. This illustration might be a little more tricky to figure out than the previous logo exercise. Rearranging your layers as you develop the illustration is easily done by dragging and repositioning the layers in the **Layers** panel. Don't forget to name your layers.

In the previous exercise chapter, we started by creating all of the simple basic shapes first. The approach here will be a little different because we don't really have many of those basic shapes to create. Instead, we have almost all custom shapes to work with. In addition, because we will be filling all or most of our shapes with color and shading, we will need to create closed path shapes for this project.

> **Closing a path**
>
> To create a closed path with the Pen tool while creating the shape, simply return to the first node as your shape's final click and the path will close itself. The Pen tool icon will change to show a small circle. Or, you can select the first and last end nodes and go to the **Close Curve** option in the context toolbar.

Pen Tool method

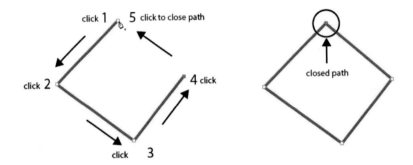

Node Tool method

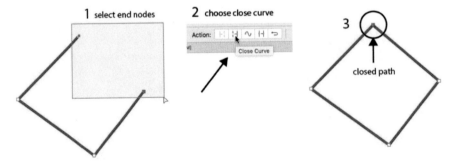

Figure 12.5 – Two methods of creating a closed shape

> **Choose layer, create shape**
>
> Once again, before creating any shapes, remember to select the correct layer or you can select an element that is already on the layer you want as a quick way to select the correct layer. If you do place something on the wrong layer, select it either in the document or in the **Layers** panel and press *Cmd* or *Ctrl* + *X*. This will cut or remove it, but it will also place it on your computer's clipboard. Then select the layer it should be on in the **Layers** panel and press *Cmd* or *Ctrl* + *V* to paste it. It will be pasted to the correct layer and it will show up in the exact same spot in your document.

The steps we will be following

The steps used to create this illustration are flexible and the order may cross over at times, but this is the general order of the process we will use:

1. Create all of the shapes with strokes only.

2. Add fills with color from the provided color palette (or your own).

3. Add shading using various techniques. For this exercise, we will use an all-vector workflow but sometimes it can include pixel painting.

4. Add lighting using various techniques. For this exercise, we will use an all-vector workflow but sometimes it can include pixel painting.

Fine-tuning and adjustments are usually done as we build each section before going on to the next section. However, they can occur at any time when needed.

Step 1 – Building the shapes

Starting with *step 1*, building all of your shapes first will give you a chance to see how the character is shaping up and allow you to edit or finesse your shapes before going on to the coloring step. Creating an illustration or anything for that matter in steps ensures that you concentrate on one thing at a time, moving forward in increments, eventually building up to a finished illustration. This is especially helpful in the early stages of a project.

I start creating these shapes using a thin magenta or pink-colored line. The color is distinctive and when it comes to *step 2*, adding color fills to the shapes, it will be easy to see which shapes I have filled and which I haven't. This comes in handy on large, complicated projects. You can use any color you wish, of course. I just happen to prefer the brightness of magenta. Make sure the lines aren't too thick as that may create some crowding in tight areas where the lines are close to each other. My line widths are set at 1 point in the **Stroke panel**.

It's time to get drawing

Let's get started building these two characters as described in *step 1*. Unlike the previous chapter, I'm not going to describe every click, as I want you to try to tackle *step 1* using the methods described and covered in the last chapter. This is a chance for you to put into practice once again building the individual shapes that will eventually become these two characters. Proceed as you did with the logo using the sketch as a guide, and remember that the fewer points you use, the smoother the curve will be.

As you progress, study the examples in this chapter of my pen work as well if it's helpful to see how I approach some of these path shapes. I prefer smooth, kink-free curves and if that's the style you are trying to achieve, hopefully, these examples will help you. Remember, fewer points or nodes not only create smoother lines, but they also make it easier to edit your paths when and if you need to.

The Pen tool

If you feel you need a refresher on the Pen tool as you start to create the shapes needed for these two characters, review the section on shape creation and the Pen tool exercises for creating straight lines and curved lines in *Chapter 11, Creating a Professional Logo*. Most, if not all, of the shapes will be based on curved lines. Some will have sharp corners, some will have smoother corners.

On the **Ricky** layer, I created the shapes that will become her face, neck, and hair. The **hair top**, **face**, and **pigtails** layers are sublayers of the **Ricky** layer.

Curve 1, curve 2, curve 3…

It goes without saying but I will say it again: try to name your layers. Not every layer will need a name, but your main or base layers should be named. Trust me, even the simplest illustration can get confusing if you're not organized. It's a great habit to get into!

If you look at *Figure 12.6*, you will notice how some of the shapes are overlapping each other. This is because when we eventually fill the shapes in with color, the areas that are behind other areas won't be seen, so we can run those shapes in behind. We do this so we don't have to have perfect borders between all shapes that butt up to each other. The numbers correspond with the numbered layers to show the hierarchy of the stacking order.

For example, the **hair top** layer (**1**) is above the **face** layer (**5**) in the layer stack, meaning it will cover up the top of her face where the face goes under her hair. This is the same for the **ear** layers (**2/3**) and the **pigtails** (**6/7**) as well as the chin area of the **face** (**5**) and the **neck** (**4**):

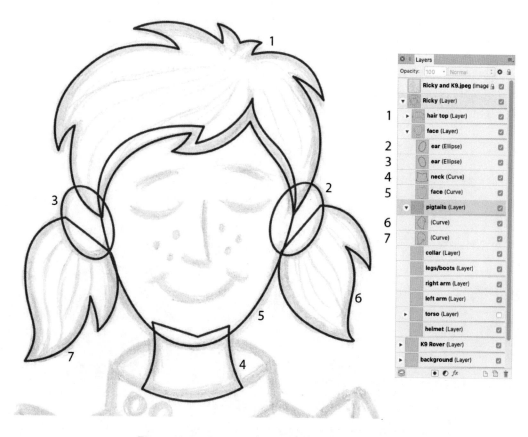

Figure 12.6 – Creating shapes with border overlaps

This will be more self-explanatory when we start filling each of these shapes with flat color, but until then, just know that while you are creating all your shapes, you should keep in mind which shape is where in the stacking order so you can add those extra areas that will be hidden.

Sometimes you'll notice certain situations where one element will need to be on a layer that isn't named appropriately or accurately for that element. For instance, for the **Collar** layer, the two shapes that make up the back of the collar need to be placed below the **neck** shape in the layer stack because they are behind the neck. In this case, I placed those two collar shapes on the **face** layer and made sure they were below the main **neck** shape layer. See *Figure 12.7*:

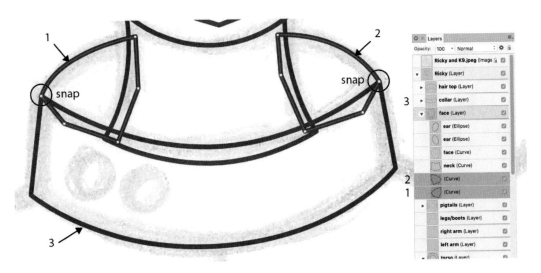

Figure 12.7 – Reordering layers for correct visibility

One thing you may notice in the layer stack is that I moved the **collar** layer up and above the **face** layer because it has to be in front of the neck. It's these kinds of changes and adjustments that you may find you have to make as you build your character's shapes.

I have also turned on snapping from the top or main toolbar for this *step 1* shape-building process to help line up corners or areas of the paths that should be directly in line with each other as indicated in *Figure 12.7*. It's not a mandatory step but it will keep your shapes lined up nicely and may reduce possible cleanup work later.

The next section I'm going to build is the torso section. I just keep drawing the shapes using the methods we covered in *Chapter 11, Creating a Professional Logo*, on creating curves with the **Pen tool** and by using any of the shape tools Affinity Designer provides, such as the **Ellipse Tool** for the two circles in her suit's center area, as well as the swoosh of the rocket insignia. You'll need to **Convert to Curves** from the context toolbar those two ellipses to cut away the parts you don't need to make the swoosh shape as shown in *Figure 12.8*.

Using the Node tool shortcut to cut path segments

There is a handy little shortcut to cut away sections of a path between two path nodes. Using the **Node tool**, if you hover over a section of a path and press the *Ctrl* key, you will see a red **X** beside the Node tool cursor arrow. Clicking the path will delete the section of the path between the two nodes. If the path only has two nodes, it will delete the whole path. Add nodes if you need to with the Node tool for cutting away sections.

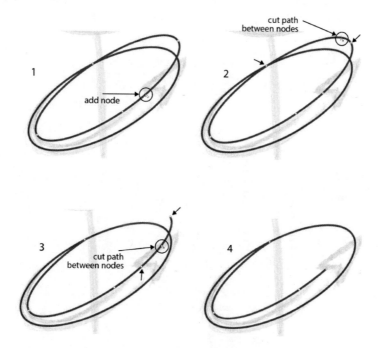

Figure 12.8 – Node tool shortcut cutting path segments

With the Torso section in *Figure 12.9*, you can see how I am subtly correcting some of the linework as compared to the sketch. Once you start constructing the digital shapes, you may want to make these types of adjustments as you go.

Also, notice how I am keeping close to the edges with my linework that will be under its neighboring shapes. This is what I call the **over/under** rule. As discussed earlier, some shapes will be in front (**over**) and some shapes will be behind (**under**), and later, when we fill these shapes with color and start shading and adding effects, there is one effect that adds shading along edges and if the edge of the "under" shape is too far away from the edge of the "over" shape, it won't work as well, so try to keep your edge creations fairly close to each other. In the case of *Figure 12.9*, the two circles in the center will be above all of the other shapes as indicated in the layer stack. When you draw your shapes, you have to determine which shape will be over or under. Don't worry if this isn't making sense at this point, there will be plenty of examples coming up in the shading section.

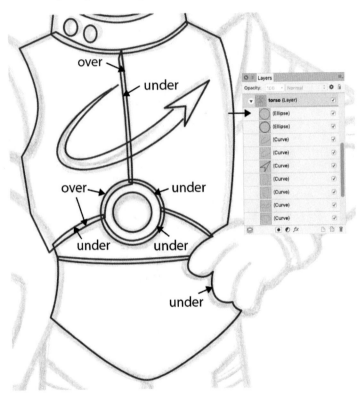

Figure 12.9 – Shape edges and the over/under concept

I went on to the arms next, adhering to these same principles of over and under. I ended up adding a new layer above the left arm for her **Left hand** because it needed to be in front of the arm. *Figure 12.10* also shows how I created the hand with just three separate finger shapes. Shape 1 provides the index finger and the hand's main shape as one shape. Shapes 2 and 3, the other fingers, will be in front and will use the same base color as shape 1. The shading stage will eventually define them from each other.

The upper-left arm notch detail was first created with the Pen tool with sharp corners. Then the Corner Tool was used to round the corners slightly, adding a nice sense of thickness to the suit. The interior lines of this detail shape, as well as the center lines of the shoulder and elbow football shapes, will be added later at the shading and lighting stages.

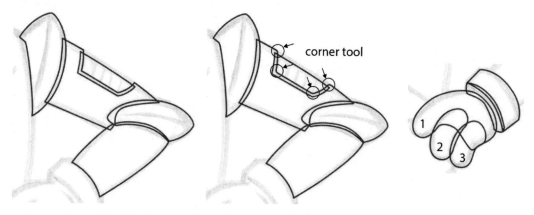

Figure 12.10 – Left arm and hand

I went ahead and completed all of the shape creation linework. In the following figures, I show you some closer views of the shapes I have created, all using the same process.

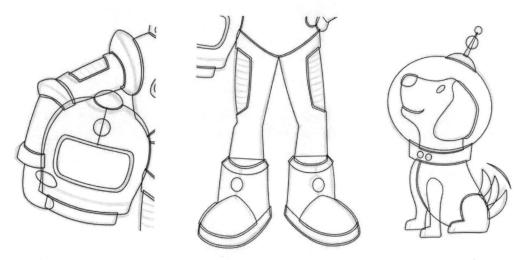

Figure 12.11 – Right arm, legs, and K9 Rover

Figure 12.12 is a screenshot of the linework for the two characters together without the sketch layer visible. I ended up reducing Ricky's head to about 90% as I thought it was a little too big after I had drawn everything in. It should fit into that helmet after all.

Figure 12.12 – Ricky and K9 Rover linework

Figure *12.13* shows the **Layers** panel's layer stack so far for Ricky and K9 Rover. As we progress with the color fill in and shading stages, some positions may shift and others may be added. Also in Figure *12.13*, I am showing the **Swatches** panel with the downloaded color palette we will be using, which you can download here: `https://github.com/ PacktPublishing/Up-and-Running-with-Affinity-Designer/tree/ main/Chapter12`.

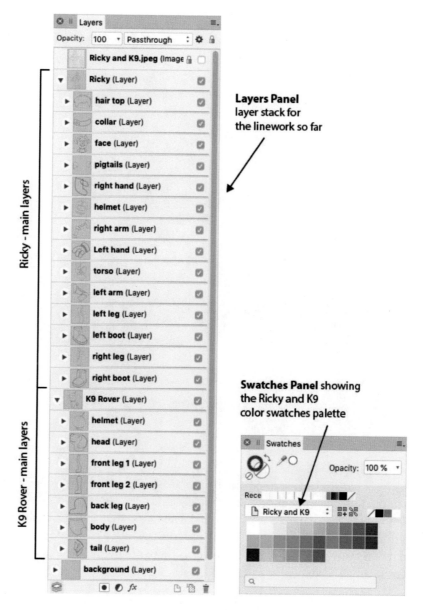

Figure 12.13 – Layers panel and Swatches panel

Step 2 – Color fills

Now the fun part – choosing colors while filling in all of our closed shapes. This is the first part of the coloring and shading stage. This is where things start to take shape fairly quickly. I went ahead and chose a few different colors from the `Ricky and K9` palette in the **Swatches** panel:

Figure 12.14 – Shapes filled with flat color

Feel free to either use the provided palette or choose your own set of colors. These particular color swatches were chosen to complement each other. I find that using a limited color range keeps a piece visually united. Using too many colors can create a busyness that makes it harder to work with and look cohesive. For color ideas and inspiration if you want to create your own palette, there are many great color-themed websites online for choosing color palettes. Go online and search for color themes or color palettes.

In this first stage, you are choosing the base colors for each shape – not too dark and not too bright because we will be adding shading and highlighting to most of the shapes using the lighter and darker colors from these swatches. Looking back at the sketch, those bold pencil outlines help the characters' individual sections stand out against each other. Later, the shading and highlights of those individual sections will help distinguish them from one another. Currently, a lot of the light-colored shape boundaries are running or blending into each other. We'll fix that soon.

As far as the process goes, don't worry about getting everything perfect straight off – we will be making lots of adjustments as we go and the forms will slowly emerge as we go along. For now, concentrate on getting a general color setup that is pleasing to your eye with some nice base colors and a few darker and lighter tones for shading and highlighting as described above.

Step 3 – Shading

Remember that "shading along the edges" technique I mentioned a few pages back? This is now the time to see what it can do. This technique goes a long way toward getting the cool dimensional feel that is currently missing with just our flat color shapes.

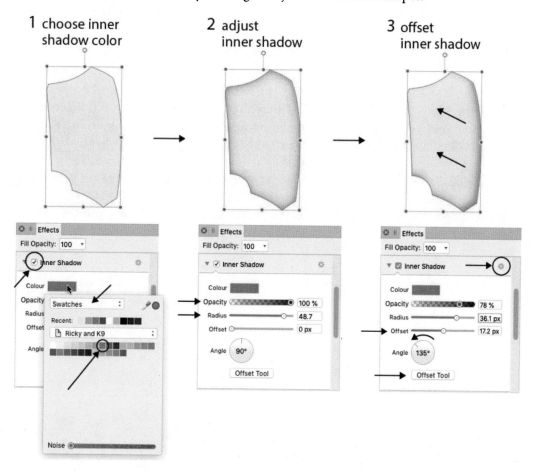

Figure 12.15 – Adding an inner shadow from the Effects panel

The **Inner Shadow** effect from the **Effects** panel, as shown in *Figure 12.15*, lets you add a shadow-like tone of your chosen color evenly all around the edges of the selected shape. It also gives you the option to assign a color to that shadow by clicking on the color swatch in the panel. This will pop up a **Color Selector** panel, and here, using the drop-down menu, you can select from all of the available types of color subpanels, including your color swatches as shown in steps **1** and **2** above. The **Opacity** slider controls the strength of the effect and the **Radius** slider controls the size of the shadow tone. The slider goes up to 100 pixels, but you can enter numbers above that in the number field to the right of the slider.

In some cases, you may want to reposition the inner shadow effect to create a wider shadow area in a specific area. The **Offset** slider in combination with the **Angle** controller allows you to do this as shown in step **3**, by moving the entire effect to a new position. Alternatively, clicking the **Offset Tool** button will allow you to click and drag on the shape itself to manually adjust the offset.

The tiny gear icon in the upper-right corner, when clicked, will open up the **Layer Effects** panel for the selected effect – in this case, **Inner Shadow**. The panel shown in step **4** is identical to the **Inner Shadow** effect panel with three new additions. It has an **Intensity** slider that will allow you to deepen or intensify the shadow effect. It has a **Scale with Object** button to ensure that if you resize the shape at any point, the **Inner Shadow** effect will scale along with it. It's usually a good idea to have this feature switched on, otherwise, you may get some unexpected results when scaling. Lastly, it has a **Fill Opacity** dropdown, which allows you to reduce the opacity of the shape's **Color Fill**. This can come in handy if you want to remove the fill color altogether but keep the **Inner Shadow** effect.

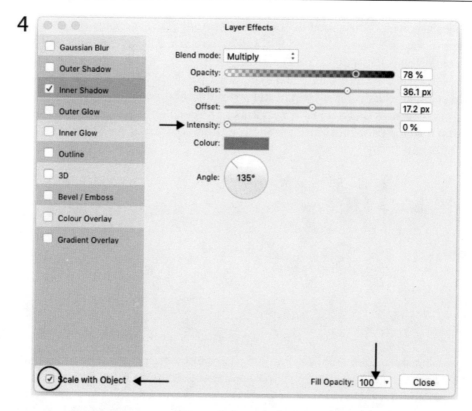

Figure 12.16 – The three extra options in the Layer Effects panel

The second important component of the shading method we will be using is the addition of **Gradient Shading** to each of the shapes to enhance their 3D quality, giving a sense of form to the shapes by approximating or mimicking the shadow areas.

> **Convincing shading relies on a consistent overall light direction**
>
> At this stage, it is important to establish an overall light direction. I usually imagine the light is coming from the upper left-hand corner. No matter which direction you choose, it is especially important that you be consistent and keep the same light direction in mind while applying these shading gradients to allow your light and shadows to be perceived as being correct.

To create a gradient, choose the **Fill** Tool from the **Tool** Panel and click and drag across the shape in the direction you want the gradient to follow. Affinity Designer will add an approximated color as the second color stop. 9 times out of 10, you will need to pick another color from the **Swatches** panel to get what you want to replace this automatically selected color, especially if you want to stick with the color swatches you already have in your color palette. This is done by clicking on the circular *color stop* that you want to change on the *gradient path* and selecting the desired color from the **Swatches** panel as shown in *Figure 12.17*:

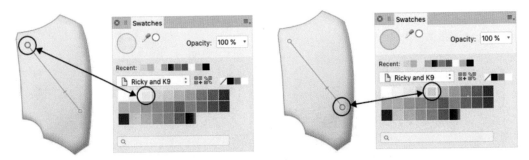

Figure 12.17 – Applying a linear gradient

Once you click on a color stop, you can drag it around to reposition it or you can add additional color stops if needed by clicking anywhere on the gradient path and then selecting or adjusting that new color stop from the color panel. You can also *reverse* the direction of the gradient by clicking and dragging the fill tool in the opposite direction or by clicking the reverse direction button in the context toolbar. There is also a **Rotate** gradient button in the context toolbar.

Notice that the gradient does not affect or change the previously applied **Inner Shadow** effect whatsoever. The two effects are independent of one another. You can also delete a color stop by selecting it and pressing the *Delete* key, however, this can only be done with color stops that are in between the two outside or original color stops. If you delete one of the original two color stops, the entire gradient will be deleted and will be filled with the remaining color stop as a solid color.

There are four types of gradients to choose from. They are **Linear, Elliptical, Radial**, and **Conical**. *Figure 12.18* shows the four types available. The handles on the gradient paths allow you to control the various aspects of each of the gradients. Click and drag them around to see how it affects your gradient. We will be using the linear gradient for most of the gradient shading work in our illustration.

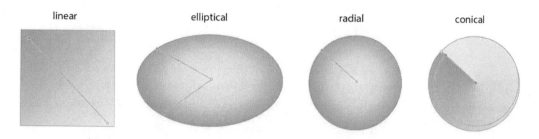

Figure 12.18 – The four different types of gradients

Using a combination of **Inner Shadow** effects and subtle **Gradient fills,** go over the entire light sections of Ricky's spacesuit and add shading as discussed while keeping in mind the light direction. Create the shadow areas, taking your time to really think about the form of each of the shapes. The arms are basically cylinders as well as the legs. The helmet is like a large sphere with a cutout opening creating a recessed shadow along its top edge.

I also decided to apply shading to her neck and the areas inside of her collar using the darker pink colors in the color palette. At this stage, keeping the shading subtle is good practice. You can always adjust as you go if you feel you need to add darker or lighter shading. As you progress, you should start to see that the initial flat shapes of color slowly become more tangible and dimensional. Generally, light and shade applied in the correct areas will go a long way toward bringing these characters to life.

Figure 12.19 shows my shading progress on the lighter areas of Ricky's suit and her neck and collar area using just **Inner Shadow** effects and **Linear Gradient** shading. The figure also shows how I achieved the three-dimensional look of her spacesuit's circular central ring. I used **3D Effect** with an accompanying **Outer Shadow** effect, adjusting the parameters to achieve a three-dimensional ring with a drop shadow. You will need to click on the gear icon in the **Effects** panel to get access to the **Layer Effects** panel's extra features. Play around with the light direction sphere in the panel to achieve the correct lighting angle. There is a great amount of control with all of the adjustment sliders available to you here. I also added a light-colored background circle inside of the ring to cover up the area where the three sections behind converge. Also notice that I have checked the **Scale with Object** checkbox so that this 3D effect scales with the object if I resize the illustration.

Speeding up your shading workflow

If you recall, you can copy and paste a selected object's attributes to another object by selecting the object you want to copy and pressing *Cmd* (Mac) or *Ctrl* *(PC) + C* to copy its color or effect attributes. Then select the object you want to have the same attributes and press *Cmd* or *Ctrl + Shift + V*. It will paste or transfer those copied attributes to the selected object. This will save you tons of time by not having to repeat the same steps over and over again.

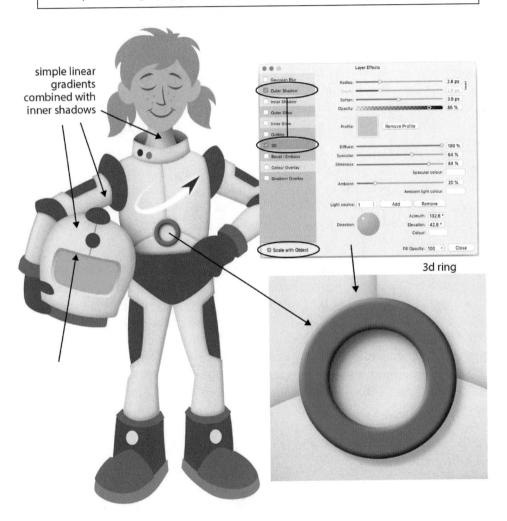

Figure 12.19 – Inner Shadow and 3D effects with Linear Gradient shading

The next step will be to recreate this same inner shadow and linear gradient shading process for the blue areas of the spacesuit, including the hands. We will then use these same methods for the space boots.

In *Figure 12.20*, you can see the same initial shading process at work in these blue areas. I pay careful attention to the light direction and keep in mind the shape or form of each of the objects. I have isolated the shorts below to show how the flat color shape (**1**), when **Inner Shadow** (**2**) and **Linear Gradient** (**3**) are applied, becomes more tangible and believable:

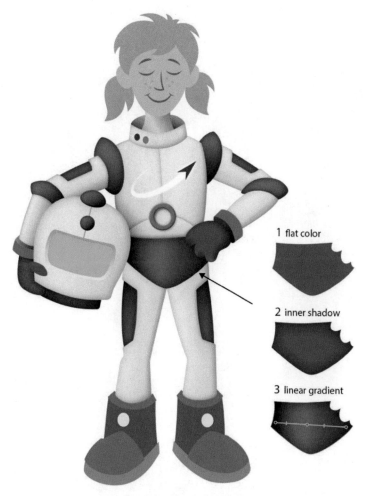

1 flat color

2 inner shadow

3 linear gradient

Figure 12.20 – Inner Shadow and Linear Gradient shading in the blue areas

When these principles are applied to all of the shapes, it forms a nice base for the highlighting and fine-tuning work to come in the next phase.

Step 4 – Highlighting

In *Figure 12.21*, I am showing in step-by-step form the two methods I used to do some of the form highlighting used in Ricky's spacesuit. This highlighting helps to give each form more structure. It can be subtle but this type of detail work really makes a difference in terms of realism.

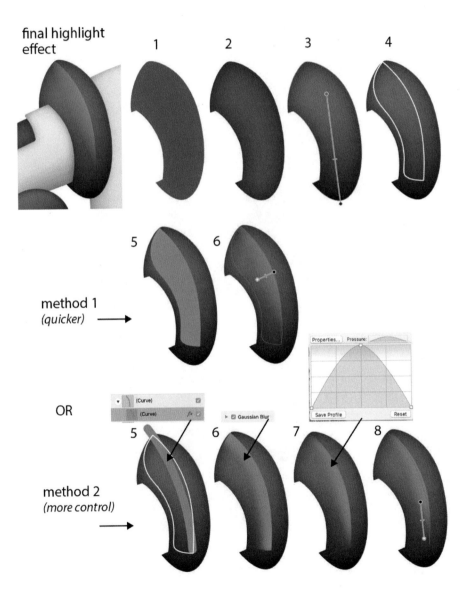

Figure 12.21 – Steps showing two highlighting methods used

Let's take a look at the breakdown of what is happening in these steps.

Steps **1** through **4** are common for both methods, with steps **1** to **3** of adding an inner shadow and linear gradient having been covered earlier:

- Step **1** – Here you start out with the base color as a flat shape.

- Step **2** – Apply an **Inner Shadow** effect with a darker color – usually a darker version of the base color. I chose a darker blue from the supplied Ricky and K9 palette.

- Step **3** – With the **Fill** Tool, drag a gradient from the base color to the darker shadow color, keeping in mind the light direction and where the shadow is likely to fall. Select each color stop on the gradient and apply a color from the color palette.

- Step **4** – Create the shape that will be the highlighted area. This highlighted area will determine to some degree the form of your object, so pay close attention to its shape.

Steps **5** onward are different for methods **1** and **2**. **Method 1** is easier and quicker and is fine for most situations. **Method 2** is a little more work but offers more control for areas that can be a bit of a challenge. The example here isn't a challenge but I wanted you to see both methods in practice.

Method 1 continued:

- Step **5** – Fill the highlight shape with a lighter highlight color. I removed the stroke.

- Step **6** – Using the **Transparency** Tool, drag the tool across the selected highlight shape until you find the highlight that feels right to you. This can take a few attempts. Essentially, you want to have a nice transparency gradient falloff with no sharp edges that give away your highlight shape.

Method 2 continued:

- Step **5** – Create a wide stroke in a lighter highlight color and nest that stroke inside the highlight shape in the **Layers** panel, which will mask it. Mine is **4.5 pts.** wide.

- Step **6** – Select just the stroke and apply a **Gaussian Blur** to it. I applied a 7-pixel blur. The combination of the stroke width and the blur width should create a nice soft highlight area. Adjust both the stroke and blur widths until it feels right.

- Step **7** – This step will fade or reduce the blur on each end of the stroke. With the stroke selected, in the **Stroke** panel's **Pressure** popup, add a central stop on the graph and drag the two end stops all the way down to effectively create a pointed tapered stroke. Comparing step **6** with step **7** shows how the two ends of the stroke are not sharp anymore and create a nice smooth fading out transition.

- Step **8** – If needed, you can apply a transparency gradient toward the end of the stroke to further fade it into the base color shape.

Method 2 can be more than is needed for most situations, but it does give you more control than just a transparency gradient will allow. The combination of the stroke width, the stroke taper, the blur width, and the ability to adjust the curve of the stroke itself offers an alternative that can comes in handy for certain circumstances.

This is the method I used for the hand and finger highlights, as shown in the next step-by-step example in *Figure 12.22*.

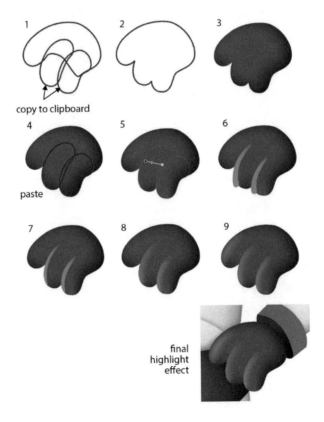

Figure 12.22 – Steps showing the method two highlighting method

Here is a breakdown of the steps shown in *Figure 12.22*:

1. Copy the two fingers to the clipboard or copy and drag them out of the way.

2. Select all three shapes that make up the hand and **Boolean Unite** them to create one shape.

3. Fill that united shape with the blue base color and apply an **Inner Shadow** effect with an **Offset**, as described earlier, to allow for more shadow toward the bottom and right side of the shape. There's no need for a **Linear Gradient** this time.

4. Paste or place the two fingers back on top of the hand shape.

5. Apply the same blue base and use the **Transparency** Tool to fade each shape to allow the dark inner shadow of the base hand layer to still show through along the bottom of the hand.

6. Create two wide strokes in the highlight blue color and **Taper** them using the **Stroke** panel's **Pressure** feature as described in *Figure 12.21*.

7. **Nest** these two strokes inside of each of the finger's shapes using the **Layers** panel.

8. Apply a **Gaussian Blur** to each of the finger highlights. Mine are 8.5-pixel blurs.

9. For the index finger, copy one of the finger line blurs and paste it inside the hand shape by selecting the blur, copying it, selecting the hand shape, and choosing **Paste Inside** from the **Edit** menu. This is just another way to nest elements inside of other elements. You could have also used the **Layers** panel to nest the shape as we've already done a few times in this chapter.

I am going to now go ahead and continue the spacesuit highlighting and details before going on to Ricky's boots, face, and hair. In the following figures, I will attempt to show processes and methods broken down for the various sections to show how to achieve some of these results for yourself. There are many ways to get similar results and it's always a good idea to experiment to find what works best for your purposes. These just happen to be the ways I have discovered over many projects and lots of trial and error. I still get stumped at times, however, and every project comes with its own challenges. Overcoming these challenges is what keeps it exciting and fun and learning something new is what it's all about.

Figure 12.23 – Ricky's spacesuit and helmet shading and highlights complete

Figure 12.23 demonstrates how multiple applications of well-placed inner shadow effects and gradients can simulate the appearance of form, light, and shadow on what started out as simple, flat-colored 2D shapes. Part of what makes this successful is not only knowing how to create these effects but also knowing where to place them. This is the sort of thing that can take time to learn and is where good reference and a keen eye and observation of the world around you can come in handy.

Next, let's look at the spacesuit shoulder details:

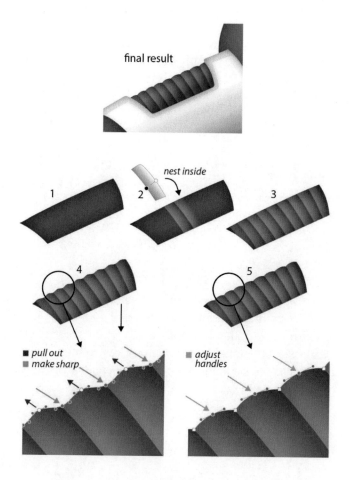

Figure 12.24 – Steps for spacesuit shoulder details

Here is a breakdown of the steps in *Figure 12.24*:

1. This is the base shape we will put our ridges into. It has a dark blue **Inner Shadow** applied to it.

2. Create a slightly curved rectangular shape as shown, fill it with a light blue from our color palette, and nest it inside of the base shape using the **Layers** panel. Add a **Transparency Gradient** to it to fade the light blue to transparent as shown.

3. Copy and drag to create multiple copies of the rectangle shape inside of the base shape. Rotate them slightly left and right as shown so they are not all exactly at the same angle.

4. Select the base shape and add the first set of new nodes using the **Node** tool along the shape border where the dark and light rectangular-shaped borders meet, as shown. These are the green arrows in step **4**. Then add a second set of nodes centered in between the first nodes. These second nodes are the red arrows in step **4**. Select all of these and pull them slightly out to create a subtle bump. With the **Node** tool still active, click on the first set of nodes (the green arrows – the nodes that weren't moved) while holding the *Option* or *Alt* key to create sharp or corner nodes.

5. With the Node tool, go back and adjust the handles of the nodes you pulled out (blue arrows) to create nice round bumps as shown in step **5**.

Tip for selecting

As you build more objects and elements and as our project gets more complex, it can become difficult to make the right selections. If you are experiencing this, try going into **Outline Mode** by going to **VIEW | VIEW MODE | OUTLINE**, or *Cmd* or *Ctrl + Y*. This will enable you to easily select anything in your file that isn't hidden or locked.

You might have noticed a pattern by now of repeating basically the same steps over and over as we create all of these different elements that make up Ricky's suit. This is the typical workflow I employ most of the time and, after a while, you will get pretty adept at it. This is good because, soon enough, you will not think so much about how to do something and start to focus your attention more on the creative or fun side of making your ideas come to life.

As you build these skills, you will find yourself taking on subject matter that might have seemed too challenging or difficult previously. By tackling each component one piece at a time, your confidence will grow with each project completed.

Figure 12.25 shows a breakdown of the **Linear Gradient** I used for the green-blue metallic components of Ricky's spacesuit. It's comprised of five colors that mimic the surface of a shiny green-blue metal. Metal can be tricky to get right, but basically, there is usually a high amount of contrast as the surface is very reflective. Ensure there is a bright highlight on one end of the gradient surrounded by darker tones and a slightly duller highlight on the other end to simulate any reflected light. Try to use colors from the color palette to keep your illustration's colors consistent.

You may have noticed in *Figure 12.23* I changed Ricky's collar to this metallic material as it looked better to me and it just made sense as this is where the helmet would attach and that would most likely be metal.

I have also added a few **Tapered** strokes of the bright-green color to mimic the highlighted edges of the metal corners, and in the case of the collar, the non-tapered stroke depicts the thickness of the metal. Notice as well the arrows that indicate the direction of the gradient. This is especially important with metal. Experiment with different directions to see what works best for each piece. Try to keep the highlight placement consistent as each piece is theoretically using the same light source direction.

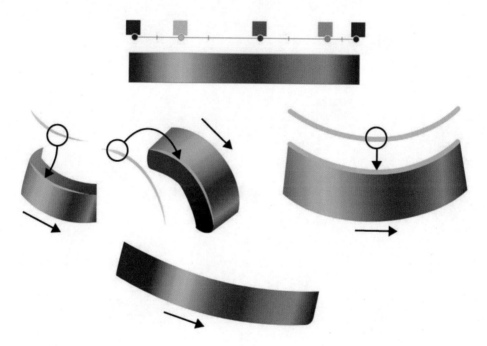

Figure 12.25 – Linear gradient for the metallic components

Let's move on to Ricky's space boots next. Here, as with the collar, I have changed my mind on the color of her boots. I found that the lighter color was more in keeping with her overall suit and I found the blue color tended to make them look more like winter boots or big slippers. Plus, I'm loving this hard plastic, reflective, lighter suit material.

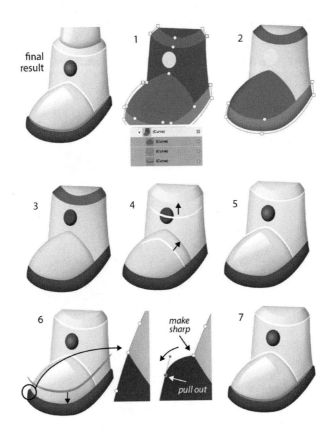

Figure 12.26 – Steps for building the space boot material

Here is a breakdown of the steps in *Figure 12.26*:

1. Select all of the boots' components and nest them inside the base shape in the **Layers** panel as shown. Using this method of nesting inside of a main or base shape allows more control over the silhouette of the overall shape and it also saves time as you don't have to worry about the precise positioning or lining up of shape borders.

2. Copy the light material (*Cmd* or *Ctrl* + *C*) or color from another similar part of the spacesuit and paste (*Cmd* or *Ctrl* + *Shift* + *V*) onto the selected base shape of the boot. Make any adjustments you need to the **Linear Gradient** using the **Fill** Tool.

3. Repeat this step for the toe section of the boot. Then select the light circle element and repeat this step again, only with the dark blue this time.

4. Create a couple of light **Tapered** strokes as shown and position one above to mimic an edge highlight and the other over the top of the area where the toe section meets the leg section as shown. Copy the light material again and apply it to the upper curved U-shape element to mimic that wide edge catching the light on the upper part of the boot. Remove the **Inner Shadow** from it and make any necessary adjustments.

5. Add a subtle soft **Gaussian Blur** light-blue highlight to the blue circle shape. Place it slightly toward the left indicating the light source from that side. Also, to create that shiny hard plastic feel, add a white or very light-colored shape as shown and apply a **Transparency Gradient** to it with the **Transparency** Tool.

6. Create another **Tapered** stroke in light blue and place it to create a ridge on top of the boots' sole strip. With the **Node** tool select the base or silhouette shape and add a couple of new nodes right where the sole meets the boot on both the front and back sides of the boot. We are going to create a bit of a bump to mimic some thickness for the sole. This adds more realism and gives the foot more of a solid feel on the ground. Add the new nodes as shown and make sure the node lies right on the intersection of a **Hard** or **Sharp Corner** node. Then select the nodes just below it and reposition them away from the boot to create a bit of a protrusion to suggest a bit of thickness for the sole.

7. This is the finished boot. A culmination of all of the preceding steps.

Here are the separated components of the helmet. Every element here but one is heavily reliant on a simple **Linear Gradient** to bring it to life. Note the different angles of each and the different colors used in each, usually a lighter to darker color within the same tonal range. A few elements are also taking advantage of an **Inner Shadow** effect. Top it off with a couple of well-placed white-to-transparent highlight fades on the helmet surface and the glass visor and when all of these shading and highlighting effects are combined, they make a fairly convincing space helmet.

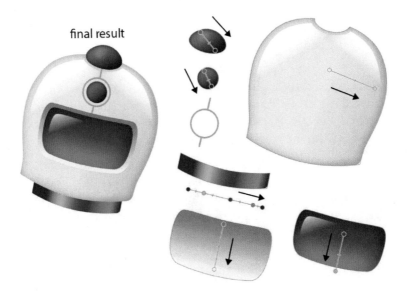

final result

Figure 12.27 – Components and effects that together make up the space helmet

Let's turn our attention to Ricky's face and hair. I want to keep the cartoony characteristics of her face so we won't be straying too far from the sketch. In other words, we aren't going to get too realistic.

As we proceed, I will be repeating the **Inner Shadow** as well **Linear Gradient** shading effects. *Figure 12.28* breaks down the steps I followed to create the final look for her face and hair:

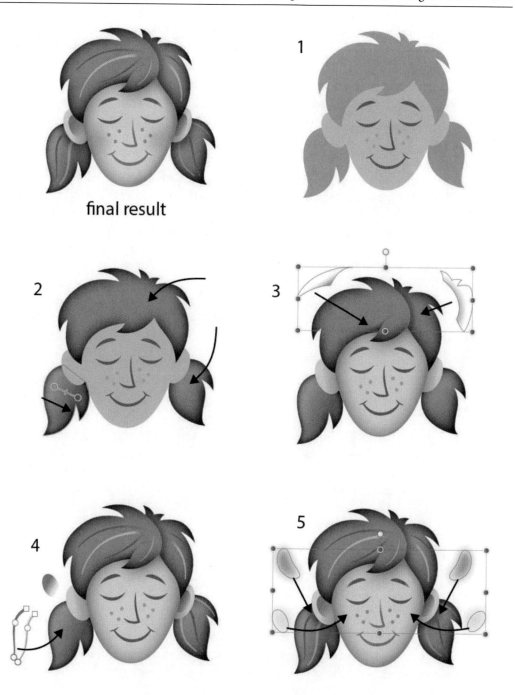

Figure 12.28 – Steps for Ricky's hair and face

Here is a breakdown of the steps in *Figure 12.28*:

1. I start out with the flat colors for Ricky's face and hair that I assigned earlier.

2. I add a dark orange **Inner Shadow** effect to all of her hair. I used an amount of 66 pixels at 100% opacity. Adjust yours to your liking. I wanted it dark enough to match the contrast of the spacesuit. I also added **Linear Gradients**, as shown, to the two pigtails but not the main hair, for some sense of directional shadow, paying attention to the light direction.

3. To add a sense of volume to her hair, I created two shapes that I used to add shadows. One creates the parting in her hair and the second a very small contour shadow for the hair that comes down in front of her forehead. Compare the differences between step **2** and step **3**. Inside the forehead contour shape, I used a linear gradient of dark orange that goes from 100% to 0% opacity using the **Transparency** Tool. For the part in her hair shadow, I used the nested blurred stroke method, again using a dark-orange color. The stroke is placed inside the shape, then blurred. Both were set to **Multiply** mode. I was finding her face a little too pink, so I lightened her skin color and added an **Inner Shadow** effect of 79 pixels to her face in a darker red.

4. I created light- and dark-orange tapered strokes and placed them as shown to depict hair flow direction loosely following the shape of the hair sections. I then added two transparent gradient ellipse shape fades to depict her inner ear shapes. These were dark red.

5. I then added two very subtle **Gaussian Blurred** ellipses for a bit of redness in her cheeks and added two dark-orange Gaussian blurred shapes behind her ears but in front of her pigtails for a bit of shadow behind her ears. Use the **Layers** panel to move the objects in front or behind one another.

> **Note**
> Depending on the size of your document, some of the above pixel numbers may not be the same for you as they were for me. Experiment for the best results.

Finally, let's take a look at our trusty four-legged sidekick, K9. He is sporting his own doggie spacesuit so there are a few similarities to Ricky regarding shading and coloring. In *Figure 12.29*, I have separated out each of the components and because I think you are most likely up to speed with the process, rather than describe each step, I will just make some notes about what is going on with some of these elements.

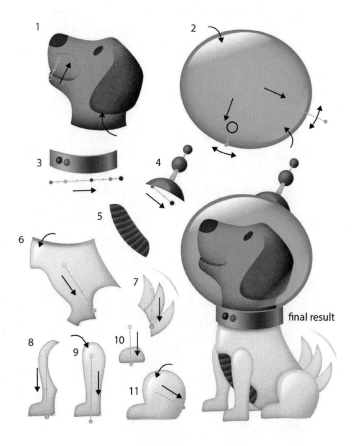

Figure 12.29 – The components that make up K9

- **Element 1**, K9's head, has a base head shape with a dark-orange **Inner Shadow** applied to it and his ear, nose, and mouth shapes are nested inside of that base shape. The ear has a transparent fade at the top that fades into the base shape color and I placed a blurred stroke inside the ear shape at the bottom to create that shadow there, which gives the ear a sense of thickness. The only **Linear Gradient** on his head is a separate shape added just above his mouth to create a sense of form for his snout.

- **Element 2**, the glass sphere for his helmet, is made up of an **Elliptical Gradient** and an **Inner Shadow** of dark blue. The smooth, glassy reflected effect is achieved with the use of a white shape with a transparent fade at the top left as well as a bright green transparent fade at the bottom right. With highly reflective surfaces, the outside edges are the most reflective. Leave a gap – don't take your shape right to the edge or the effect will be not be the same.

- **Element 3** is just another instance of the same metallic **Linear Gradient** used earlier.

- **Element 4** uses a **Linear Gradient** as well as a small light-blue circle shape with a **Gaussian Blur** for a soft highlight.

- **Element 5** is another carry-over of styling from Ricky's spacesuit reconfigured to conform to a little doggy spacesuit.

- **Elements 6 – 11** all have similar combinations of mid- to dark-pink inner shadow effects and linear gradients. I have indicated with arrows the directions of the linear gradients. I also added a few white transparent gradient fades to mimic the reflective highlights of the hard plastic spacesuit material, also indicated with arrows.

All of these elements put together make up our interstellar sidekick K9 Rover.

Figure 12.30 shows our two finished characters, showcasing the culmination of all of the drawing, shading, and highlighting work we have covered in this chapter:

Figure 12.30 – Finished Ricky and K9 Rover

Hopefully, this final outcome demonstrates the powerful capabilities and potential of Affinity Designer for this type of illustration.

I thought it would be fun to break away from the stark white background so I placed our two characters in an actual environment. In *Figure 12.31*, I created a very simple space scene background to place them on:

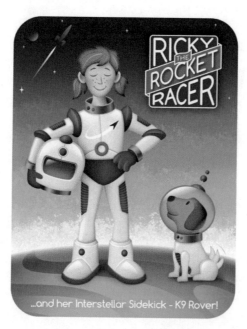

Figure 12.31 – Ricky and K9 Rover as a poster, advertisement, or package design with the logo

I imagine it could be a poster or a toy advertisement, or maybe a package design for the lid of a tin box/container, perhaps containing tin toy versions of Ricky and K9.

For those readers who might want to create something similar, I have broken down the process I went through to create the background step by step in *Figure 12.32*:

1. Hide the **Ricky** and **K9** layers and on a new layer entitled **Background**, create a full-page vertical **Linear Gradient** using four color stops: a dark blue, a mid-blue, the brightest green, and white.

2. In **Pixel Persona** create a new pixel layer above the gradient layer, choose the Paint Brush Tool, and a fairly textured brush from one of the supplied brush categories. Mine was from the **Sprays and Spatters** category. Reduce the **Opacity** of the brush to around **50%** from the context toolbar and, working from the bottom, going from light to dark, sample the lightest color from the gradient below and paint in a curving arc manner. Gently paint in the lightest color, then sample the bright green from the gradient and continue, following the example in *Figure 12.31* for a visual guide. We will cover more pixel painting in the last chapter, *Chapter 13, Rocketing into the Pixel Cosmos*.

3. Create a large **Ellipse Shape** and fill it with a bright-to-dark green **Elliptical Gradient**. I added a white **Inner Glow** to it as well so that it blends the hard edge of the shape into the white pixel-painted background somewhat. The effect makes it feel a bit like a glowing atmosphere.

4. Copy and paste one of the stars from the previous chapter's logo file into this file and place them accordingly, making sure to mix up the sizes a bit. Create a few swirls with the Pen tool, nest them inside of the planet ellipse, and fill them with bright green. Use the **Transparency** Tool to fade them into the base planet as shown.

5. Add the small flying rocket and the main logo type from the previous chapter position as shown. Create a small planet and fade it into the background using the **Transparency** Tool. I added the wording at the bottom Sidekick K9 type.

6. Unhide the **Ricky** and **K9** layers.

7. With a soft, round brush, add dark-blue pixel-painted shadows beneath each character as shown in the closeup of step **7**. The key to getting this right is adding the shadows very softly, reducing your brush opacity to approximately **20%**. Finally, on the top layer, add a white, rounded rectangular border by using a rounded rectangle-shape tool and a larger normal rectangle. Select both and perform an **Xor Boolean** operation to them to cut a hole through the larger rectangle. Adjust it to fit.

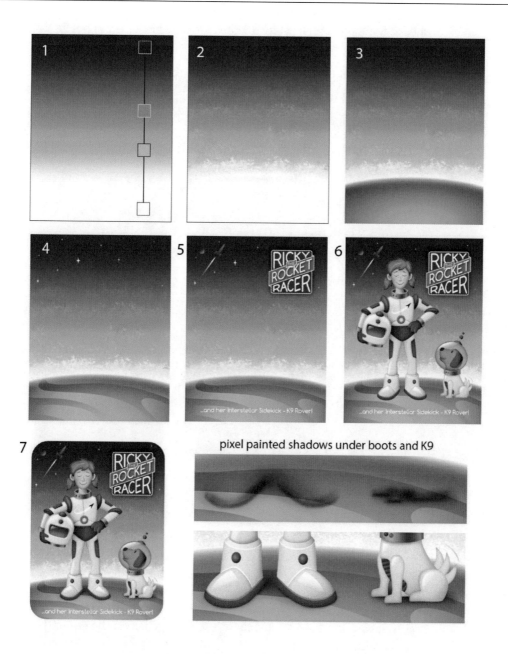

Figure 12.32 – Steps for creating the space background

Here is a screenshot of the **Layers** panel stacking order for the background portion of this illustration:

Figure 12.33 – The layer stack for the space scene background

Note **white border** is above everything in the **background** layer.

Adding noise for a retro feel

To repeat or recap this step from the end of the previous chapter, to add a nice quick retro feel to your work, add some noise to give it a subtle grain or texture. The easiest way to do this to the whole piece is to add a new vector layer to the top of your layer stack, drag out a rectangle-shaped tool shape that covers the entire piece, and fill it with white. Select the white rectangle and change **Blend Mode** on the **Layers** panel to **Multiply** at **100%**. Go to the **Color** panel and, with the white rectangle still selected, click on the **Opacity** color swatch to switch it to **Noise** as covered in *Chapter 5, Main Studio Panels and Managers*. Then, adjust the amount of noise to your liking. Because the white rectangle is set to **Multiply**, you will only see the noise generated, not the white rectangle. Unfortunately, the effect is a little too subtle to show up well in a screenshot, so I haven't included one here.

Summary

Well, we sure covered a lot of ground in this chapter! Our journey took us from building the paths and curves based on a concept sketch all the way up to a fairly realistic, stylized couple of fun characters. We utilized the skills learned from the previous chapter and put them to good use creating a more advanced illustration.

We learned how a cohesive color palette can contribute to giving overall harmony to an otherwise complex illustration. We discovered how to transform flat, 2D colored shapes into dimensional surfaces with the use of shading and highlighting. We explored using **Inner Shadow** effects and **Linear** and **Elliptical Gradients** to describe form and shadows from a consistent light source. Not least of all, with the exception of part of the background, we created all of this using an all-vector workflow, with the advantage of making it easy to continue to refine it at any time while maintaining its resolution-independent nature, allowing it to be used at any size.

In the next and final chapter of this book, we'll complete the last practical exercise. We'll be discovering Affinity Designer's **Pixel Painting** shading workflow while creating Ricky's retro rocket. This exercise will illustrate the pros and cons of a slightly different approach to the all-vector workflow of this chapter. The countdown has started – it's almost time to blast off!

13
Rocketing into the Pixel Cosmos

Welcome to the thirteenth and final chapter of *Up and Running with Affinity Designer*. In this third exercise chapter, we will continue to build on what we have learned in the previous two chapters, and this time we will tackle creating Ricky's racing rocket. The finished illustration project should look something like the example in *Figure 13.1* and utilizes a combination of Designer Persona and Pixel Persona workflows:

Figure 13.1 – The finished rocket illustration

As you can see, this final illustration is slightly different in appearance from the previous exercise. In this illustration, we are adopting a hybrid workflow, taking advantage of the vector features as well as the pixel painting features of Affinity Designer.

Prerequisites and expectations

The goal of this third exercise chapter is to switch gears a little and see how the shading and lighting process, using a slightly different approach, can bring perhaps a more painterly feel to add a nice metallic, roughed-up look to our weary rocketship. Over the course of my day-to-day illustration work, I tend to use a combination of these two workflows and it always amazes me how seamlessly the two personas work with each other.

We will start out once again by building our base shapes using the **Shape** tool and the **Pen** tool, and we'll organize these elements using the **Layers** panel. This time, instead of using **Gradients** and **Inner Shadow** effects to shade and enhance our object's form and shadows, we'll use **Pixel Painting** along with some **Bevel/Emboss and 3D Effects** for an altogether different approach for our final look. One of the advantages of this approach is that it can sometimes speed up the process as the painting method allows a little more flexibility and doesn't require some of the pre-planning steps that an all-vector workflow can have. Additionally, it can also offer a few more creative expression possibilities with its array of brush categories and options. Plus the bevel and 3D effects produce some pretty convincing results in a matter of clicks, saving you even more time.

These bevel and 3D effects are available in both the Designer Persona and the Pixel Persona, but up until now, we haven't really used them so I thought we'd make use of them in this chapter. As it turns out, they are ideally suited for what we need to create on Ricky's rocketship.

We will start as we did in the previous chapter, by placing the rocket illustration sketch shown in *Figure 13.2* into Affinity Designer as a guide, referencing it as we create the illustration shape by shape.

Let's get started – downloading the sketch

Okay, let's make a start on this final practical exercise project. To follow along using the provided rocketship sketch, you will need to download it from the download link and save it to somewhere on your hard drive where you will be saving your Affinity Designer file for this project. The sketch can be downloaded from the following link: `https://github.com/PacktPublishing/Up-and-Running-with-Affinity-Designer/tree/main/Chapter13`.

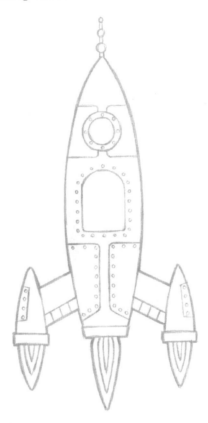

Figure 13.2 – Ricky's rocketship sketch

Document setup

Once you have the sketch downloaded, let's create the Affinity Designer document that we will be using to build the illustration. With Affinity Designer open, go to **FILE | NEW**. For my setup using this sketch, I am once again going to start out with an **8.5 in x 11 in** vertical format. If you need to resize the document after you create it, go to **FILE | DOCUMENT SETUP** and reconfigure your options.

Refer to *Figure 13.3* for the document settings that I chose for this logo project. I'm using a vertical version of the **Letter** size at **300** DPI using **Inches** for **Document units**. Similar to the previous chapter, I'm not using the **Create artboard** option and I've set **Image placement policy** to **Prefer Linked**. I'm also again going with **RGB/8** for **Color format** and an sRGB profile, and I'm deselecting **Transparent background** without any **Margins** or **Bleed** settings:

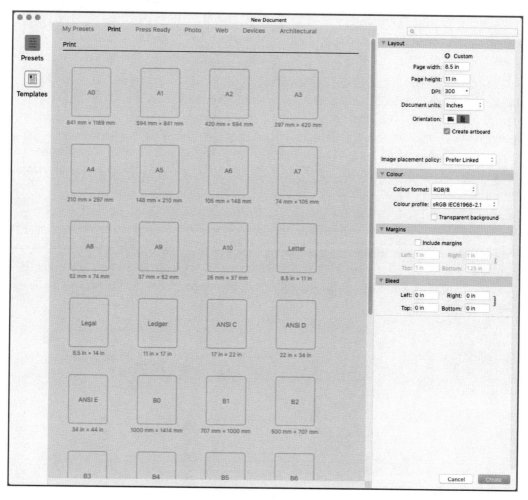

Figure 13.3 – My document settings

Keep in mind that we will be working with a lot of resolution-dependent pixel painting in this one so make sure the resolution you choose for your document is not too low. 300 DPI or above should be fine. Use a higher resolution if you want something poster size or larger than 8.5 x 11 inches.

Placing the reference sketch

Once you have your document created, let's add the sketch image by going to **FILE | PLACE** or clicking on the **Place** Tool in the **Tools** panel and selecting the sketch to place it in our document.

Once again, scale the placed sketch up or down to fill the document window if you need to. Use the **Move** Tool to select it and drag on the corner handles *without* the *Shift* key pressed to scale it without stretching it. Then in the **Layers** panel, I reduced the **Opacity** of the layer to **50%**, changed the **Blend** mode of the layer to **Multiply**, and then locked the layer. In the final finished image, the rocketship has been rotated. We will do this at the end of the process. It's much easier and better to create all of the elements before rotating, so keep it straight vertically for now.

Once in place and locked, we are going to use the sketch as a guide to draw all of the shapes and lines on layers below while still seeing the sketch because it's on the top layer. The **Multiply Blend** mode of the sketch layer allows us to see through the sketch as we build the rocketship. If we need to hide the sketch for any reason, we just have to hide the sketch layer in the **Layers** panel. Locking the sketch layer prevents us from accidentally selecting or moving it.

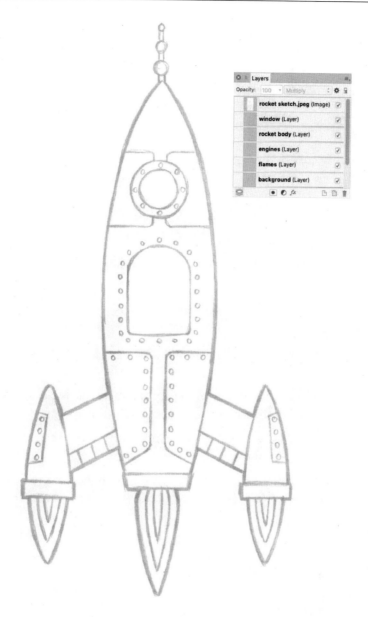

Figure 13.4 – The sketch in the document with the main layers set up and named

Creating the layer stack hierarchy

As mentioned in the previous two chapters, when determining the layer stack, review the sketch and decide how best to divide up the layers. *Figure 13.4* shows how I've decided to break up the layer stack.

I have left the sketch layer at the top of the stack, as explained earlier. The rest of the layers are placed from top to bottom in the order that they will appear in the illustration, with the background layer at the bottom of the stack. This illustration at this point doesn't appear to be as complex as the previous chapter, which is reflected in the current number of layers. We will, however, be adding many more sub or nested layers as we begin to create and then paint our elements, so that number will increase. Don't forget to name your main layers.

Similar to the building process in *Chapter 11, Creating a Professional Logo*, we will be able to use a lot more of Affinity Designer's basic shapes to create most of the rocketship's components.

The steps to create this illustration

The steps we are going to use are flexible and the order may cross over at times, but this is the general order of the process we will use:

- Step 1 – Create all of the shapes with strokes only. Nest shapes inside of shapes where it makes sense for easier control of their boundaries and visibility.

- Step 2 – Add base color fills with color from the provided color palette (or your own).

- Step 3 – Add shading using mostly pixel painting methods. We may use some vector methods as well for certain areas.

- Step 4 – Add lighting using mostly pixel painting methods. We may use some vector methods as well for certain areas.

- Fine-tuning and adjustments are usually made as we build each section before going on to the next section. However, they can occur at any time when needed.

Let's look at these steps in detail.

Step 1 – Building the shapes

As in the previous two chapters, I start creating the rocketship's shapes using a thin magenta or pink-colored line. For this one, I'm going with the line width set at 2 points in the **Stroke** panel.

Drawing the rocketship

Using the method described in *step 1*, I created all of the various components on the appropriately named layers as seen in *Figure 13.5*. Notice the panels I have nested on the **main rocket shape** and **engines** layers:

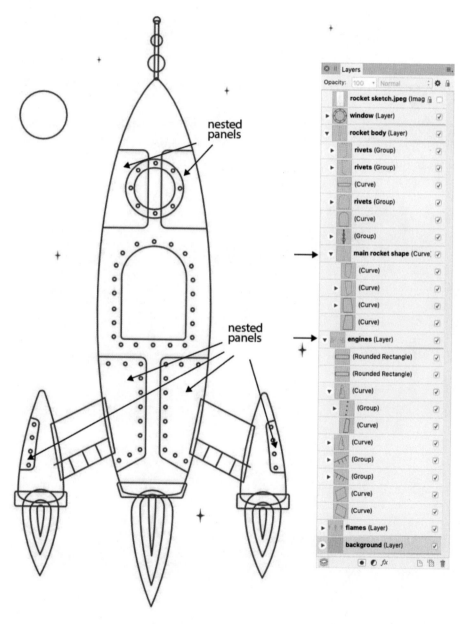

Figure 13.5 – All of the rocketship paths drawn

Some useful building tips

- For nice round corners, draw the shapes with sharp corners first then select the corners and using the **Corner** Tool from the **Tools** panel, apply a suitable amount of rounding to them. This way you can still edit them if need be.

- To ensure elements line up nicely, enable snapping. This will help in lining up those rivets and ensuring the distances between them are equal.

- Group elements such as the rivets sections for easier transforming and coloring.

- Create one side of the **Engine Assembly**, then copy, drag, and **Flip Horizontal** for the other side.

- To create the nice sharp point and smooth curve of the **Main Body** shape, use two ellipse shapes and apply an **Intersect** or **Divide Boolean** function to cut away the outer shapes, leaving the inner shape as shown in *Figure 13.6*:

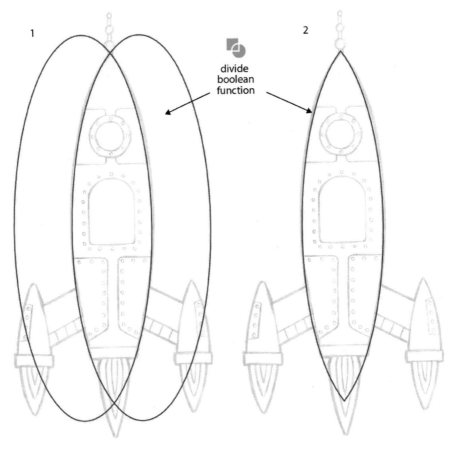

Figure 13.6 – Using two shapes to create one with the Divide Boolean function

- Creating the rounded doorway can be done using an **Add Boolean** function or using the **Rounded Rectangle** Tool from the **Tools** panel. Here I used a **Compound Add Boolean**. A Compound Boolean is a way of using the first four Boolean functions non-destructively. To do this, select both of the objects you want to Boolean. Press the *Alt* or *Option* key while clicking on the Boolean icon in the upper toolbar and this will create the Boolean but leave the objects intact. This allows you to continue to reposition or transform the objects without committing to a destructive shape:

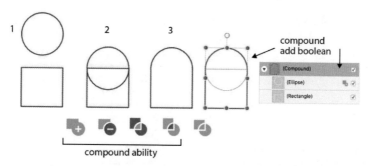

Figure 13.7 – Method 1 – using the Compound Add Boolean function

- The second method is to use the Rounded Rectangle Tool and adjust each of the corners independently from the context toolbar:

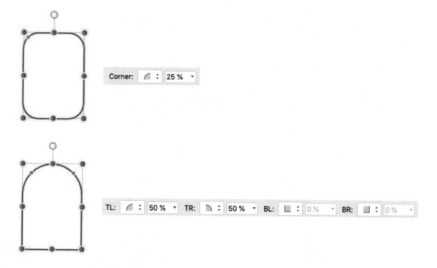

Figure 13.8 – Method 2 – using the Rounded Rectangle Tool

- A very handy method for editing separate objects at the same time yet independently is to use the **Transform Objects Separately** feature located in the context toolbar when two or more objects are selected. I used this feature to edit the width of the two lower elements of the engine assemblies. Another practical example would be if you wanted to reduce or enlarge the size of all of the rivets at the same time but didn't want to move them from their positions. You would first select them all and choose the transform objects separately to scale them. This is a very powerful and handy feature.

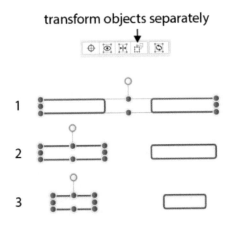

Figure 13.9 – Transforming objects separately

Step 2 – Applying base colors

Step 2, applying base colors, will be pretty straightforward for this simple rocketship. Feel free to color yours how you see fit. I thought I would separate the panels and the engines out from what will be the base metal of the main body. I am once again using the `Ricky` and `K9` color palette from the last chapter. If you need to re-import the palette, go to the **Color** Panels upper-right menu flyout and choose **Import Palette**, then choose either **Application, Document**, or **System**. Either will work for our purposes. Navigate to where you downloaded it to and click **Open**. We will also be using the Greys Palette that comes shipped with Affinity Designer.

With the Greys palette visible, we will start with the rocket's main body. Select the main rocket shape or main body layer and then select a mid-tone gray color to fill it with. Before we start pixel painting and shading values, we'll establish an overall color scheme for each component, then when it comes time to shade with the pixel painting method, things will go more easily and faster. You could pixel paint each of these shapes with a flat base color but this method is quicker with fewer steps involved.

For my rocket, I wanted those nested panels to be the dark red from the `Ricky and K9` color palette. To access that palette, just click on the **Color** panel's palette **Name** dropdown and navigate to that palette. To select those nested panels inside of the rocket's main body shape, you can either select them in the **Layers** panel or *double-click* on one of their paths to select one panel. Double-clicking gives you access to nested shapes inside other shapes. While you have this access, go ahead and *shift-select* the other nested panels and then choose the darkest red in the `Ricky and K9` color palette. They should all get filled with that color, although you may need to change the target to **Fill** and not **Stroke**.

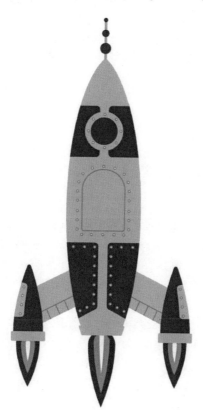

Figure 13.10 – The rocketship filled in with flat base colors

---

Copying styles

Remember at this first stage, you can copy and paste your elements' styles to other objects by copying with *Ctrl* or *Cmd* + *C* and then pasting with *Ctrl* or *Cmd* + *Shift* + *V*. This won't work with pixel painted areas, so take advantage of it at this first stage if you can.

In *Figure 13.10*, you can see how I divided up all of the shapes with mostly the red and grays discussed earlier. I also added dark blue to the round window and some orange and almost the lightest red to the flame areas. The plan I have in mind is to create metallic-looking colors with carefully placed highlights and shading, as always, with a light source direction in mind. This will be a hybrid approach with a combination of a vector flat base color and pixel painting shading and highlights.

Steps 3 and 4 – Pixel painting – shading and highlighting

Let's get started painting. Once you are happy with the general color direction, switch Personas to the **Pixel Persona** by going to the upper-left top corner and selecting the **Pixel Persona** button. Depending on your UI setup, some of your panels may have shifted around or disappeared after switching Personas. The main panels we will be using are **Brushes**, **Color**, **Layers**, and **Swatches**, and the context toolbar for adjusting our brush options. A good general rule of thumb to follow is to use a light touch while painting.

Shading and highlighting are covered at the same time here because, a lot of the time, while painting that is how you will proceed. It's just part of the natural flow of decision-making with pixel painting, so we will tackle them simultaneously.

Some useful painting tips

- **Opacity** – I usually paint with a **50%** or lower opacity setting on my brushes, or sometimes I reduce the **Flow Opacity** as well and start off with subtle strokes. You will find it easier to control the application of paint this way. The number keys on your keyboard are shortcuts for the Opacity slider: *1 to 9 are 10 to 90%; 0 is 100%*.

- **Rotating** – Rotating your document can make it easier to apply certain paint strokes for more control or a smoother look. Go to **VIEW | ROTATE LEFT** or **ROTATE RIGHT**. I've set these to *L* and *R* shortcuts. It rotates in 15-degree increments.

- **Tablet** – Access to a drawing tablet and pen can also make the painting process seem more natural or intuitive, although it's not mandatory. I used a mouse for this exercise.

- **Layers** – Use additional **Pixel Layers** to build up areas if need be. If you paint everything on the same layer, it may be difficult to correct any mistakes. It's also great for experimenting with different techniques or approaches without jeopardizing work that you've already done. I usually keep my shading, highlighting, and texturing paintwork separated on different layers.

- **Other Tools/Brushes** – Use other tools such as the **Eraser** or **Dodge** and **Burn** tools from the **Tools** panel or experiment with more textured styled brushes from the **Brushes** panel for different looks.

- **Straight lines** – Use *Shift* while painting to create straight lines.

- **Brush size and hardness shortcut** – Use the shortcut *Ctrl + Option* or *Ctrl + Alt* while dragging **Left** and **Right** to **Resize** your brush, or with the same keys pressed, dragging **Up** and **Down** to adjust the **Hardness** of the brush.

- **Sampling colors** – Use the color sampling shortcut while painting to grab or pick a color from the document. Pressing *Option* or *Alt* and dragging will bring up a magnified pixel viewer that you can **Color Pick** the underlying color from to be your new **Active Color**.

Bringing it all together

In *Figure 13.11*, I'm showing the completed painted rocketship with notations on what was done on it to transform it from the flat 2D color stage to a full-fledge, dimensionally shaded, somewhat realistic rocketship.

If you compare this to *Figure 13.10*, you will see just how much can be achieved with a combination of pixel painting and **3D** and **Bevel** effects in Affinity Designer. You can choose, of course, what level you want to take yours to. I was going for a classical retro rocket look complete with space wear and tear and that rough and ready textured look of many miles logged out there in the cosmos.

The process in brief

All of the larger areas of metal, including the red panels, both engine assemblies, and the wing struts, were hand-painted in the Pixel Persona using 2-3 pixel layers as follows: a soft, dark initial shadow layer above the flat base color layer, then a highlight layer above the shadow layer, and finally a texture layer above the highlight layer. All of the rivets were created using the **3D** and **Outer Shadow** effects. The panels, door opening, and bare-metal housings above the flames all have **Bevel** effects. I used a few white, tapered, and Gaussian blurred strokes along the fuselage and engine assemblies for a subtle metal reflection to enhance the roundness of these shapes. I will break down some of these process steps visually in the coming pages.

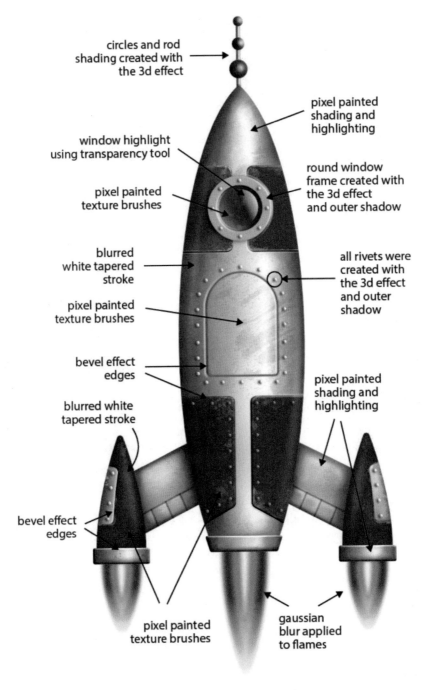

circles and rod
shading created with
the 3d effect

pixel painted
shading and
highlighting

window highlight
using transparency tool

round window
frame created with
the 3d effect
and outer shadow

pixel painted
texture brushes

blurred
white tapered
stroke

all rivets were
created with
the 3d effect
and outer
shadow

pixel painted
texture brushes

bevel effect
edges

pixel painted
shading and
highlighting

blurred white
tapered stroke

bevel effect
edges

pixel painted
texture brushes

gaussian
blur applied
to flames

Figure 13.11 – The finished rocketship with notations

If the image in *Figure 13.11* looks a little overwhelming, I apologize. That wasn't the intention. I just wanted to make sure I pointed out the main techniques that were used to shade the rocketship. Each step of the process is taken one at a time and when seen altogether can seem like a ton of work. It is a bit of work but the effort is worth it and it is actually a lot of fun bringing it to life.

Steps for painting in the Pixel Persona

- In order to pixel paint in Affinity Designer, you first need to be in the **Pixel Persona**.

- Select the flat-colored base layer you want to paint on and click the **New Pixel Layer** button at the bottom of the **Layers** panel.

- This will create a new pixel layer immediately above the flat color layer. Click and drag the new pixel layer underneath and slightly to the right of the flat color layer to nest it until you see the horizontal gray bar shift to the right. When you let go, it should be slightly indented to the right, just below the flat color layer. Make sure the gray bar is horizontal, not vertical when you drag it before you let go. Vertical is a different type of mask.

- Now, because the new pixel layer you moved is nested, any painting you do on this pixel layer will be kept inside the base layer's boundary. You don't need to worry about keeping within the shape. It will be masked. If it isn't, check to see that it is indented below.

- With the new pixel layer active, proceed to paint using the **Paint Brush** Tool from the **Tools** panel. Open the **Brushes Panel** and choose an appropriate brush for what you need. They are categorized depending on the sort of look they produce. For the rocketship, I used mainly brushes from the **Basic** and the **Textures** brush categories.

- Repeat this process for each new pixel layer. Keep your workflow efficient and flexible by not painting everything on one layer in case you need to correct mistakes or make changes.

- To continue painting on a pixel layer after you've deselected it, you must reselect it in the **Layers** panel to activate it again, otherwise, Affinity Designer will automatically create a new pixel layer for you.

Breakdown – main body painting workflow

Let's break down a few of the main steps, starting with the main body element.

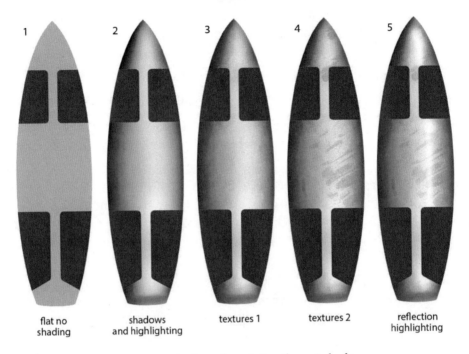

Figure 13.12 – Steps for painting the main body

- Step **1** – Select the main body or the gray area layer.

- Step **2** – On a nested new pixel layer, using a soft basic brush and low opacity setting, start to paint in the shadow areas in a dark gray color, paying attention to the light source and surrounding shapes as a guide for placing the shadows. Add a smooth central, low-opacity white highlight to suggest the roundness of the form.

- Step **3** – On a nested new pixel layer, add subtle texturing with a texture brush to add interest and wear and tear to the surface. Use a variety of gray colors.

- Step **4** – On a nested new pixel layer, continue with a slightly different type of texture brush that is more aggressive or pronounced.

- Step **5** – On a nested new pixel layer, add a more pronounced reflection highlight with a soft basic brush.

Breakdown – doorway opening and red panels

Let's break down the door opening and red panel workflow:

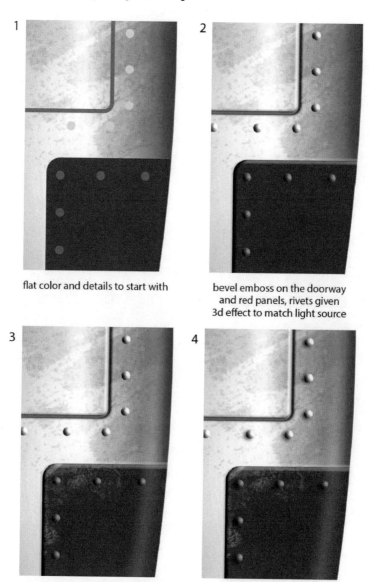

1   flat color and details to start with

2   bevel emboss on the doorway and red panels, rivets given 3d effect to match light source

3   pixel painted shading and texture on red panels, tapered and blurred white stroke reflected highlight

4   outer shadow effect added to all rivets to match light source

Figure 13.13 – Steps for door opening and red panels

- Step **1** – Start out by selecting the elements you want to apply effects to.

- Step **2** – I added a **Bevel / Emboss** effect to the doorway opening. Since the doorway opening metal material is the same as the rocket, I didn't give it a fill so that the rocket material can show through; it just has a stroke. When using the **Bevel** or **3D** effect, always consider the light direction and adjust accordingly in the **Layer Effects** popup after clicking on the gear icon in the **Effects** panel for each effect. In this case, the round sphere icon indicating the light direction seems to be the opposite of what I wanted. Some of these effects may behave differently from what you are expecting. Always go by what you see in the preview of the actual shape.

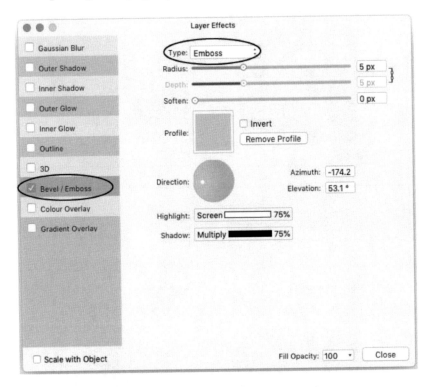

Figure 13.14 – Bevel / Emboss settings for the door opening

For the red panels, the same **Bevel / Emboss** effect was used with some slight modifications to the settings and the addition of a **3D** effect as well, as shown in *Figure 13.15*. Note the ability to change the **Profile** curve used for the **3D** effect. You have a great amount of control with all of these **Emboss** and **3D** effect settings. It is a lot quicker and much more flexible than if you tried to pixel paint these types of effects by hand. They really come in handy for this type of work and will save you a ton of time and they look great.

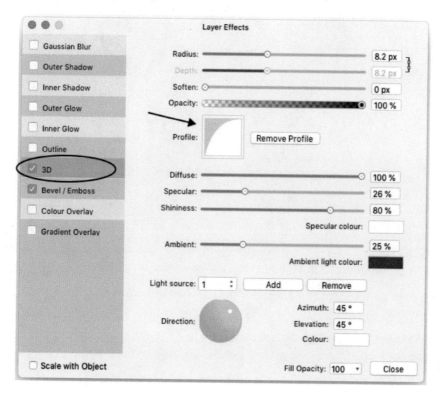

Figure 13.15 – 3D effect settings for the red panels

- Step **3** – Using a dark red color and a soft **Basic** round brush, I added some shading to the panel to change it from that flat look to a more rounded look as the panel is supposed to be wrapping around the rocket. Then I added some subtle **Pixel Painted** textural details to the panels with **Texture Brushes** to give them a bit of an aged look to match the bare metal of the main rocket body. Finally, over top of the panel and the main body, I added a tapered, curved, blurred white line for a bit of a reflected highlight to really sell that metallic feel. It's subtle but very important.

- Step **4** – The **3D** effect rivets were looking like they were floating so I added an **Outer Shadow** effect to them paying attention to the light direction for consistency.

Breakdown – window

Let's take a look at the breakdown of the window creation:

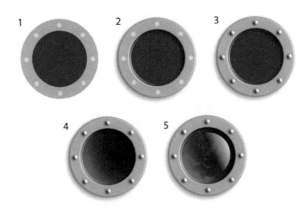

Figure 13.16 – Various steps for creating the window

- Step **1** – Start out by selecting the elements you want to apply effects to.

- Step **2** – I added a **Bevel / Emboss** effect to the circular window frame. I also added an **Outer Shadow** effect for that cast shadow on the lower left.

- Step **3** – I gave the rivets a **3D** effect and an **Outer Shadow** effect.

- Step **4** – To make the window glass area less flat, I pixel painted with a soft **Basic** round brush a deep, dark-blue area at the top right and a soft, lighter-blue area at the bottom left. This just adds a nice sense of depth to the glass.

- Step **5** – Continuing to paint on a new pixel layer, I pixel painted a bit of texture to carry over that consistent feel of the rest of the rocket's surfaces. I then added a white circle and faded it to transparent using the **Transparency** Tool. Note: to access the **Transparency** tool, you'll need to jump back into the Designer Persona.

Hopefully, you are seeing that with just a few clicks and a little planning, once you know what some of these effects and simple pixel painting methods can do to take those flat color shapes to the next level, you will be encouraged to experiment using these techniques in your own work.

Figure 13.17 shows a few closer views of other areas of the rocketship and they employ the same methods we just covered:

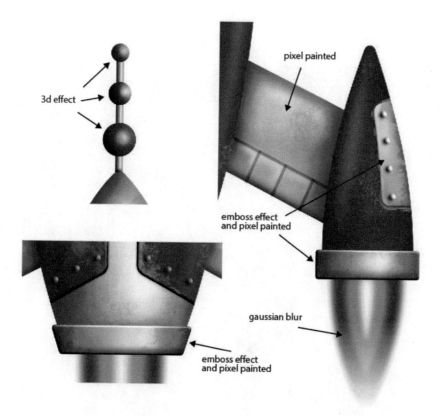

Figure 13.17 – Various effects and steps for the wing struts, engine areas, and retro rocket pointer

Pros and cons – a win-win situation

All processes have advantages and disadvantages and strengths and weaknesses. Fortunately, with Affinity Designer, you don't have to sacrifice one method over another. You have both at your disposal in a very convenient, easy-to-use interface.

This last chapter has shown how we can switch between the two personas with ease, using the Designer Persona's vector and effects prowess for what it does best and then exploiting the Pixel Persona for its amazing painting and texture abilities.

The wear and tear look of the rocket surface would have been much more difficult to achieve without the ability to use the power of painting and the use of different brushes.

Why settle for one when you can have two? Use both Personas to your advantage and see your creative possibilities take flight!

The final illustration in *Figure 13.18* brings together both of these Persona workflows to achieve an image only Affinity Designer can achieve seamlessly in one application.

Figure 13.18 – The finished rocket illustration

With the rocketship finished, I added the space background as a background layer. I then rotated the rocket by selecting all of the layers that make it up and rotating them as one unit. Happy travels!

Summary

This concludes the end of this third exercise chapter and brings us to the end of this book. If you made the thirteen-chapter journey all the way to here, congratulations for sticking all the way to the end! If you skipped around the book, that's cool too. I hope it whet your appetite for more and I'd encourage you to check out some of the other chapters' content for lots of great tips and tricks.

In this final chapter, we learned how the Pixel Persona's painting workflow can add a whole new level of dramatic visual difference to your project. The combination of pixel painting with bevels and 3D effects as well as other vector effects and methods were all covered in this chapter. It's really the culmination of all that we have learned throughout the course of this book.

Although we may not have covered every single aspect of this extensive program, I hope that through all of the chapters and exercises we did cover, you have gained some lasting knowledge about this amazing application and will be able to confidently go forward and continue this journey creating your own Affinity Designer masterpieces.

Affinity Designer, no doubt, will keep on improving, adding new features, and increasing its user base over the years to come. With this book, covering the basics and the fundamentals of how to get up and running, you will be well equipped to take advantage of this amazing software's trajectory.

I'd love to see what *you* create with Affinity Designer. To stay in touch, find or follow me online at:

Instagram – instagram.com/kevincreative/

Website – www.kevincreative.com

Behance – behance.net/kevincreative

Dribbble – dribbble.com/kevincreative

Thank you for coming along for the ride. I hope it wasn't too bumpy! ;-) – Kevin

`Packt.com`

Subscribe to our online digital library for full access to over 7,000 books and videos, as well as industry leading tools to help you plan your personal development and advance your career. For more information, please visit our website.

Why subscribe?

- Spend less time learning and more time coding with practical eBooks and Videos from over 4,000 industry professionals

- Improve your learning with Skill Plans built especially for you

- Get a free eBook or video every month

- Fully searchable for easy access to vital information

- Copy and paste, print, and bookmark content

Did you know that Packt offers eBook versions of every book published, with PDF and ePub files available? You can upgrade to the eBook version at `packt.com` and as a print book customer, you are entitled to a discount on the eBook copy. Get in touch with us at `customercare@packtpub.com` for more details.

At `www.packt.com`, you can also read a collection of free technical articles, sign up for a range of free newsletters, and receive exclusive discounts and offers on Packt books and eBooks.

Other Books You May Enjoy

If you enjoyed this book, you may be interested in these other books by Packt:

Mastering Adobe Animate 2021

Joseph Labrecque

ISBN: 978-1-80107-416-2

- Gain a solid understanding of Adobe Animate foundations and new features
- Understand the nuances associated with publishing and exporting rich media content for various platforms
- Make use of advanced layering and rigging techniques to create engaging motion content
- Create dynamic motion by using the camera and variable layer depth techniques

Mastering Adobe Photoshop Elements 2021 - Third Edition

Robin Nichols

ISBN: 978-1-80056-699-6

- Identify the five parts of Elements and set up your computer, camera, and monitor
- Import, organize, and keep track of your imported media library
- Develop advanced image retouching skills
- Discover how to add text and graphics to photographs
- Cultivate your understanding of multi-image, multi-layered editing techniques
- Develop illustrative skills with the many drawing tools available in Elements 2021

Packt is searching for authors like you

If you're interested in becoming an author for Packt, please visit `authors.packtpub.com` and apply today. We have worked with thousands of developers and tech professionals, just like you, to help them share their insight with the global tech community. You can make a general application, apply for a specific hot topic that we are recruiting an author for, or submit your own idea.

Share Your Thoughts

Now you've finished *Up and Running with Affinity Designer*, we'd love to hear your thoughts! Scan the QR code below to go straight to the Amazon review page for this book and share your feedback or leave a review on the site that you purchased it from.

https://packt.link/r/<1801079064>

Your review is important to us and the tech community and will help us make sure we're delivering excellent quality content.

Index

Made in the USA
Middletown, DE
13 June 2022